CHINA'S
WATERGATE

Political and Economic Conflicts, 1969-1977

LEO GOODSTADT

Distributed in the U.S.A., CANADA and MEXICO
by

 Humanities Press

Atlantic Highlands, N.J.

VIKAS PUBLISHING HOUSE PVT LTD
New Delhi Bombay Bangalore Calcutta Kanpur

VIKAS PUBLISHING HOUSE PVT LTD
5 Ansari Road, New Delhi 110002
Savoy Chambers, 5 Wallace Street, Bombay 400001
10 First Main Road, Gandhi Nagar, Bangalore 560009
8/1-B Chowringhee Lane, Calcutta 700016
80 Canning Road, Kanpur 208004

Printed at Dhawan Printing Works, 26-A Mayapuri, New Delhi 110064

CHINA'S WATERGATE

BY THE SAME AUTHOR

Mao Tse-tung—The Search for Plenty

PREFACE

In 1972, President Richard Nixon spent the summer with a single ambition: how to get a second term in office. His campaign to win the presidential election ran smoothly enough except for a stupid blunder. Nixon's political staff were concerned to monitor their opponents' activities. A plan was hatched to plant an electronic bug in the campaign offices of Nixon's rivals. The men hired to carry out this illegal contract were caught by the police, and the Watergate Affair had begun. Richard Nixon won the election. His most trusted aides were convicted of a variety of crimes linked to the Watergate break-in. President Nixon struggled to escape responsibility for a conspiracy to cover up the facts of the case. In the end, Nixon was forced to hand over the presidency to the almost unknown Gerald Ford. President Ford retained the services of Nixon's apparatchik, Dr Henry Kissinger. The new President also decided that Richard Nixon ought to be saved from the final disgrace of trial and probable imprisonment by a free pardon. Gerald Ford proved an honest but ineffectual President, heavily dependent on Dr Kissinger who finished up with a more distinguished reputation than either of the two presidents whom he had served.

In 1971, on the opposite side of the Pacific Ocean, a similar drama was staged. The second most important figure in China's communist hierarchy was accused of seeking to seize power from his master, Chairman Mao Tse-tung. The conspirator was an undistinguished personality, except as a general, named Lin Piao. In September that year, he fled from Peking only to die in a plane crash in the Mongolian Republic under circumstances of the greatest mystery. The rise and fall of Lin Piao marked the triumph and tragedy of Mao Tse-tung. Because of Lin Piao, Mao's authority over the Chinese nation crumbled. Before he died in 1976, Mao had been the object of demonstrations demanding his removal no less dramatic than the calls for President Nixon's impeachment. Mao had an apparatchik known to the world as Chou En-lai, who finished up with a reputation as distinguished as that of Mao Tse-tung at the height of his influence. Mao's successor was no better known to the Chinese nation than the man who replaced Nixon as President had been to the American people. And it fell to Mao's successor, Hua Kuo-feng, to protect the reputation of Mao Tse-tung when his widow, Chiang Ching, and three other politicians, popularly identified as the most ardent Maoists, were branded the "gang of four" and placed under arrest.

The history of the remarkable events which led to Mao Tse-tung's reduction in stature and the elevation of Chou En-lai to the rank of China's most beloved leader is narrated here as closely as possible to the way in which Chinese themselves understood the drama of the decade from 1966. Specialists in contemporary China studies will recognise how much of the account is drawn from official, published, Chinese sources and how much is based on the news that China keeps out of its news media. Only at the very end of the narrative is every verse and chapter noted precisely in a section on Peking's case against the "gang of four." Peking is never slow to pronounce a verdict on leaders who have fallen out of favour. The Chinese Government is much shyer about formal publication of the full background to such verdicts even when great numbers of its citizens already know what the leadership will only commit to print after considerable delay. The aim of the chapters which follow is to explain the drama which culminated in the denunciation of Mao Tse-tung's widow and her associates while the world waits for the Chinese authorities to decide how much they can prudently put on the public record.

LEO GOODSTADT

CONTENTS

CONTENTS

CHAPTER ONE

THE END OF A DYNASTY AND
A DOWAGER EMPRESS

FOR THE HUNDREDS of tough-looking Chinese officials, with hardly a young or female face among them, each phrase and gesture of the afternoon's performance would follow a script they knew by heart. Every member of the audience had attended scores of criticism sessions and knew all too well how carefully rehearsed the entertainment would prove. In ordinary circumstances, most of the thousand or so present on this grim December day in 1976 would have found a plausible excuse to avoid leaving the warmth of their offices and travelling through the biting winter wind to witness the public humiliation of yet another group of China's leaders. Almost all those checked so meticulously by the massive security cordon before entering the auditorium could have justified their absence by urgent state business, for only the most prominent Communist Party and government officials had been issued with passes to attend. On their desks, even crucial files would have to wait, nevertheless, because this criticism session marked the wheel of fate come full circle to slake a lust for revenge which had long ached for satisfaction.

As the audience settled down in its chairs, three men and a lone woman were pushed on to the rostrum. The youngest of the men was manacled, his hands pinioned behind his back. He might lash out at the officials on the stage acting as impresarios if he were not handcuffed, so the audience explained to one another in whispers. A similar precaution had been taken with the thin, haggard woman in her sixties whose temper was rightly feared still. She was granted the concession of being allowed to keep her manacled hands in front instead of being strapped behind her back.

The crowd felt no compassion for the four lonely individuals about to be vilified in front of onlookers who would need little encouragement to express a violent hatred for the prisoners. Once upon a time, the bulk of the crowd would have worn a look of deep respect at a confrontation with any of the four. They had been counted among the mightiest in the land. The woman was Chiang Ching, widow of Mao Tse-tung, the man whose word had swayed China's progress from 1949 till his death in September 1976. The young man condemned, like Chiang Ching, to wear manacles had been plucked in 1973 from the obscurity of a minor post in Shanghai to become a Vice Chairman of the Communist Party. He had made his name, Wang Hung-wen, notorious as a symbol for insubordinate sentiments which showed respect for neither age nor experience. The other two men had climbed in 1967 almost to the summit of power during the tempests of the Cultural Revolution. One, Chang Chun-chiao, had emerged as Deputy Premier after proving his mettle in crushing radical extremists, worker-anarchists and criminal gangs in Shanghai, China's largest and most sophisticated city. The final member of the "gang of four" was Yao Wen-yuan, the man who had been given the job of acting as the country's intellectual policeman and editor of all its national news media.

The cream of the Chinese establishment had not come to witness a trial. All four were self-evidently guilty, and nothing too monstrous could be alleged against the three men and their female accomplice. The audience itself had lived in fear from July 1966 till October 1976 of being subject to precisely the ordeal which the "gang of four" would now endure. The audience had come to believe that this nightmare through which they had lived for a decade was engineered deliberately and maliciously by the "gang of four." The audience contained a large proportion who had actually suffered as victims of harrowing public criticism sessions. They had been reviled and frequently assaulted on a host of trumped-up charges. Pity and sympathy were not virtues to be practised on this winter's day of dreadful cold.

The prosecution's witnesses were called forth by the practised masters of ceremonies and recited their lines well. Indignation in the hall remained under control since the accusations had been

widely publicised in advance. But the impresarios had a surprise
in store for the crowd. Finally called on stage was a small
group of medical personnel. They had tended the late Prime
Minister Chou En-lai as he approached his death in January
1976. They narrated how Chou's wife, who was keeping her
vigil by his bedside, had been summoned away on the pretext of
the most urgent official business. As she left, a merciless Chiang
Ching slipped into Chou's room and ordered the nurses and doctors
to leave her alone with the dying man. The witnesses went on
remorselessly with their account of how they had suspected
Chiang Ching's motives and peered through the glass window
above the door. They had seen and heard Chiang Ching badger
Chou En-lai, stricken with terminal cancer, about whether or not
he had been responsible for sending some book or other to her
husband Mao Tse-tung. They had dared to rush back into the
room only when Chou was struck by Chiang Ching.

Among the audience, near the front, was an old man who
looked too feeble to be capable of the least physical exertion.
Almost any literate Chinese could have put a name to the bulky
veteran dressed in the baggy uniform of the People's Liberation
Army—Defence Minister Yeh Chien-ying, Communist Party
Vice Chairman and one of China's most revered generals. The
description of what Chiang Ching had imposed on Chou En-lai
as he lay helpless and so close to death proved too much for
Yeh. His indignation pumped energy into him as he searched
feverishly for a missile to hurl at the four on the stage.
With nothing obvious to hand, Yeh was inspired to take off a
shoe. He sent it spinning at the four miscreants. Almost at once,
the air was filled with flying shoes. The "gang of four" were
led away, physically unharmed but well aware that the next few
months would bring a gruesome round of similar sessions at
which the hatred of the onlookers would be far more genuine
than at almost any denunciation rally held in China since Mao
Tse-tung had come to power in 1949.

Many in the audience tried to see if another general was
present among the hundreds who filed out to brave the cold once
more despite the heaters in the squat sedans with drawn curtains
which would shuttle most of them back to their offices. This
second general was Hsu Shih-yu, an outstanding combat commander with little interest in politics and even less taste for

ideological rhetoric. Hsu was responsible for the major southern military region with his headquarters in Canton. But for 20 years until January 1974, he had commanded a coastal region which included Shanghai and had its headquarters in Nanking. Most of the army officers in this region owed their careers to Hsu Shih-yu's appreciation of their talents. Few of his former subordinates could deny him their total loyalty. The first week of October 1976 saw Hsu travel to Nanking on a journey which sealed the fate of Chiang Ching and the other three, which is why the crowd was interested in glancing discreetly at him before leaving the auditorium.

Peking in September 1976 had heard rumours that Shanghai, long identified by the public at large as the base of the "gang of four," contained army units on the verge of mutiny. The plan was, so the central authorities had heard, for regular and militia units to seize Shanghai and declare their support for Chiang Ching and eventually start a campaign to capture the capital. Hsu Shih-yu was able to assure himself in Nanking that his presence and voice still commanded respect and affection among the region's officer corps. At the end of the first week of October 1976, he had neutralised the potential threat from dissident troops around Shanghai. Hsu felt the short trip from Nanking to Shanghai to be unnecessary. He quashed the mutiny before it began with a mere phone call during which he pledged his reputation to an ambitious handful of Shanghai officers that he would take no more than two hours to destroy them and any military force they might care to field against him. Hsu's promise was enough to convince the would-be dissidents to lay down their arms. On October 7, 1976, in order to guarantee that the central Government did not lose control of Shanghai even momentarily, Hsu had all normal train traffic diverted. The railways were monopolised by army units dispatched to ring Shanghai, move on strategic points and encircle the few military units of doubtful loyalty.

These moves meant that the Politburo and the new Communist Party Chairman, Premier Hua Kuo-feng, could take Chiang Ching, Party Vice Chairman Wang Hung-wen, Deputy Premier Chang Chun-chiao and Yao Wen-yuan into custody without fear of military confrontations on their behalf or declarations of local autonomy in protest against their arrest. In fact, Shanghai would have risen in rebellion, almost certainly, if the city had been seized in the name of the "gang of four" since the city disliked the quartet more intensely perhaps than any other part of China. But the capital was taking no chances.

Analysis of both national and local reports of what followed the arrest of the four strongly suggests that their detention came as a considerable surprise. Although a showdown seems to have been feared as a future possibility, none of those close to the "gang of four" seems to have anticipated that Hua and the Politburo would strike so soon or with such efficiency. As Hua Kuo-feng boasted later, not a drop of blood was shed in the operation to overthrow the "gang."

For Chiang Ching, in particular, her fate had a tragic irony. She had expected, as had most ordinary Party members, to be given the rank of honorary Party Chairman out of respect for her husband's memory. Hua Kuo-feng was expected to retain real control over Party affairs with a suitable title and to relinquish the burdens of the Prime Ministers's Office to Chang Chun-chiao. It was inconceivable to most Party members that Hua could hope to run both the Government and the Communist Party. Chang Chun-chiao was the only Deputy Premier under the age of seventy with the qualifications to take over as prime minister, it was believed. Rumours and wall posters had predicted just such appointments for some three weeks after Mao Tse-tung's death. Instead of being promoted, Chiang Ching and Chang Chun-chiao, together with Wang and Yao, were transformed into the "gang of four," villains whose crimes were greater possibly than had been laid at the door of any public figure since the establishment of the Communist Party's rule in 1949.

Chiang Ching did not accept her detention without protest. She went on hunger strike and was threatened with forced feeding which did not intimidate her much. She capitulated, however, when informed that if her hunger strike continued, she would be taken before an audience composed of students from two institutions in the capital, Peking and Tsinghua Universities. Their undergraduates had been led to believe that some dozen of their classmates had been used by the "gang of four" and then secretly executed and their bodies cremated on Chiang Ching's orders to ensure no embarrassing witnesses would be left to gossip. Chiang

Ching capitulated and actually requested an improvement in her daily rations, which was authorised.

Chiang Ching's husband was equally unlucky. Mao Tse-tung had wanted to die in Peking. Fate denied him this final favour. He had laboured hard to win an honourable chapter to his memory in China's history. Before his death, his reputation had already become the victim of a meticulous destruction. His associates and his successors had waged a protracted campaign to minimise his prestige and discount his contributions to China's independence and progress. The father figure of modern China could not repel the ravages of personal misfortune, miscalculation and the conspiracies of men who seized the levers of power as his physical strength ebbed through age and disease. Mao Tse-tung left the world a lonely and embittered old man. His closest comrades were no longer at hand. Many were dead or senile; a considerable number had been disgraced in Mao's own name. Within his family he could find small comfort as the wife, Chiang Ching, whom he had married at considerable cost in power and prestige, had betrayed him, or so he was convinced. The Communist Party, which had enshrined absolute obedience to his precepts in its constitution, had come to ignore his wishes and distort his directives.

The battle to destroy the authority of the almost legendary Mao Tse-tung began in 1966 at the very moment when he seemed to have achieved his greatest triumph. The most intimate details of the conspiracy against Mao are obscure, and the identity of many of the actors in this remarkable political intrigue can only be guessed at. Yet the existence of a grand strategy to destroy Mao as a major force in Chinese life is beyond question. The men who contributed most to his downfall were: his former official heir, Lin Piao; the Prime Minister, Chou En-lai; an old adversary, Teng Hsiao-ping; and, by accident, his wife and Deputy Premier Chang Chun-chiao. The conspirators' main base was Shanghai at first; they took time to gather overwhelming support in the capital. Although the struggle against Mao Tse-tung involved personal ambitions and vendettas, at stake were conflicts nearly as old as Chinese civilisation, as well as the perpetual problem of administrators about how far they can rely on appeals to reason rather than on intimidation to guarantee that the public obeys their commands.

The final act in the drama was staged after Mao's death. Its details cannot be graced with a very dignified description, as the various steps taken by Mao's successors revealed a great deal of cynicism and no great affection for Mao Tse-tung at any level of Chinese society. However, the ultimate hostility displayed towards Mao Tse-tung was latent rather than overt in origin, and the disrespect exhibited towards him was the last stage in a long-drawn-out programme to denigrate Mao Tse-tung.

After Mao Tse-tung's death in September 1976, the rulers and masses of China almost drowned in their floods of tears and oceans of eulogies. The Government quickly decided that Mao Tse-tung was to enjoy a veneration of a spectacular nature. Every word ever written by the late Chairman, the Communist Party Central Committee proclaimed, must be collected for inclusion in the "Complete Works of Mao Tse-tung." If the undertaking to print for posterity every sentence ever penned by Mao were honoured literally, the speeches, articles, essays, directives, cables, minutes, inscriptions and jottings involved would fill several score of volumes. China would be buried under the millions of words which Mao had poured forth so prolifically. He would become more impossible to study than Lenin, whose published writings—30 fat volumes published by Moscow between 1928 and 1937—are too much for most admirers to peruse in full. Deep acquaintance with Lenin's more obscure writings was taken by China's most distinguished leaders in 1968, for example, as convincing evidence of a provincial plot to set up a rival organisation to Mao's Communist Party. Lenin is studied today mainly as the author of two- or three-volume "Selections" or a few, short, graphic tracts. Much the same fate was obviously intended for Mao Tse-tung, thus curtailing his influence as China's major political philosopher in at least a hundred years, if not for several centuries.

With Mao Tse-tung Thought consigned to moulder on the mustier library shelves, the Peking leadership turned its attention to Mao's human remains. He was to be embalmed and placed in a shrine to which the nation could come on pilgrimage. This plan seemed an attempt to perpetuate the memory of Mao in a spectacular but reverent manner and bestow a sort of immortality on him by preservation of his corpse from decay. A similar scheme had been entertained for Sun Yat-sen, the leader of the 1911 revolution which overthrew the country's imperial rulers and launched the nation on the path towards Mao's China. Sun's embalmers failed to protect the nation's first president from decay, and he was buried eventually in the humble soil. Common features of Chinese society are its accurate folk memory, and an interest in the more morbid details of bodily processes, a popular topic of lively conversation. The announcement that Mao Tse-tung would not lie in a grave but would be placed in the hands of embalmers aroused considerable interest in the gruesome aspects of what must be done to a body to preserve it. Such discussions of the corpse of Mao Tse-tung were a direct assault on his dignity, however unintentional the participation of the population at large.

Not without good cause had Chou En-lai insisted that he be cremated and his ashes scattered across the countryside. Mao Tse-tung had requested similar treatment for his remains. Not without reason had the Communist Party's leaders rejected his wishes. The failure to inscribe the mausoleum's foundation stone with Mao's name led first to speculation and them to open suggestions that Mao should share his memorial with shrines dedicated to Chou and to the Communist Party's first Commander-in-Chief, Chu Teh. These calls marked a further step in reducing Mao Tse-tung's prestige. As these decisions to mummify both the political and physical remains of Mao Tse-tung were publicised throughout the nation, elite units of China's toughest combat divisions provided cover for a delicate security operation, the arrest of the "gang of four," a group of national personalities headed by Mao's widow, Chiang Ching. This move required some courage by the country's rulers. Mao Tse-tung was not a full month dead; the traditional mourning period, during which a dead man's family must fulfil certain social obligations to commemorate the deceased, was not nearly ended. In addition, a man's wife in Chinese society belongs to his family and abandons her own family far more completely than is true in Western society. All Mao's immediate relatives of his own generation were dead except for his fourth wife, Chiang Ching, which made her the senior member of the Mao family. Her arrest was an affront to her husband's memory which defied all normal Chinese conventions.

She appealed to Wang Tung-hsing, commander of the praetorian guard, a man responsible over some 40 years for Mao's personal safety. Her pleas were rejected. Wang proclaimed that his duty was to guard the lives of the Party Central Committee and its Politburo members in particular. He owed no personal loyalty to Mao, to his widow or his household. Wang Tung-hsing could not have saved Chiang Ching in any case. His units could not have resisted the rest of the armed forces. The army's opposition to Chiang Ching and the others taken into custody was guaranteed by the popularity of the man who inspired the arrests, the veteran general and Defence Minister, Yeh Chien-ying. The detention warrants were actually signed by the acting head of the Communist Party, Hua Kuo-feng, not just as a matter of protocol but because Hua had ample cause of his own to insist that Chiang Ching and the "gang of four" be imprisoned.

On her head was to be heaped every mistake and misfortune experienced by China since 1966. Had the economy too often seemed to put revolutionary slogans before the people's welfare? Chiang Ching and her accomplices had wantonly distorted Mao Tse-tung's teaching on the role of revolution during the struggle for prosperity. Had men grown old and bent in the service of the Communist Party and the Chinese masses been pilloried merci-lessly? Chiang Ching and her fellow conspirators had been bent on usurping power even from Mao himself. Had the country en-dured constant disruption of industrial discipline and a decline in unity between the armed forces and the rest of the nation? Chiang Ching and her clique had engineered dissension and disharmony to enhance their careers in the ensuing anarchy. Had the urban population grown weary of the constant upsurges of violent intimidation by political factions ready to use force against the lawful administration and ordinary citizens? Chiang Ching and her fellow-plotters had egged on such factions to split the Communist Party and erode the authority of the legitimate administration. Had the normal chains of command within the Party and the Government been ignored constantly and Peking's directives defied? Chiang Ching and her supporters were busy building a rival secret Party structure of their own. Had the Chinese been bored out of their minds with the monotony of revolutionary operas, films, novels and newspaper stories, all constructed around unchanging and unbelievable tales of superhuman dedication by unflawed heroes? Chiang Ching and her cabal had tried to project an idealised portrait of themselves and to manipulate the news media to indoctrinate the population with their tainted views.

How had Mao Tse-tung passed his days while his wife plotted on such a gross scale? The first denunciations of Chiang Ching and her unholy associates saw a spirited effort to exonerate Mao from blame for his wife's misconduct. He had seen through her diabolical strategems and ordered her to desist, it was claimed officially. She had not complied with his instructions. He had denounced her clique, but they had persisted with their plot. His criticisms of their manoeuvres and his instructions to stem the damage they inflicted on the country were either distorted or suppressed. Mao was powerless, surrounded by such fiendish ambitions, and censored so ruthlessly that he could not reveal the sins of his wife and her partners in crime to the masses. Yet every explanation of how Mao had been defied, tricked or ignored sullied his image still further. Mao's impotence confronted with his wife's machinations was a tale only the most gullible could swallow. After all, Hua Kuo-feng was appointed, the official accounts claimed, first Prime Minister and then Communist Party Chairman by Mao personally in defiance of his wife's opposition. Here, Mao was portrayed as in full control of the situation.

Yet on a host of other major issues from 1966 till his death, China was asked to believe, Mao had been forced to abdicate control over his own wife and three relatively junior members of the Party power structure whose original appointments he had endorsed. On any reasonable interpretation of life at the top in Peking in the decade from 1966, the sins blamed on Chiang Ching and the "gang of four" by the official news media were in reality criticisms of Mao himself. On policy matters, the indictment against the "gang of four" made no sense unless Mao Tse-tung's name was substituted for those of the "gang." In addition, Mao himself had drawn special attention in 1971 to the grave consequences for a political leader unable to keep his wife and her ambitious interference under control. His remarks on the topic added a sardonic note to the Chiang Ching affair.

The fear that the sophisticated elite would reject Mao Tse-tung's innocence of all complicity in his wife's acts led to discreet hints designed especially for the intellectuals' consumption. Mao had been coerced into going along with his wife, the press recounted, and had been deceived by spurious documents. Attacked by traitors so close to him, Mao had no option but to "step aside" and remove himself from the frontline of the power struggle. Otherwise, he would have been unable to avoid a stab in the back. To any informed and shrewd Party member, government official or citizen, the truth was that Chiang Ching had acted very much as her husband desired. When she had not complied with his express wishes, she had done what Mao had predicted, and he had hoped to profit from her apparent defiance. Not until the last years of his life, did a rift emerge between husband and wife, and then not for political reasons.

Chiang Ching started out as an actress; she returned to the stage in 1966. Like every talented actress, she knew the value of a good director, a post filled by Mao till almost the very end. Only then did Chiang Ching fall for the old temptation of seeking to star in a performance to be produced and directed entirely by herself. The fact of the matter was that Mao Tse-tung chose, for reasons of his own, to protect his wife from open criticism until his death; to use her; and to maintain in powerful positions the three men condemned as her chief accomplices. The reluctance to blame Mao Tse-tung and to find other scapegoats for the follies and misdeeds of a decade had an important precedent in post-1949 China. Stalin was never openly denounced by Peking although slyly criticised for years in China before his condemnation by Moscow in 1956. Mao dared not denounce Stalin who had annointed Mao as a true communist leader. In 1976, China's new leaders found it convenient to appear as Mao's legitimate heirs and thus avoided overt attacks on Mao Tse-tung himself. His widow's arrest was just as effective in the context of Chinese politics as an open denunciation of her dead husband.

The population expressed no resentment at the moves by their leaders to diminish Mao Tse-tung's stature. Nor were they perturbed by the haste with which the Prime Minister, Hua Kuo-feng, was proclaimed as the new Party Chairman nominated by Mao himself, an appointment which Chinese respect for mourning rites might have suggested could be postponed for a few weeks. The populace gave every sign of extreme joy at the

startling developments in the capital. The detention of Mao's
widow was hailed in terms which left no doubt about the univer-
sal hatred in which she was held. To judge from popular reaction,
the others taken into custody with her were no public favourites.
From October 22, 1976, the crowds in the country's major
cities swept into the streets in a carnival mood, joking and
laughing as they waited for their turn to shout "strike down
Chiang Ching" and her accomplices and wave their fists. Fire-
crackers were let off by the thousand, a usual festive custom but
also a ritual to scare away the ghosts of the dead as well as
devils. Mao Tse-tung's portrait was much in evidence but
covered with red bands, a symbol of happiness, instead of the
white or black ribbons which ought to surround a dead person's
photograph. The atmosphere was like a second liberation of the
nation or the ecstasy which marked the 1945 surrender of
Japan.

The loathing for Chiang Ching was particularly violent.
Staid Party members giggled over scandalous tales of her
amorous frolics, and a piece of doggerel went the rounds which
translates roughly:

> Fear not the heaven's fall
> And fear no earthly might.
> Fear only for the telephone call
> That may disturb the night.

This verse was inspired by Chiang Ching's alleged exploits with
a senior member of the Ministry of Sports. He had been at his
daily work-out after finishing in the office when he received an
urgent summons to the phone. Chiang Ching demanded his
presence at once. He was not dressed appropriately for such an
interview, he protested, and he would need time to bathe and
change. The business would not wait upon his toilet, he was
informed, and a sedan car was already outside for him. He put
a track suit over his singlet and shorts and was driven to Chiang
Ching's residence, so the tale goes. Here, Chiang Ching, dressed
in a revealing, sheer-nylon wrap, expressed her astonishment
that a healthy athlete should fear a chill so much as to cover himself up in a track suit. He removed the offending garment, upon
which he was told he did need a bath. He was led by Chiang

Ching to a room whose door the hero locked with care. To his surprise, after he started the shower, another door opened. He was joined by a naked lady, somewhat past middle age. The hero of this scurrilous tale did not rejoin his wife for three days; by which time, he was allowed some rest and recuperation. He was a satisfactory gymnast, for he was summoned more than once by phone thereafter to pander to the appetites of a rather elderly lady. The story's wide circulation reflected Chiang Ching's lack of public esteem and the unsavoury reputation which had clung to her since her years as an actress in Shanghai.

Among the mass of misdeeds of Chiang Ching and the three men arrested with her were certain capital charges, for which some parts of the country demanded the death penalty. These accusations embraced alleged disloyalty to Mao Tse-tung and a plan to launch a military coup in order to seize power and to instal Mao's widow as the country's ruler. The first allegations against Chiang Ching of betrayal of her husband also involved claims that she would not let him die in peace, and of acts which endangered China's foreign policy interests. Peking propaganda exaggerates profusely but can rarely be caught out in a barefaced lie. In Chiang Ching's case, her husband had been disturbed on his deathbed. On July 28, while in the throes of his final illness, a massive earthquake struck northern Hopei, the province in which the capital is located. Peking itself shuddered during the tremors, and considerable damage was done to the older part of the city. Mao Tse-tung was removed for his own safety from Peking and died outside the capital. Hence the accusation that Mao was not allowed to face death undisturbed on his own bed.

The second charge, about Chiang Ching's threat to the country's diplomatic policy, was born of indiscretions during her lengthy interview with an American author, Professor Roxane Witke, to whom Chiang Ching spoke frankly and not very cheerfully about the Mao household. The publication of reports overseas based on Professor Witke's interviews did nothing to enhance Chinese prestige abroad. Greed for unsavoury gossip about life in the Forbidden City was exploited to the full by the news media abroad. On the basis of this unfortunate incident, Chiang Ching's encounters with foreign delegations to China could be represent-ed as unauthorised and dangerous intervention in Chinese con-

tacts with the outside world. In March 1975, Chiang Ching
made a secret speech on foreign policy which was leaked to the
outside world with no deletion of its highly uncomplimentary
remarks about Vietnam's communists. Once more, Chiang Ching
appeared to have threatened Chinese diplomacy in a highly
sensitive area.

As with the cases built up against most Peking personalities
disgraced since 1949, the very first charges against Mao's wife
were those closest to the facts. Subsequent denunciations are
usually embroidery on the first allegations, or sinister construc-
tions manufactured out of the quite guileless words and deeds of
the condemned leaders. In Chiang Ching's case, the first indictment was of special importance because the accusations implied
that Mao Tse-tung was incapable of controlling his wife even
when the national interest was at risk. Mao's fading physical and
mental powers throughout 1976 were no excuse as his regiment
of bodyguards recounted in its eulogy for him that, right up to
his death agony, Mao's faculties and political acumen had been
alert.

But Peking remained anxious to preserve a facade of respectability, with the new leadership presented to the people as
appointed and approved by Mao Tse-tung before his final illness.
This tactic was Peking's answer to the problem of legitimacy in
political life. A delicate conjuring trick was required to inherit
Mao's political legacy without being bound by his more inconvenient or embarrassing bequests—notably a Politburo contain-
ing the "gang of four." Similarly tortuous manoeuvres had
succeeded in the past. In 1966, Head of State Liu Shao-chi had
been cast into utter ignominy as "China's Khrushchev" and a
latter-day worshipper of Confucius. Liu was more than Head of
State. He was Mao's apparent heir; and before 1966, no public
suggestion had ever been voiced that Liu Shao-chi was anything
other than Mao's most loyal comrade. The Communist Party's
Secretary-General, Deputy Premier Teng Hsiao-ping, was
denounced as Liu's arch-collaborator. No one had the temerity
to inquire how Chairman Mao had allowed his Communist
Party to fall into the hands of such a villain as Teng. To compli-
cate matters further, Teng had been allowed to make a triumphant return from his enormous disgrace in 1973. (Liu Shao-chi
had fallen victim to cancer meanwhile.) No one was impertinent

enough to ask how this reversal of the 1966 verdict on Teng Hsiao-ping could have been possible.

Mao Tse-tung survived the overthrow and denunciation of his closest officials in 1966 and later survived their political resurrections. He even managed to survive, but only just, the death in 1971 of his "closest comrade-in-arms" and official heir, Defence Minister Lin Piao. Lin was vilified as the instigator of a plot to kill Mao Tse-tung and seize power. No one demanded in public how Lin Piao had managed to induce Mao to endorse him as "Mao's favourite son," although Party members could not be prevented from posing this question in private. The same excuse was employed to exculpate Mao in the case of Liu Shao-chi, Teng Hsiao-ping, Lin Piao and Chiang Ching and the "gang of four." Mao had tried patiently to teach these sinners the error of their ways but they had refused to confess and repent. This excuse had worn a trifle thin by 1976 when Mao's widow, Chiang Ching, and the rest of her associates were arrested.

CHAPTER TWO

SOVIET PLANS FOR CHINA AND
ITS PRIME MINISTER

WHILE MAO TSE-TUNG was still alive, a veritable galaxy of eminent communists were castigated as traitors both to Mao Tse-tung and to China. Mao gave every sign of sincere conviction that he was the target of a plot which had lasted for several years. At various points, he believed he had eradicated the chief conspirators only to find later that a fresh group had gathered to plan his downfall. At length, a conspiracy theory became part and parcel of the Maoist view of life at the top. An obvious reaction to this phenomenon is to argue that over the years, Mao grew paranoic rather than senile.

However, a feature of the allegations brought against almost every leader hurled into disgrace is that they were in the service of the Soviet Union. As a matter of historical record, Stalin had tried energetically to control the Chinese Communist Party for over twenty years until it came to power in 1949. Almost without exception, Stalin's designs for the Chinese communists were catastrophic. If Mao Tse-tung had not won the bitter factional struggle against the Chinese dispatched by the Kremlin to lead the communist revolution in China, the Communist Party would have been exterminated in almost all probability. For nearly ten years, Mao was locked in battle against Stalin's agents within the Chinese Communist Party. As a revolutionary leader himself, experienced in subversion generally and the stratagems practised by Stalin in particular, Mao had no reason to believe that his victory in the fight to lead the Chinese Communist Party had made genuine converts out of his old pro-Soviet antagonists. Moscow's ambitions towards China were demonstrated from 1945 to 1954 by Soviet occupation and ruthless exploitation of various parts of northern China; by the prices demanded from

Peking for the arms and materials supplied by Moscow during the Korean War; and by the discovery in 1954 that Kao Kang, a major military and economic administrator, was a Soviet agent. Soviet subversion warrants a degree of paranoia from potential victims.

A reasonable conclusion would be to accept Peking's rogues' gallery and see Mao's China as under attack from a conspiracy which resembled an onion: each skin peeled off—or pro-Soviet leader purged—revealed another underneath. However, this sort of simplistic reading of events falls down when the evidence mustered against each of Mao's supposed opponents since 1949 (except Kao Kang) is weighed with any care. The men thrown into the dustbin of history and branded as Russian lackeys had records of hostility towards Soviet claims on leadership of the communist world and vigorous resistance to any compromise over China's total independence of any foreign power. The pro-Soviet charges have a hidden significance which does not embrace treason of the conventional sort. The true charge against disgraced leaders, such as Liu Shao-chi or Lin Piao, was not lack of patriotism but of sympathy for the wrong side in the split which began in the Chinese Communist Party as soon as Stalin assessed it as a band of revolutionaries he ought to take seriously and, therefore, bring under Moscow's control.

Soviet communist leaders are denounced by Chinese communists as "revisionists" who believe in buying public support for official policies with material benefits and who want to resurrect through a system of cash and material rewards the class system which the Russian Revolution in 1917 intended to overthrow. (The Sino-Soviet polemic embraces far more complex arguments than this simple summary, of course.) This side of Peking's quarrel with Moscow is well known. The other side is not noticed so frequently: the Chinese condemnation of the Kremlin's use of physical violence against its own citizens and those unfortunate enough to live under Russian garrisons in Eastern Europe.

Peking during Mao Tse-tung's leadership denounced not just "goulash" communism in the Soviet Union but the Russian leaders' use of the knout. Condemnations of Chinese Party leaders denounced as anti-Maoists have included since 1966 the twin charges of a desire to use material benefits to corrupt or bribe the masses and the use of intimidation against individuals loyal to the Chinese version of Marxism preached by Mao. The exploitation of human greed or fear was wrong, according to Mao Tse-tung, because almost everyone, even those who began with heretical views, could be induced to adopt an unselfish attitude towards their work and social responsibilities. A handful would need punishment for stubborn anti-Chinese or anti-communist activities. But persuasion and education not coercion and corruption were the proper way to induce China's citizens to cooperate with the Government's political and economic programmes.

While Mao Tse-tung still enjoyed national respect, public defiance of slogans or directives issued in his name was unthinkable. His name rallied support for mass campaigns although even Mao could not prevent his shrewd subjects from developing a cynicism about the Mao Tse-tung personality cult or stop the average citizen from resisting ideological movements once boredom with repetitious catch-phrases set in. The use of force against the population's recalcitrant elements critical of official plans was hardly ever necessary, taking the country as a whole. (Exceptions to this happy state of affairs were inevitable from time to time, and force became a more important factor as Mao Tse-tung was enfeebled by age.) However, Mao Tse-tung, in common with Chinese in general, believed the nation to be composed of sensible and decent human beings who would respond to reason and resist intimidation.

The role of force in politics is a general problem and a question of great significance in Chinese culture, as will be discussed later. Here, all that needs to be said is that the Chinese Communist Party contained a large group who had survived through the support of the peasantry as they struggled to win power before 1949 and who had watched their Japanese and Chinese foes alienate the population through the use of terror. This faction, together with those whose rural experience had taught them that peasant goodwill counted for more than attempts to terrify the eighty per cent of the 900 million Chinese who live in the villages, formed Mao Tse-tung's natural allies. On the other side was a group which saw development as a struggle which called for the same tight discipline which wins wars. This second faction believed the nation's need for social and economic development was too urgent to waste time on persuasion of anyone who doubted the administration's wisdom. After all, cooperation with official instructions would bring its own rewards in the form of higher incomes and other tangible benefits. By definition, this latter faction was "revisionist" and pro-Soviet in its outlook. But these distinctions in background and experience did not put officials into two, tidy, quite separate groups. Some former guerillas, for example, who had relied on the peasants as their truest allies during hostilities were transferred to cities where they became part of the urban bureaucracy, forced to satisfy the demands of their city constituents. Such varied careers led to shifting alignments within the power structure.

The split within the Chinese Communist Party was regarded by Mao Tse-tung as the unavoidable result of China's pre-1949 class structure, of the corruption of Party members and of the influence on China of foreign capitalism and Russian revisionism. Mao Tse-tung should have paid closer attention to the way in which Chinese culture had been split for two thousand years on the rural issue. He should have recognised the irresistible temptation in times of natural disaster (almost yearly occurrences in some part or other of China) to use a combination of material rewards and coercion to induce the public to employ every ounce of energy in overcoming calamities and adversities. He should also have noted with greater clarity how the tight discipline demanded by a Communist Party of its members compared to ordinary citizens led many Party members to believe in the virtues of severe control over the individual as a solution to all problems. Yet the way in which Mao found himself throughout most of his career at loggerheads with the Party of which he was the official Chairman showed his basic mistrust of the average member's attitude towards ordinary people, a point which Mao also worried over in many of his essays.

Moreover, the cleavage within the ranks of Party members was a dynamic and not a static feature of Chinese politics, with individuals able to swop sides constantly—irrespective of age and origins—in accordance with changes in economic conditions and personal judgments about the extent to which any crisis or, indeed, major problem was an emergency serious enough to require desperate remedies even at the expense of Maoist orthodoxy. The split at the top could also be seen in divisions reflected at every level of the Party as the different grades of Party committees tried to solve their specific local problems. Background and experience sorted the leadership into basic factions. Economic pressures kept the various shades of opinion for and against the merits of the Maoist approach in a constant state of flux as rival groups in the Party won recruits or lost adherents. Thus, a man yesterday counted with the angels could today become a pariah to the Maoists; the errant leader of today could change his opinions and soon join the Maoist camp after a sincere self-criticism. Yet, it must be emphasised, no Chinese leader had the slightest intention of becoming a Russian puppet or making China into a Soviet satellite. The clash was between ideas not over high treason.

The fluid character of the Party Central Committee and its Politburo, until 1975 at least, explains why various individuals, such as Mao Tse-tung's wife, Chiang Ching, and her close associate, Yao Wen-yuan, could be genuinely committed to Mao and the defence of his ideas and yet form links with groups far from enthusiastic about many of his radical innovations. Only in the last few months before their arrest did Chiang Ching and the rest of the "gang of four" seemingly become locked into a block opposed by a majority of the Party Central Committee. Until this point, individuals mistrusted by Mao and members of Mao's entourage had been able to find common ground on a great variety of issues. Similarly, after the arrest of the "gang of four," the tide of trends and events carried Party leaders closer to some of their comrades and then away again as each new problem to be resolved by Peking initiated fresh discussions and debates inside the Politburo.

A single figure was involved in every struggle within the Chinese Communist Party from the first bid by Mao Tse-tung to establish his mastery over its destiny until Mao's reputation lay in ruins. This same figure became the sole member left of the band of leaders selected by Stalin to ensure the Chinese communists took their orders from the Kremlin. In every way, this man was a total contrast to Mao Tse-tung, and he stood to gain most from the dismissal in disgrace of Mao's closest associates. He had been less involved in terms of time in guerilla combat than Mao, though he was an experienced leader of peasant insurrections. He alone of the inner leadership at the heart of the Peking administration had a known record of (urban) terrorism similar to that practised by the Soviet secret police. Above all, he was the apparatchik, indifferent to ideology but obsessed with policies, business and the efficient conduct of administration. This natural antagonist of Mao Tse-tung was none other than Chou En-lai. He was the greatest survivor of the Chinese communist revolution, and to him went new power and enhanced authority as one potential rival followed another into political oblivion. By his death in January 1976, Chou En-lai's stature among his own people had risen to a height far superior to that enjoyed by Mao Tse-tung, an achievement which must rank among the wonders of modern political history.

Chou En-lai never concealed the Kremlin's original hopes for his support or Mao Tse-tung's misgivings about who commanded Chou's ultimate loyalties. Chou hailed from the world of minor scholars and officials and had the charm and manners so valued by this class. Mao Tse-tung came from the coarser world of the peasants even though his father had more money than most. Mao himself went through the normal educational system from primary school to the post-secondary level; Chou, academically speaking, idled away his time abroad after secondary school. Chou En-lai's public speeches were never his personal compositions. He spoke always in his official capacity and his utterances represented a collective Party or official stance. His private conversations were either devoted to specific affairs of state or were discourses, especially as he aged, filled with an attractively expressed personal and practical philosophy. His acknowledged ideological contributions were non-existent. He accepted official policies and fed them into the national administrative machine which was his pride and joy. His protests over specific policy proposals seem to have strayed rarely, if ever, from voicing the bureaucracy's doubts and hesitations as to whether a particular programme could be implemented in practice.

Mao turned his back on the intellectuals, a group to which he belonged by educational background, ability and instinct and whom he had much prized in his earlier years. Chou guarded the interests of this elite, for he recruited from its ranks the brainpower which his government machine needed. Chou also realised that the influence of China's intellectuals was of extraordinary significance, and he wanted their support. Mao Tse-tung was not unaware of the impact which intellectuals commanded. His decision was an attempt to destroy their prestige rather than to woo them. Finally, when in control of the underground movement in Shanghai, Chou had never baulked at the use of brutality. Mao, by contrast, seems unique among communist revolutionary leaders in his lack of stomach for physical extermination (although he sometimes found it expedient not to insist on rigid enforcement of his directives against arbitrary violence and executions).

Inevitably, the relations between Mao Tse-tung and Chou En-lai were more complicated than has been depicted in this brief and simplistic account. But it is clear that decades of the closest working associations between the two men had not created in either a fixed image of each other. Their views and judgments of one another varied with events. Periods of trust and collaboration mingled with intervals of suspicion and resentment. Their relationship was not the frozen and contrived posturing of king and courtier. The two were politicians of a very high order, each with a particular and personal part to play in Chinese affairs. Mao preferred the realm of ideas and weighed Chou's worth in terms of usefulness and Maoist ideology. Chou was concerned with the world of administration and assessed Mao from the standpoint of usefulness and practical results. As it happened, the two were able to postpone a permanent rupture because Chou was the superb bureaucrat and amenable to Mao's philosophy; while Mao was a unifying force whose basic doctrines could advance the nation's economic and social development. The two were personalities in their own right as well as politicians. Mao Tse-tung eventually lost his ability to dominate lesser mortals because age, infirmity and political misfortunes eroded his charisma. Chou En-lai, in contrast, grew old gracefully, mellowed and displayed a human warmth which proved more durably attractive to the Chinese than the hysterical adulation cultivated by Mao Tse-tung.

The moderate image which Chou En-lai presented to the outside world in particular should not be allowed to distract from the more sordid side of domestic power politics. Indeed, Chou employed his external prestige to shield himself from attacks at home, particularly in 1967. Furthermore, although Chou came to be eld in the highest esteem as a superb diplomat, almost all the fo eign policies with which he was personally involved were either ruinous or simply unfruitful. This accusation can be tested with a few famous forays by Chou into the realms of personal diplomacy. As part of Peking's effort to win the support of the non-aligned Afro-Asian nations at their first conference in 1955 in Bandung, Chou En-lai exerted all his talents both at the Conference proper and at meetings with individual leaders especially those from Asia. China temporarily won a new image; yet solid support for its international posture failed to materialise. Southeast Asian states, in particular, shed none of their mistaken mistrust of China's territorial ambitions towards them. Chou had a special relationship with Pandit Nehru, India's first Prime Minister. In 1962, the two nations went to war. As a result, the Soviet Union with whom China had by now quarrelled publicly and bitterly had within its grasp an Indian ally along China's southern flank so that Peking had to face potential pincers' pressure on two borders. In 1964, Chou made an African tour. He spoke of the continent's revolutionary potential, which frightened his hosts and created a substantial backlash against Peking among the often fragile, newly-independent African nations.

When the Cambodian leader Prince Sihanouk was overthrown by a palace coup in 1970, Moscow refused to lend him Russian hospitality. Chou made Sihanouk his own protégé and sought to transform the Prince into a world statesman. In this way, North Vietnamese designs on the rest of Indochina were to be contained, as Cambodia would be headed by a man who would owe everything to the Chinese. Sihanouk participated on Cambodia's behalf in a summit conference of the Indochinese communist administrations and insurgent groups at a venue in southern China during 1970. This meeting was also Chou's work, intended to fortify the impression of Chinese support for the war against the Americans. Chou was supposed to understand the realities of class struggle; he failed to see that the Cambodian communists would not tolerate Prince Sihanouk's influence once they had won power. Sihanouk simply disappeared in 1975, and the Vietnamese communists were the dominant force throughout Indochina. Communist Vietnam looked to the Kremlin and to its satellites for material support and took a decidedly unsympathetic attitude towards Chinese diplomatic sensitivities. Chou's Indochinese 1970 summit and his personal patronage of Sihanouk were wasted investments. Most important of all, the summit conference in

1972 with President Richard Nixon was an idea which Mao Tse-
tung claimed he had forced through against the advice of China's
Foreign Ministry whose master, in fact though not in name, was
Chou En-lai.

US Secretary of State, John Foster Dulles, refused to shake
Chou's hand at the 1954 Geneva Conference to end the first
Indochina war. The American Secretary of State was a boor on
this occasion. But he could argue that lack of politeness had not
prevented him from achieving his objectives (with minor exceptions), namely the prevention of Soviet expansion without leading the United States into either a conventional or nuclear war.
Chou was polished and urbane, admired and applauded. Yet at
the end of his life, his diplomacy had failed to produce any
committed sympathisers in Asia other than Pakistan and Sri
Lanka. In Europe, China could regard only Albania as an ally.
In Africa, the closest admirers of China were the Tanzanians,
but they were certainly not lined up with the Chinese who had
built a showpiece railway for Tanzania. China's influence in the
Arab world and the American hemisphere was insignificant. No
peace treaty had been signed with Japan. Taiwan remained
unincorporated into the rest of China. The United States declined to accept the Chinese conviction that disarmament negotiations with the Soviet Union were a snare and delusion. A
million Russian troops remained on China's northern frontiers,
with many Soviet divisions within easy reach of the capital.

However, Chou En-lai could afford to ignore the disappointments of diplomacy as he contemplated his domestic coups. After
all, as each head rolled, metaphorically, Chou always came closer
to total power. Head of State Liu Shao-chi was a man of
considerable ability and a fair match for Chou, particularly as Liu
could count on the support of the gifted Teng Hsiao-ping, the
Communist Party's Secretary-General. Both Liu and Teng had a
vast array of officials right across China who looked upon the
pair as their patrons. Liu and Teng had a much wider circle of
grateful clients in the power apparatus than Chou, whose concern was with the central administration. Liu and Teng were
ruined at the start of the Cultural Revolution in 1966. Defence
Minister Lin Piao was elected secretly as official heir to Mao
Tse-tung in 1966, a post to which he was nominated formally in
1969. Lin also wanted to become Head of State which would

have made him Chou's master. Lin's death in 1971 meant only Mao Tse-tung could take Prime Minister Chou to task. True, such figures as Chu Teh, the nation's greatest military commander in modern times, could cut Chou down to size with no great difficulty. These heroic names, nevertheless, were for the most part rare and too old to find the energy for political in-fighting or else they were admirers of the Prime Minister.

Very wisely, Chou packed all major official positions in his gift with men whose careers had been built up through Chou's backing or who had been selected or approved for preferment by the Prime Minister. Even the "gang of four's" Chang Chun-chiao, boss of the Shanghai administration and viewed overwhelmingly (but not by Chou) as too radical in outlook to suit the Premier, had explained in 1967 the trust and reliance he reposed in the Prime Minister. No particular difficulty arose in 1974 when Chou went through the list of candidates to be announced as deputy premiers in January the following year and found Chang's name included. The Premier could employ a man with the Shanghai leader's adroitness and cool head. By 1975, China had two masters, Chairman Mao and Premier Chou. Adulation belonged to Mao, though more as a matter of form than fervour. Admiration belonged to Chou, mostly because he radiated reassurance that the country was on the threshold of a new and better era. To have climbed on to a pinnacle equal in eminence to that on which Mao reclined was all the more astonishing since the Prime Minister's ascent was not the product of the kind of massive personality cult which had made Mao into a colossus. Chou En-lai was the final foe within the Maoist fortress, whom Mao himself had long feared and whose glories rioters proclaimed during urban upheavals in April 1976.

CHAPTER THREE

THE DESTRUCTION OF THE COMMUNIST PARTY

THE SLIDE FROM greatness began for Mao Tse-tung in 1966, a year in which his words, thoughts and deeds became the objects of almost religious veneration. To his slogans were ascribed by the news media miraculous powers which could only be believed through a sublime act of faith. Not given as a society to formal religions, the Chinese found the prescribed rituals for invocation of Chairman Mao's name and veneration for quotations from his works not much to their taste. Steps were taken by wilier spirits to cope with meetings during which tests of individuals' familiarity with Mao Tse-tung Thought were on the agenda. Everyone was allotted in advance a definite chair and hence a particular verse from Mao to recite by heart. This practice was now being condemned. The attitude which it indicated was of ancient origin. Chinese are said to be by tradition largely Confucians and to engage universally in ancestor worship. However, Chinese have never made a deity out of the very human philosopher, Confucius; nor have they imagined their dead grandfathers and more distant ancestors to be gods. China has built a society which has survived so much of human history that a solid practicality underpins the nation's general attitude to the lives of the renowned and humble alike, and the tendency to indulge in fantasy gets short shrift.

The Mao personality cult was brought to an abrupt end by its own object who expressed his opinion that though politically useful in the consolidation of his political power, the cult had become tasteless if not empty rhetoric and ritual. The steps Mao Tse-tung took at the end of 1970 to curtail the extravagant public respect showered on him came too late. The stream of accounts of cures from acute medical conditions, of passionate heroism, of scientific discoveries and of prodigious courage and morality inspired by Mao Tse-tung Thought had taken on overtones of pious parody if not direct satire. If the official press and radio from 1966 to 1969 were taken at their literal word, mankind knew no woes which the correct application of Mao Thought could not cure. Since the peasants in particular, but workers and bureaucrats as well, had to be lectured frequently for flagrant neglect of Mao's directives during the most intense periods of his cult, a fair inference is that Mao Thought for many was an exhibition of respect for a myth rather than a man or, worse still, a matter of lip service not conviction. Mao himself observed that a third of those who hailed his name were hypocrites, while another third merely followed the fashion of the moment.

In 1966, Mao Tse-tung's principal concern was the lack of respect he enjoyed within the ranks of the Communist Party and officialdom. He had grown more and more perturbed since 1961 at what he perceived to be a drift toward Soviet-type policies in the conduct of the economy. This trend had begun in 1959, the first of three dreadful years during which natural calamities beset the country and the danger of famine stared a very hungry population in the face. To add to Peking's burdens, the Soviet Union, its principal trade partner and source of aid, had abrogated unilaterally its aid agreements during these three grim years. All Russian technical personnel were withdrawn and carefully took home blueprints, technical manuals and other data needed to complete unfinished projects and operate new plants. The pressure of the emergency was such that the Chinese Government followed Lenin's example when confronted by comparable disasters in the infant Soviet Union. Ideological principles could be sacrificed with impunity provided that the practical expedients adopted produced more grain and other necessities. Incentives came back into vogue, while the central administration demanded a high degree of discipline to minimise waste and to grasp the greatest possible control for Peking over the nation's resources.

These policies were a serious compromise with Maoist tenets and opened the door to imitation not just of Lenin but also of Khrushchev, the man China damned as the personification of the Kremlin's betrayal of true communism and its adoption of goulash and the knout as basic political principles. Mao Tse-tung backed the programme of grain and daily necessities at all costs, even jettisoning his basic precepts, at the height of the emergency. By 1962, China was past the worst, and the economy was on the road to recovery. Mao urged that the time had come to abandon the compromises born out of the direst needs and to abandon all imitations of the Soviet Union. He was paid scant heed.

If anything, more Soviet-type practices flourished unabated. A senior economist (Sun Yeh-fang, "China's Lieberman") called for the introduction of the same profit-based criteria recently adopted by the Russians to boost economic efficiency. Bureaucratic privilege and abuses were rampant. Industrial workers were subject to tight management though compensated with a rich variety of cash and other incentives. The peasants were allowed great latitude as to how they met their obligations under state economic plans and still greater scope to indulge their irrepressible taste for private enterprise activities in their free time. China seemed likely to go even further than the Soviet Union in tampering with the essentials of Marxism, as Mao Tse-tung viewed matters, and to become a second Yugoslavia, a nation so close to capitalism as to make no difference to the Maoist. This tendency is part of the explanation for the way in which China conducted much of its early debate with the Soviet Union in terms of violent attacks on the Yugoslavs.

The Cultural Revolution can be seen as a movement with almost as many origins and aims as there are commentators on the storms of 1966 to 1969. Given the vast panorama against which the campaign was waged and the enormous cast which took part in the drama, most of the very diverse interpretations have their uses because they capture certain aspects of the upheaval's tangled web of personalities and motives. The Cultural Revolution is thus in need of no detailed review here. Its importance in the account of Mao Tse-tung's ultimate fate lies first in Mao's own basic goal in encouraging the movement designed to destroy China's administrative machinery; and secondly in a handful of characters' reactions to various phases of the Cultural Revolution.

In 1966, Mao Tse-tung wanted power. This desire to control affairs was unusual. He had no ardent desire to run the Government. Routine administration held no attractions for him.

Marxist philosopher, elder statesman, mentor of the masses and guardian of the nation's political purity were his favourite occupations. Secondly, Mao Tse-tung had tried to convert the country's ruling elite to his views by conventional means on several occasions before 1966. Communist Party conferences, Central Committee meetings and debates, published essays and secret speeches had been his first weapons. He had made little headway. Thirdly, he had no desire to seize power for its own sake. His sole gratification was the opportunity he would obtain to divert China's communist administration back to a virtuous course safely removed from the wiles of Russian revisionism.

The destruction of the country's administration, both state and Party, which was Mao Tse-tung's first clarion call was not a simple strategem. Quite the oppos te. The onslaught launched against every form of authority oiather than tht of Mao's own name illustrates a key feature of Chinese political life. The campaigns which punctuate each year as predictably as the change in seasons are exercises designed to reap the maximum profits for those who mastermind them. The Cultural Revolution was no exception. The downfall of as many officials of any significance as could be accomplished by all means short of murder was a short cut to mass popularity. The Chinese bureaucrat is a creature of tradition who frequently behaved after 1949 with as little respect for the public as his predecessors in the imperial mandarinate. Officials remained more often feared and resented than respected in Mao's China. The overthrow of those who had used their offices arrogantly was a goal to which the Chinese masses would rally with glee. The disgrace of a sizable proportion of the bureaucracy also meant a reduction in the country's administrative overheads, a long-cherished ideal for Mao Tse-tung.

Next, for ordinary citizens to cross-examine, criticise and decide the fate of their former official overlords was an introduction to democracy of a most basic and rare order. Mao hoped that the experience of airing grievances and reviewing bureaucratic records would be so traumatic for his people that the sort of repressive elitism tolerated by the Russians would become anathema to the Chinese. Widespread plucking out of men in power also meant that those engaged in the pro-Soviet conspiracy against the Chinese version of Marxism could be swept out of the

Communist Party and the Government. Their removal would put an immediate halt to the anti-Maoist policies they had espoused or implemented. Furthermore, the inefficient leaders, the failures and those promoted beyond their capacities could be weeded out with considerable benefit to the future administrative system. A savage jolt to the bureaucracy would weaken attachment to conventions and precedents; undermine vested interests and cliques within the power structure; and allow novel experiments to be tested as substitutes for more orthodox administrative structures. Mao Tse-tung would be rid of men he disliked or distrusted and at liberty to insist that his ideas prevail in shaping policies and programmes for the future.

Mao Tse-tung's appeal for mass criticism of the leadership was popular enough in 1966 but gave no guarantee of success in overcoming his opponents within the elite. This group did not take long to realise they were in danger of losing their jobs and that few had any hope of making a deal with Mao and switching to his side. Men such as Head of State Liu Shao-chi and Party Secretary-General Teng Hsiao-ping had not risen to the top without learning how to destroy their rivals. From 1962 onwards, they had refused to bow to the spirit of Mao Tse-tung's directives and had not hesitated to alter even the letter of Mao's instructions in the pre-1966 Socialist Education Movement. They were unlikely to capitulate meekly in 1966. However, Mao Tse-tung had one prime advantage in dealing with these two figures in particular. They had been entrusted with abolition of rural abuses which both the peasants and village administrators exploited for personal gain. The drive was called the Socialist Education Movement (and sometimes the "Four Cleans"). Liu especially bungled badly. Minor officials were dealt with far too harshly, arousing their resentment. Not enough attention was given to convincing the peasants that they ought not to tolerate bribery, petty intimidation by officials, illegal profit-making enterprises run by individuals and such social ills as arranged marriages tied to the feudalistic dowry system. Despite their heavy-handed tactics, Liu and Teng had not established new moral standards in the countryside with its 650 million inhabitants. The pair were vulnerable on an impartial scrutiny of their performance in the massive, peasant, agricultural sector.

Logic is not the most cogent ingredient in political struggles;

a rational argument is often the least persuasive. To back an assault on this pair, as well as others earmarked for denunciation, Mao Tse-tung expected to be able to move from criticism based on factual analysis to the psychological disintegration of a host of individuals as men able to function in the political arena. Mao banned physical extermination of his enemies; he had no qualms about their mental destruction. Many critics of the Cultural Revolution insist that the humiliation heaped on officials, often after physical abuse and considerable intimidation by unruly mobs, left scars from which they could never hope to recover and that their treatment was more cruel than any physical punishment. The local news media in every part of China have referred repeatedly since 1969 to the timidity of officials; to their fear of being subject to the same sanctions as they endured in the Cultural Revolution; and to their desperate anxiety, in consequence, to avoid taking responsibility for the conduct of affairs.

This topic is raised because of a document released as part of the dossier to show that Lin Piao, Defence Minister until killed in a 1971 air crash, had plotted to murder Chairman Mao Tse-tung to whom Lin Piao was official heir. The document claimed that Mao drove his aides, members of his family and adversaries to the verge of mental breakdown. One facet of Mao's private character was the enormous emotional force he radiated in personal encounters. Few could escape being overwhelmed by Mao's personality, as records of closed Communist Party meetings, for example, reveal. His total domination of the proceedings flowed from a mixture of candour, ability to play with different moods and the vehemence of his rage — crushing in its force by the care with which it was steered towards particular targets. Small wonder that nearly all the top Party leaders were persuaded at some time or another to make damaging self-criticism before their colleagues after they found themselves in conflict with Mao.

Mao Tse-tung demanded in 1966 that the masses be unleashed by the million and given control of schools, colleges, offices, factories and other institutions with no concern for the danger of anarchy or disruption. He appears to have assumed that these moves would encounter stubborn resistance from the Communist Party elite, and a brutal verbal and emotional confrontation would ensue. On past performance, Mao would emerge the victor if only by a small margin. The more vitriolic the debate, the more crippled he would leave the opposition's leaders and the less able they would be to undertake any future burdens of responsibility. Within Chinese family and working environments organised on hierarchical lines, similar confrontations between elder and younger generations or seniors and subordinates may be observed. But Mao's style involved, seemingly, more than appeals for the deference due to rank or age.

Mao Tse-tung had a gift for calculating how to strike down an antagonist during some encounter so as to leave him derelict, bereft of friends even amongst his natural allies. The opponent felt isolated from the rest of the group, a rejected minority of one; and then he could be smothered by Mao's pent-up hostility. The end of a confrontation saw humiliated individuals totally bested by Mao in debate and forced to swallow whatever unflattering descriptions Mao chose to hurl. The classic example of Mao's strategy was the 1959 Lushan Party Conference where Defence Minister Peng Teh-huai began a criticism of Mao's policies with a massive display of courage and integrity. By the close of the meeting, Peng had been dismissed and was glad to have an opportunity to write his own confession.

The Cultural Revolution of 1966 was a unique event. Never before had the leader of a ruling Communist Party dared to smash the Party machine and seek to make popular adulation his power base. The personality of Mao Tse-tung, who had conceived this plan, was no less peculiar. Mao's zeal for apparently unlimited political and social destruction to allow him to start the construction of a new China was viewed with alarm by the bulk of the current power-holders. The first moves to launch the Cultural Revolution had come in late 1965 and ran into immediate resistance. Strenuous opposition had gathered by early 1966 to Mao's vision of a nation controlled by its masses and in which its leaders would be compelled to accept public scrutiny of their performances and accept abject humiliation if the crowds so decreed. Party bosses fought hard to thwart Mao's grand design. The mass media in the capital, for instance, gave as little coverage as they dared to the new Mao campaign. Head of State Liu Shao-chi struggled to divert the Cultural Revolution away from its goal of mobilisation of the nation en masse and to keep it under some measure of orderly control through his Party functionaries. Local Party leaders could afford to challenge the Cultural Revolution more brutally than their Peking counterparts who had to meet Mao's wrath face-to-face.

At the same time, some leaders, notably the Chou En-lai club, had calculated that Mao must win the 1966 struggle. They declined to oppose him and his inevitable victory. The Communist Party and the Government broke up into rival camps, which eased Mao's task in seizing domination of the Chinese political scene.

To conquer his adversaries, Mao Tse-tung had to be sure of a face-to-face encounter. Otherwise, his ability to dominate the Party leadership could not be exercised. The tribute paid by the Lin Piao dossier (the "571" documents as they have been called) to Mao's capacity to take virtual possession of his foes' minds also made a mention of his ability to manipulate events to his maximum advantage. Head of State Liu Shao-chi was the foremost personality on the 1966 list of those to be purged and awoke to this reality. Liu decided to outmanoeuvre Mao by convening a meeting of the Central Committee in accordance with Communist Party rules for a date on which Mao and the bulk of his supporters would be absent from the capital and unable to return to Peking in time.

Mao Tse-tung at this juncture miscalculated badly and became a hostage to Defence Minister Lin Piao. The Party Central Committee split in a big way, and a high percentage of its membership faced merciless ruin; a real danger existed of armed resistance by Mao's opponents. The country was brought to the brink of civil war. Army commanders sympathetic to the two rival groups in the Central Committee began to march on the capital. Mao gave himself over to Defence Minister Lin Piao in the belief that Lin could deliver the military strength needed to crush any attempt to thwart Mao's will. Mao was to regret later that he had left himself at Lin's mercy. Lin was to prove the block on which Mao Tse-tung would stumble and on which Chou En-lai would erect his political bastion.

Mao Tse-tung's decision to rely on the armed forces was peculiar. It betrayed an unusual loss of nerve and also a gross misreading of a key personality in the drama. He normally thrived on the tension of crises. In 1959, Mao had been faced with a recalcitrant Defence Minister whose popularity with the troops was of sufficient dimensions to raise the spectre of an army mutiny. Mao's response was such lofty contempt for the prowess of the country's generals that the threat of mass insubordination disappeared instantly. Mao said that if the troops rejected their duty and refused to obey him as Communist Party Chairman, he would happily return to his old guerilla fastness and raise a new revolutionary army and capture Peking for the second time in his life. In 1966, Mao demonstrated no such disdain for the power of the gun as divisions were mobilised to defend those bent on holding a Central Committee meeting in his absence at which he would be stripped of his Party posts. He lost control of the situation and allowed Lin Piao to mobilise troops to intervene.

Less damaging in the long run but harder to comprehend was Mao's ignorance of Teng Hsiao-ping's character. As Party Secretary General, Teng was the key to the quarrel over the meeting's date.

Teng must have known how Mao nursed a grudge against him for he had long spurned the custom of paying court to Mao as the nation's elder statesman. However, Teng Hsiao-ping had been a general in the People's Liberation Army with a distinguished combat record, a life-long Party member and the only man in China to have been Acting Premier when Chou En-lai had been abroad. Civil war was the last sort of betrayal a man such as Teng could contemplate. Teng had a moral integrity which would shame most politicians. The record shows how Teng decided that Mao Tse-tung was entitled to his chance to get to Peking and participate in the vital meeting. The crisis was over. The troops returned to their barracks. Mao won a bare majority in the Central Committee. Teng went into disgrace as the price of his virtue along with Head of State Liu Shao-chi. Teng Hsiao-ping went into the political wilderness neither dishonoured nor crushed. He had followed the tradition of famous Chinese officials who did not hesitate to defy the imperial will to carry out their duties honestly. Such historical personages have become folk heroes. One of them, Hai Jai, had been made the hero of a play designed to satirise Mao Tse-tung. The Maoist counter-blast to this drama in November 1965 marked the first public broadside in the campaign which the next year became known as the Great Proletarian Cultural Revolution.

Lin Piao was now the dominant figure on the scene. He was a remarkable man despite his absurd appearance. Although Lin perceived Mao Tse-tung's ability to crush mentally and emotionally his opponents, Mao seemed unsure of his own capacity to control Lin Piao. Perhaps Mao Tse-tung was assessed with such cool objectivity by Lin Piao that the latter was able to counter Mao's dominance and even to unnerve him. It was hard for Mao Tse-tung to reverse the situation and cow Lin Piao since Mao seems not to have invested much effort in a detached analysis of the other man's character. Mao had seen no reason to perform such an exercise, although he had certain misgivings about the Defence Minister. Nevertheless, Lin cultivated a reassuring image of utter dedication to Mao and his teachings.

In his role of Minister of Defence, Lin Piao had made the army adopt a book of quotations from Mao's writings as its spiritual drill manual. The Mao personality cult began in the army and was spread by Lin on the eve of the Cultural Revolution to the population at large. A campaign was launched to get the civilians to model themselves on the troops. This movement to learn from the army also offered a plausible excuse for infiltrating into government departments and official posts a large number of military personnel. Not until too late, after the Cultural Revolution had started, did Mao Tse-tung appear to realise he had to live with two quite different versions of Lin Piao. Lin seemed Mao's most dedicated vassal; yet Mao was suddenly no longer wholly convinced by Lin. The single-minded, Maoist, professional soldier turned out in 1966 to have an intellect of his own which was far from simple.

Mao grew uneasy at Lin Piao's special study of violent power seizures and at a 1966 lecture in which Lin had expounded how much of Chinese history was a chain of coups against the central government. Mao was very sensitive on this score. For some still unexplained reason, the 1956 uprising in Hungary became a Maoist nightmare. A host of articles at the start of the Cultural Revolution warned that Mao and his supporters were resisting elements allegedly anxious to imitate the Hungarian uprising. The same argument was resurrected in April 1976 after riots in several Chinese cities. In the wake of Khrushchev's secret 1956 speech retailing the crimes of Stalin, unrest and disorders were not confined to Eastern Europe. As Mao related in 1957, China

too had experienced unrest, though on a minor scale. Yet somehow, Mao Tse-tung seemed to interpret Hungary's 1956 overthrow of its communist masters as awesome testimony to the
fragility of a communist party's hold over the minds of its
subjects.

Lin Piao apparently knew that his discussion of power seizures
would disturb Mao Tse-tung but he was not deterred. Lin
seemingly wanted to distress Mao. A remarkable side to the Lin
Piao documents analysing Mao's power to drive men mad was
the cold assessment of Mao. Lin reduced him to clinical terms
and seemed to have hit upon a formula for dealing with a man
whom Lin regarded as far from normal. One technique, seemingly, was to play upon Mao's fear of being overthrown by force.
Another was to pander to what Lin regarded as overweening
vanity. (Mao was inordinately sensitive to criticism and probably
more insecure than vain; hence Mao's bouts of self-deprecation
recorded in various secret speeches and confidential political
writings.) Fortunately for Lin, good soldiers will parrot with
every sign of enthusiasm almost any set of slogans or extracts
from the official manuals if drilled by seasoned platoon commanders. Lin Piao was able to point to the armed forces as
testimony to his devotion as they were models of fervent flattery
of Mao Tse-tung Thought. Finally, Lin Piao adopted a posture
of extreme personal humility towards Mao and avoided scrupulously ever being seen to differ from Mao Tse-tung. Such were
his tactics, at the outset at any rate. Lin Piao, in short, had put
Mao Tse-tung in the category of an emotional invalid whose
main needs were to be humoured, reassured, applauded and yet
kept under control with the occasional deliberate inflammation
of Mao's suffocating political anxieties.

Lin Piao was a brilliant soldier but a limited politician. He
was no great success as an amateur psychiatrist. His humility
soon degenerated into a sort of servility so repulsive to any on-
looker, to say nothing of Mao himself who knew how to discount
adulation, that it actually aroused suspicion instead of providing
a constant assurance of utter fidelity. In addition, Lin Piao simply
proved incapable of dominating environments where the military
chain of command no longer operated. He was soon revealed
as unable to rely even on the armed forces to carry out the task
for which they were to have been trained before 1966: acting as

the standard bearers in the creation of a new Maoist China.

However, Lin Piao was not without an understanding of politics. Unlike Mao Tse-tung, Lin realised that administration is a skill which cannot be left to amateurs or haphazard, make-shift arrangements dreamt up by the most influential demagogue of the day posing as a representative of the masses. Mao conti-nually weakened his own position by a refusal to recognise that politics can be split into two parts. First come the ideas, goals, criteria and the philosophising. A brilliant mind can produce a wealth of new concepts and grand designs based on a realistic appraisal of national needs and available resources. But all will remain sterile theory until drafted into an action programme which can be turned over to professional administrators to be implemented. The most lucid and compelling political essay is verbiage until fed into a government machine geared to translate theory into practice. Since Mao disliked bureaucrats and felt the masses had unlimited talent when made responsible for running their own affairs, he never took sufficient care to see that his Thought was reinforced by the administrative machinery requir-ed to make official policies truly reflective of Mao's own teachings. His writings often hinted at an astonishment on his part that the logical force of what he prescribed for China had not led to the instant adoption of his proposals.

Since Mao Tse-tung had retired from the Government (as opposed to the Communist Party) in December 1958, he could afford to produce the theory and let others worry about practi-calities. The Cultural Revolution, however, was a denunciation of the administration for not having applied Maoism to every aspect of its work and an attempt to dispense with normal government procedures. Bored by the trivia of running the central Government, Mao had small right to complain that his influence was not manifest in the bureaucratic establishment. But complain with great bitterness Mao Tse-tung did, both as he prepared for the Cultural Revolution and after he launched the campaign.

Lin Piao's shrewdness in establishing a Maoist camouflage for the armed forces before 1966 and his care in preventing the breakdown of the military Communist Party apparatus were indications that he foresaw an administrative vacuum if Mao's Cultural Revolution managed to wreck the civilian Party and government structures. Into this no-man's-land, Lin Piao hoped to lead his troops.

But both Mao Tse-tung and Lin Piao had overlooked Prime Minister Chou En-lai. He had no reason to love Mao, for Chou had been forced to step down as Party leader and to play second fiddle to Mao ever after. The People's Liberation Army was Chou's creation; the propaganda machine claimed otherwise until after Mao's death. Chou could live with Mao despite these ancient defeats. Mao was a creative ideologist; Chou had no interest in ideological speculation. Mao abhorred administration; Chou thrived on making the Government tick like clockwork. He possessed an insatiable appetite for the minutiae of files and official routines. At formal banquets, Chou was often observed ignoring the food; a file on his knees, he literally corrected commas on one document after the other.

CHAPTER FOUR

CHOU EN-LAI'S STRUGGLE FOR SURVIVAL

AS LONG AS Mao Tse-tung left the job of keeping the central Government in business to Chou En-lai, the Prime Minister was quite satisfied. He would take his policy speeches for insertions and deletions in Mao's own hand. He was always deferential towards Mao but never fawned in public. As both men aged, Chou found the strain of pacifying a querulous Mao an ordeal. Mao's irritability could be mollified only by a stream of humble chatter, and Mao could frequently be induced by his Premier to endorse policies and directives only by lavish application of flattery. This relationship Chou kept very private. He might not be able to conceal his disagreement with Mao at a meeting. But Mao could count on Chou's vote. During the Cultural Revolution, Chou never voted against Mao at any of the tempestuous Politburo or Party Central Committee meetings. Chou's open differences with Mao were not concerned with principles but reflected the fears of Chou's ministerial minions that they could not cope with the practical problems of some proposal Mao was pushing. When Mao reached out in 1966 to destroy the administration, he had strayed into a world which Chou regarded as uniquely his own. Worse still, Chou's only usefulness was as a superb bureaucrat. Without a bureaucracy, Chou was not worth his salary.

Every fresh step towards less formal or orthodox methods of administration made Premier Chou En-lai increasingly dispensable. The steadier the drift towards anarchy, the more redundant Chou became and the more apparent that no central Government was functioning. Unlike the more faceless bureaucrats, Premier Chou could not drop discreetly out of sight and wait for the inevitable counter-reaction to the mounting tide of chaos and indiscriminate crime and violence. Nor was Chou as

strongly placed as humbler members of the official machines.
They had personal ties with the men who led the crowds to
besiege government offices. These links were based, in many
cases, on years of benevolent patronage and a calculated distribution of favours. Many rioters, if not the majority, were indebted to a petty Party or government mandarin for some past act
of friendship especially at village or municipal neighbourhood
level. For once, the advantages lay with the humble and lowly
for they could identify more easily with excited mobs intent on
seizing control in the names of Mao and the masses; they also
had clients in their debt.

Chou En-lai's personal popularity was also in jeopardy. He
lacked the network of local appointees and protégés which Party
Secretary-General Teng Hsiao-ping had built up over the years
by adroit exploitation of the Central Committee's right to
nominate Party office-bearers at all levels. In practice, Teng
had a veto over minor functionaries, and his approval was
essential for nominations to the more senior posts in the Party
hierarchy. Chou's network depended on the links and associations of his ministers and their senior subordinates in Peking's
central government offices. He had allies and admirers throughout the elite and among intellectuals; unfortunately most of
these were hard pressed by their own battles to stay alive
politically. He had also become a complete civilian. He lacked
the protection that his military record might otherwise have
lent him. Former Commander-in-Chief of the armed forces Chu
Teh, for instance, had no difficulty as a legendary soldier in
coping with hordes of vitriolic critics in the Cultural Revolution
who suspected correctly that he viewed Mao in very human
terms. The army let the word get about that any Peking crowd
which fancied a tilt at the aged warrior would find themselves
jousting with the sharp end of bayonets commanded by Chu's
old comrades. This friendly advice was taken literally, and criticism of Chu Teh remained verbal and he escaped the public
humiliation and physical indignities many were anxious to
inflict on the proud old man known as "the warlord."

Chou En-lai could not switch to the extremist side and
support the assaults on officialdom as did other personalities
with various degrees of success when they donned Maoist
uniforms. To abandon the bureaucrats in the front line of the

official positions under siege in Mao's name would have amounted to Chou's abdication of all control over events and deprived him of the only group on whose support he could rely absolutely, since their fate and his fortunes were inextricably linked. A brief glance at the way Chou En-lai solved the immediate crisis of personal survival reveals a great deal about his character and style.

The Prime Minister could not hope to buy his way out of trouble and throw all and sundry among the most prominent administrators to the wolves baying for blood in the capital. Yet he dared not condemn the selection of some scapegoats to appease the mobs. The choice demanded superb judgment. The case of Foreign Minister Chen Yi was a perfect illustration of Chou's approach. The Foreign Minister was another hardened veteran of the revolutionary wars, still held in the highest respect by the troops and the officer corps. He hailed from Szechwan, whose pride and joy he was, an affection he reciprocated towards the 90 million inhabitants of the country's largest province and China's "rice bowl." Others beside the peasants felt deeply attached to him. He had proved to Shanghai, the nation's largest, most sophisticated and industrialised city with an urban population of over five million, that the Communist Party was not made up of ogres. As Mayor from 1949 to 1958, he had won the trust and cooperation of the Shanghainese who remembered him with esteem even after he was promoted to Foreign Minister. In addition, Chen Yi prevented the outside world in 1966 from dismissing China as gripped by some national insanity. Foreign diplomats, their families and embassy buildings were attacked with a savagery which suggested the Peking mobs viewed diplomatic missions as the outposts of alien invaders. Chen Yi managed to convey to the foreign diplomatic community his deep revulsion at the refusal of his countrymen and their temporary leaders to observe the minimal obligations of international law, to say nothing of ordinary diplomatic courtesies.

The wilder revolutionaries wanted Chen Yi's head. The protocol and privileges attached to the conduct of relations between sovereign states were grotesquely capitalist in the extremists' eyes. The Foreign Ministry was also a prize worth its capture, an official department whose business was transacted with a secrecy only marginally less than that of the defence establishment to which it was closely related. No great effort is required to surmise why, too, Defence Minister Lin Piao or his cronies would want to see the conquest of the Foreign Ministry. In any debate over China's military strategy, the defence experts' views could not count on unconditional acceptance; foreign affairs specialists also had opinions which would not automatically dovetail with those of the High Command.

Most important of all, perhaps, was Chen Yi's refusal to treat the wild men of 1966 and 1967 with the awed reverence they aroused in other targets of their riotous criticism. Chen Yi derided them; mocked their Maoist credentials; and refused to keep silent when disgraced colleagues from the Party Central Committee were falsely accused. Chen Yi's personal courage and sense of honourable conduct were dangerous; other officials might imitate his example. Half the fun of the first two years of the Cultural Revolution was the manner in which men of distinguished and unblemished records were compelled to indulge unresistingly in self-abasement and self-condemnation, for almost any imaginable and imaginary crime, by the climate of fear and swelling tumult, often when confronted by mere youths. Chen Yi's recalcitrance was an insult to Mao's Red Guards and their adult counterparts. In addition, he was a senior member of the Chou En-lai clique. A grovelling confession from the Foreign Minister was a vital step towards making the Premier's position untenable. And Chou En-lai did not lack for enemies in the extremist proletarian climate of 1966 and 1967 on account of his polish and air of impeccable breeding. He had political rivals as well.

Whatever Chou En-lai's personal belief in Chen Yi's merits as Foreign Minister, an office whose principal responsibilities the Premier consistently declined to delegate, Chou was stuck with the old soldier from Szechwan. The demands for his dismissal had to be resisted. Chou could not afford to lose the indirect support which Chen Yi rallied to the Prime Minister from so many important groups: the army, Shanghai and Szechwan itself. Furthermore, Chen Yi's outrageous jokes at the expense of the Maoists seemed to appeal to Mao Tse-tung himself. Eventually, the Red Guards demanded Chen Yi's head, and physical confrontations between the Foreign Minister and the mobs became unavoidable. As the pressure mounted for a purge of Chen Yi in 1967, a desperate rescue operation was mounted. Mao's wife, Chiang Ching, and Mao's political confessor, Chen Po-ta, a prominent ideologue and editor of the Party's theoretical publication, *Red Flag*, were called out to snatch Chen Yi from the political cannibals.

Chen Po-ta's remarks to the extremists are of some significance. Chou En-lai had not tried to defend Chen Yi, said Chen Po-ta. Chou En-lai was not to be attacked, therefore, on charges of seeking to conceal an anti-Maoist from the masses' wrath. He, Chen Po-ta, had been the Foreign Minister's shield and was willing to be examined as to his Maoist credentials, an offer with which the youthful mob very wisely declined to close. They had to taste a little blood, nonetheless, and an urbane senior diplomatic official of gentlemanly bearing, Chiao Kuan-hua, found himself among their prey for a spell. Chiao was compensated subsequently by his appointment in January 1975 as Foreign Minister. Chiao was close enough to Chou En-lai. Mao Tse-tung had commented once that Chiao Kuan-hua's role in life was drafting the Prime Minister's speeches. Chou could have sent him out of harm's way on a mission overseas. The Premier decided, instead, Chiao was more useful to him under fire at home in Peking. Chiao did not escape from the Red Guard attacks until 1968. Fate proved unkind to him, however, for he fell into disgrace once more in 1976, this time for his links with Mao's widow, Chiang Ching, the extremists' heroine in 1967. This shift in fortunes is an illustration of the political ebbs and flows which carried individuals from one group in the Party Central Committee to another, a striking characteristic of Peking politics. Chen Yi had died in the meantime of cancer aggravated, according to popular belief, by the energy drained out of him in resisting the extremists.

Chen Po-ta explained why Premier Chou En-lai was to be guarded even more closely from mob attacks than Foreign Minister Chen Yi. Through Chen Po-ta's comments about the Prime Minister to the Red Guards, another aspect of Chou's style came to the fore. Chen Po-ta observed that the Premier served Mao Tse-tung and the Central Committee well, a claim which could have been made on behalf of almost everyone hurled into disgrace during this period. Furthermore, Chen Po-ta asserted, Chou was important to China's international prestige as he was highly regarded overseas. Chou En-lai throughout his career always found time to meet even obscure foreign visitors as well as the world's notables on pilgrimage to Peking. Chou cannot be depicted as intellectually curious about foreign nations or to have felt the same fascination for them as Mao Tse-tung (who even wanted one African visitor to explain how skin colour varied from one part of the continent to another). Chou En-lai's accessibility to visitors from abroad was tactical; receptions of foreigners were newsworthy both inside China and out. By 1966, Chou's lack of a string of foreign triumphs to justify his diplomatic role had not prevented him from becoming synonymous with the civilised face which Chinese communism wanted to present to the outside world.

Why did this attribute, carefully cultivated by the Prime Minister, weigh so heavily when Peking mobs were treating foreign diplomatic staff as badly as China's own Head of State, Liu Shao-chi? Chinese missions abroad seemed to make their first duty the conversion of their embassies into fortresses from which Maoist storm-troopers could sally forth to entertain the residents of such diverse cities as London, New Delhi and Djakarta with a taste of the excitement raging in the Chinese capital. Mao's followers were not much concerned about alien attitudes towards China. Mao, however, was. His wife explained, for instance, that the reproduction of Mao Tse-tung's image (by the million everywhere as statues, portraits, busts and badges) must be handled with care. Reverence towards her husband was not her anxiety but the need to ensure that tasteless or unartistic images of Mao did not cause him and the country ridicule overseas. Thus, a combination of Mao's sensitivity to international opinion and the willingness of his wife and of such a figure as Chen Po-ta to speak up for Chou won him a breathing space. His assiduous cultivation of a diplomatic posture had bought him time during a period when events moved so fast that popular heroes were created and ejected from grace with astonishing speed. (Chen Po-ta went into utter disgrace four years later with no kind words on his behalf, as far as is known, from Chou.)

The suggestion that, in China, Chou En-lai was not the object of the same admiration in 1966 and subsequent years as he enjoyed abroad is sufficiently peculiar to warrant further elaboration. The largest test of his abilities in 1967 was an army mutiny at Wuhan, a modern industrial centre and a key link between north and south China. Its 3.5 million inhabitants have to survive a summer of almost unbearable heat. Wuhan is thus known as one of China's "ovens," not inappropriately, since the climate was disregarded in choosing the city as an ideal location for iron and steel plants. While the physical and political temperatures rose during the summer of 1967, the garrison's patience wore thin with a rabble led by demagogues who wanted to control Wuhan. The local commander mobilised extensive support from the work force, and the city was taken over by the army and its civilian allies. Peking could not tolerate open mutiny by the soldiers.

The Maoist insistence that the Chinese nation as a whole had "the right to rebel" while demanding at the same time solid discipline from the troops had a rational explanation. The masses were Mao's divisions; he believed in their virtue and in the merits of the rough democracy they adopted. The soldiers were under Lin Piao's command. They had to be kept under the Defence Minister's tight control against the day when the armed forces would be the only organisation still intact and capable of occupying politically the scorched earth which the swing to anarchy would produce, or so Lin Piao believed. He would have the country's destiny, at that point, entirely in his hands. The Wuhan rebels had to be crushed with the utmost rigour. Gunboats were sent up the Yangtze River, just as Britain would have done before 1949 on the outbreak of a similar insurrection in a major Chinese city. This Victorian reaction was reinforced with the more modern paratrooper, and airborne units were flown in. Yet the first attempt to resolve the Wuhan scandal was typically Maoist: personal negotiations between Peking's representatives and the mutiny's leaders and a bid to persuade them to board a plane for the capital.

Wuhan and its garrison were not in a Maoist frame of mind. The two emissaries from the Party Central Committee were Public Security Minister Hsieh Fu-chi and a propaganda official and prominent extremist, Wang Li. Peking's plenipotentiaries were treated with the same scant ceremony as foreign ambassadors in the capital. They were summarily arrested; beaten up;

held in custody; and had to listen to crowds demanding they be dispatched to a better world. Chou En-lai had begun to adopt the role of mediator and trouble-shooter for the central Government when warring factions refused to be reconciled and give up violence. The Premier, with considerable aplomb, caught a plane to Wuhan to negotiate the rescue of the two captives (one of them the country's top policeman).

The news of Chou's impending arrival stirred Wuhan to renewed activity, and the city readied itself to put Chou En-lai under lock and key. Because not all the units in the Wuhan area had joined the insurrection, Chou En-lai's pilot was tipped off in time to make an unscheduled landing at an alternative airfield. The Prime Minister was able to elude his would-be captors and enter Wuhan safely. Once physically in contact with the rebels, Chou's talent for radiating charm and persuasiveness, which could verge on the hypnotic, was employed to the full. The Wuhan commander meekly boarded a plane for Peking and wrote a self-criticism. Mao Tse-tung, seemingly, intervened to save him from the conventional penalty for mutiny. The Wuhan incident demonstrated that the Peking mobs who tried to capture Chou En-lai in his office were not simply worked into a frenzy by ambitious anti-Chou fanatics on the extreme left. Wuhan revealed Chou to be no more popular with the anti-extremist elements.

Certain other facets of Chou En-lai's behaviour deserve a mention during the greatest crisis of his career, a series of perils at least as menacing as any he had experienced physically or mentally during the Pacific War and the revolutionary campaigns before and after World War II. Kwangsi Region in southern China is dominated by a minority people. Its political elite was thoroughly mixed up in the less reputable battles for control of China which prevailed from 1911 to 1949. Most Chinese know very little about this remote area, other than its attractions for the privileged few as a vacation land of scenic delights and strange tribes. Kwangsi assumed a special importance in 1966 because, through it, ran the railway line which formed Hanoi's lifeline when North Vietnam came under intensified American military pressure in the last Indochina War. The railway carried both Soviet and Chinese supplies to feed, clothe and arm the North Vietnamese population and its troops in the field. During the Cultural Revolution, Kwangsi's wilder spirits judged their own needs to be at least as urgent as those of China's Vietnamese allies. Rival Kwangsi factions waylaid trains and stripped them of the arms and ammunition intended to enable Hanoi to defeat American armies. Chou En-lai had to solve this problem.

Moscow was outraged by the failure of supplies to arrive safely in North Vietnam; Peking was embarrassed at reports that not even relief for its gallant little neighbour defying the armed might of the United States was safe from the ravages of the Red Guards. Chou did not command arbitrarily that interference with the trains must cease forthwith. He did not use immediately army units to shoot down political bandits who were sabotaging both China and North Vietnam. He talked interminably with the Kwangsi faction leaders he had brought up to the capital. He wanted to win by persuasion because this tactic would win him Mao Tse-tung's general endorsement and, equally important, because he had no desire to extend Lin Piao's influence by calling on the Defence Ministry for soldiers to resolve Kwangsi's civil war. Very significantly, Chou was not foolish enough to try to issue imperious decrees or to use bluff or intimidation in dealing with the Kwangsi factions. Official commands were universally disregarded in China at the time. The fragility of a central leader's authority and the autonomy of local chieftains were facts of life beyond concealment. Chou did not fall into the trap of seeking to employ tactics doomed to failure. Chou needed successes to survive; hardly anyone was still around to listen to excuses for failure other than Mao Tse-tung and Lin Piao, neither of whom had any reason to mourn if yet another bureaucrat fell by the wayside and, in this instance, through his own incompetence. Kwangsi was handled gradually and gently until Chou felt he could insist on protection for trains without jeopardising his own position.

Not forgotten were the intellectuals. The average university was beyond protection. The vast academic establishment under the Chinese Academy of Sciences was a different matter. At the outset of the Cultural Revolution, Mao Tse-tung had instructed that among the angels were to be counted intellectuals with records to their credit of solid contributions to knowledge Chou En-lai employed this directive liberally to keep as undisturbed as possible the academic cloisters where Chinese nuclear, ion, space and electronic technology, to pick some random examples, flourished in well-equipped laboratories backed by libraries whose access to literature from any quarter of the globe was unrestricted. Because Chou was able to play the humble instrument of Mao's personal directive and save many academic luminaries, the Prime Minister kept the goodwill of the intellectuals. Even those mauled by sadistic marathon sessions of public criticism in the ordinary universities continued to draw their salaries wherever Chou's words still carried weight; and university teachers continued to have unrestricted liberty to read as their tastes dictated even if the state had to import expensive treatises to keep their intellects occupied after their summary ejection from the lecture halls.

Chou En-lai's toughest rearguard action was fought to retain a semblance of economic administration. The reasons for this dangerous display of interest in a side of national life under the fiercest scrutiny and criticism by the Maoists more than justified the risk of Chou being identified with industrial and agricultural policies over which a large number of leading administrators had already been broken. As a superb bureaucrat, Chou En-lai could not ignore the power which went to the man who controlled the nation's ledgers. No matter what the policy or programme and no matter how practically its implementation has been planned, its costs must be covered. The man who has a close grasp of the accounts is in a position to advise that a specific policy is laudable but too expensive. The same man also has a base from which to insist that some measure with which his colleagues disagree must be undertaken to ensure the resources they seek for their own pet projects. An official explaining how one sector is locked into other branches of the economy and who runs through the financial arithmetic of the national accounts and government budget may be advocating surreptitiously a great number of political commitments. Yet the dollars and cents recorded in a ledger are not easily used as a pointer to personal ideological loyalties, for public consumption at any rate. (In reality, a fair test of a government's real aims, rather than its promises, is the way in which it commits the funds and other resources at its disposal. Ledgers, nonetheless, are not the stuff of which political manifestos are fabricated.)

Hence, economic controls meant political influence for Chou En-lai in the future.

A second consideration was the state of the Chinese economy. With reasonable weather, the peasants had adequate surpluses to sell to the urban areas in return for manufactured goods of every kind. But industry was grinding to a halt. Incentives related to a factory worker's output were outlawed, ending the system which had prevailed since the early 1950s except for minor interruptions. The labour force had no financial inducement to ignore the excitement in the streets. Wages were paid whether workers reported for their shift or took the day off for political agitation. Normal management, work routines and production became virtually impossible in most urban workshops as factions swayed backwards and forwards in their struggle to win the power which would belong to whichever clique seized control of a factory. The Red Guard newspapers published detailed accounts of the good life enjoyed by national leaders before 1966 as well as current political scandals, which did not encourage individual industriousness.

The supply of factory products to the villages could not keep pace with demand under these conditions. The peasants were not prepared to feed out of charity the urban areas whose lawless ways the countryside refused adamantly to imitate except in the vicinity of cities and major towns. The Government was forced to pump an extra RMB 10,000 million into the peasant economy through adjusting prices to favour the farming community between 1966 and 1970. Since the total cash income distributed to the peasant population annually appears to be precisely this same sum, Peking was paying a high price to keep the peasants contented: an extra twenty per cent annually in rural purchasing power.

This state of affairs could not last indefinitely. Whoever won the battle for Peking would want to rule. The victorious faction would have to establish its credibility through putting the economy in order. By defending a skeleton economic administration, Chou En-lai was ensuring that he would be as indispensable as ever during the years ahead in running the central Government with little interest in what ideological line he was supposed to honour.

Another factor was the reality behind the threat of economic

disintegration. Factory workers distracted by factions on the
rampage and the removal of all symbols of management and
discipline from the workshop, combined with profit-minded
peasants, did not mean that the authorities could not get their
hands on any resources. A great number of factories were no
longer under central control which seriously affected the budget
since ninety per cent of state revenue at the end of the 1960s
came from profits and taxes paid over to the state by industrial
enterprises. But resources were still flowing to the central authorities. They needed administration. Their allocation could
bestow considerable influence on an economic overlord, especially when the volume of resources to be shared out had dropped
while pressure groups such as the peasants needed to be bought
off. Chou En-lai may not have started out the Cultural Revolution with large numbers in his debt. He was taking care not to
allow this sorry state of affairs to continue so long as he could
keep an economic administration together.

Finally, Chou En-lai was a dedicated man. He could have led
a far more comfortable life by devoting his considerable intelligence and magnetic charm to personal enrichment in his youth
as a capitalist. He lived instead in a world of war, of gross
physical discomfort as a guerilla; of intrigue and betrayal as the
Communist Party's negotiator with its adversaries. He had his
dreams: a vision of a modern, prosperous China equal in economic power to any state in the world. He could see the creation
of such a nation undertaken by a Leninist apparatus, ready to
regiment a society scarred by a century of foreign aggression,
peasant uprisings, warlords and natural disasters, a Leninist
machine designed to compel people to perform miracles to
achieve modernisation. Stalin had undertaken just such a task.
Mao Tse-tung had put his finger on the basic weakness of the
Stalinist system: its disregard for the need to win popular
cooperation for official plans especially from the peasants.
Stalin had been deceived, perhaps, by his own personality cult
into believing he was infallible. Chou had no personality cult,
and he had learnt humility the hard way. He had learnt to
swallow his pride for over a quarter of a century rather than
collide head-on with Mao Tse-tung.

Chou En-lai had seen since 1949 a host of mass campaigns
which a man of affairs might well regard as the sacrifice of even-

tual prosperity for a mess of political pottage. After every previous traumatic takeover by the ideologues, reality had reasserted itself; the technocrats had resumed control; reason had returned to the economy. The outstanding experience of this process of advance and defeat for the ideologues was the 1958 Great Leap Forward which could not be sustained the following year in the face of catastrophic natural disasters compounded by the dissolution of professional economic management. On past performance, the Cultural Revolution would end up no differently. Most strikingly, Mao Tse-tung himself had fought hard at an acrimonious Central Committee meeting in 1959 to save the reputation of the economic and financial ministers even to the point of exonerating them from responsibility for the excesses of the Great Leap Forward the previous year. Chou had good grounds for confidence that economic issues would be the top priority once the crowds grew bored with attacking bureaucrats and one another. He could also anticipate that, in the end, Mao would be forced to turn to the economic specialists under Chou's control as had happened in 1959.

These ideas which Chou En-lai entertained were quite obvious to any observer who stopped to inquire, for instance, why the banking system with the bulk of its staff came through the Cultural Revolution virtually unscathed. The bankers worked for Finance Minister Li Hsien-nien, a trusted member of the Chou brains trust. Li had stressed in the economic depression which followed the reversal of the Great Leap Forward that the banking system was the central authorities' watchdog over the entire economy, down to the remotest farm and tiniest factory. At some point, every individual and economic enterprise had to use cash. Currency could only be issued by the bank branches, which also had the right to freeze funds whenever any doubts arose over the propriety of the purpose for which they might be employed. The banks were empowered to restrict to very narrow confines cash payments by every type of enterprise and institution. Continuous monitoring of the flow of paper money and constant inspection of branch accounts gave the banking system an uninterrupted flow of data about the state of the economy; regional shortages and surpluses; loyalty to Peking's directives; and the likely extent of illegal factories, contracts and markets. The banking system could also be used to wipe out a local administration by freezing all its accounts.

Mao Tse-tung's opponents discovered this side of the coin in January and February 1967. The bankers backed the Maoist camp's drive to end the power struggle through a quick victory by confining the right to draw money from bank accounts to Mao's supporters. The chief features of banking and its personnel are that its criteria are conservative, disciplined, non-democratic and politically neutral; so that the system continues on much the same basis regardless of the ideological colour of its political masters. Li Hsien-nien and his banks were too vast an influence not to be kept going at all costs. Hence Chou's concern with their survival.

Chou En-lai's selection of who should be protected in the economic field was also telltale. Li Hsien-nien and his financial specialists were one category. Finance Minister Li was a national figure with connections throughout the army and the bureaucracy and was highly trusted by Mao Tse-tung. Yu Chiu-li, Minister of the Petroleum and Chemical Industries, was far more difficult to defend. Yu's approach to petrol production was as completely non-Maoist, so it was claimed, as could be imagined. Oil at any price and by any means was Yu's motto. The storm he aroused was monumental. But Chou En-lai went to extravagant lengths to ensure that Yu survived. Chou even brusquely told one forum eager to topple Yu that the Minister was far too engrossed in the solution of economic planning exercises to be distracted from his work for a single day. In the prevailing chaos, this assertion by Chou was a shameless lie but no one had the nerve to contradict the Premier. Yu was too busy, Chou insisted, to take time off to listen to the Maoist masses, a fair comment probably, but totally at odds with everything that Mao Tse-tung was preaching at the time. Chou even risked an open clash with Mao's wife, Chiang Ching, on the oil industry and its protection from Red Guard critics aware of its non-Maoist tendencies. Chou did not dare to lose Yu, not on account of his planning expertise but because of the oil industry's customers. Through Yu's success in chasing growth by every means, the Prime Minister could meet the armed forces' petrol needs and maintain a thrust in the petro-chemicals sector which contributes to almost every form of industrial activity—from the manufacture of weapons and fertilisers to the production of textiles and transistor radios. Petrol was a vital bargaining counter for the Prime Minister.

All the while, Chou En-lai never ceased to talk, to cajole, to bully and beg the leaders of provincial factions out of their violent frame of mind. The Premier visited them on their home ground or took them to the capital. The flow of words was remorseless as he tried to induce rival cliques to amalgamate and forego violence. He made himself the most accessible, visible and attentive of the Peking leadership and established a personal relationship with many of the country's most powerful local power groups. While his unremitting mediation to damp down violent disputes over the right to rule in many parts of China won Chou the reputation of a moderate and practical individual, the Prime Minister did not neglect the need to show himself as always in step with the staunchest of Mao Tse-tung's supporters. He never hesitated to turn up at mass rallies to commemorate the fall from grace of some old colleague or comrade. He was as abusive of those disgraced as any Red Guard. Chou also showed his affection for Mao himself, for his wife and for Lin Piao; loud shouts were heard from the Premier wishing the Maoist leadership a long life and on their adversaries, ignominy and dismissal.

Throughout 1966 and 1967, Chou En-lai tenaciously pursued his own survival. The true quality of the Prime Minister, both as a politician with his own ambitions and as a Chinese concerned with the nation's wellbeing, became increasingly impressive from 1967 onwards. Chou wanted to stay alive politically, but for specific individual and patriotic purposes. He was determined to emerge from the anarchy with the human resources and sufficient administrative machinery to restore the country to normal, once China tired of revolution round the clock. Chou saw his roles as first the moderator, then the conciliator and finally the architect of reconstruction. If circumstances did not permit him to safeguard the careers of all his followers, he had to steel his soul and allow the non-essential members of his team to be devoured by the extremists. But Chou En-lai fought doggedly to protect the individuals on whom he depended for his own safety or for the success of his plans for China after restoration of order and stability.

By the end of 1967, Chou's own position was no longer in

danger. In the years which followed, reconciliation and reconstruction were the priorities to be achieved through the activities of the administrative machinery he had preserved. As a measure of his ability, Chou En-lai's performance from 1966 was spectacular in its conception of his own and the country's needs. Mao Tse-tung had launched the daring experiment of the Cultural Revolution and let loose chaos on China. Chou so planned matters that he moved steadily towards a position where only he or Lin Piao would be able to rescue the nation from the anarchy which Mao had aroused.

CHAPTER FIVE

THE ARMY AND NATIONAL ANARCHY

LIN PIAO WAS not idle as Chou En-lai showed his mettle. Lin Piao could only take over China by solving a complex political equation. First, law and order had to break down completely. Secondly, the normal machinery of the police and internal security forces had to disappear. Thirdly, the troops had to feel their own survival would be threatened unless they intervened to restore peace and stability. Soldiers are not generally enthusiastic about shooting down civilians. In China, the Communist Party had gone to exceptional trouble to break the old warlord mentality by constant indoctrination of the armed forces in their obligation to act as servants of the people and to accept the Party as their supreme commander. China's armoured divisions were not about to station their tanks in every provincial capital at a mere nod from the Defence Minister. A military takeover could be engineered only if both China and the armed forces seemed on the brink of collapse.

Disorder in 1967 was undeniable. The police and internal security system had ceased to function. Typical of Mao Tse-tung's distaste for the Kremlin's approach to the masses were his denunciations during the Cultural Revolution of the Public Security Bureaux and the country's law-and-order apparatus. The most effective police, he had stated previously, were the people themselves, which is true of village life everywhere but in urban areas is an invitation to the criminal elements. The police system was attacked by his supporters as essentially repressive. Conventional police and internal security operations virtually ceased.

If the politicians failed to restore order through speeches, persuasion and negotiations, Lin Piao could hope, they would be forced to turn in the last resort to the troops. Chou En-lai was

talking non-stop but his initial achievements were meagre. Mao
Tse-tung went on a grand tour of five provinces and Shanghai
during the summer of 1967. He purred with optimism and received tumultuous tributes. Yet he failed to pacify the crowds
incited by ambitious local demagogues to fight with every sort of
weapon to win power. Mao's provincial expedition seemed
successful as an endeavour to learn at first hand what was going
on rather than to exercise personal leadership in the country's
key areas. But Lin Piao could see signs that the politicians were
beginning to brace themselves to act in concert to compel
the country to return to normal. After all Mao Tse-tung, Chou
En-lai, Chiang Ching, Chen Po-ta and a host of others, with
diverse views on the merits of the Cultural Revolution, had
begun to speak with a single voice by mid-1967 on the necessity
to end violence and unite the factions. Anarchy had forced the
civilian leaders to ignore ideological differences for the time
being and turn their attention to pacification of the urban areas.

Lin Piao saw an even more urgent cause for alarm. He had
reason to suspect that his technique for handling the intractable
Mao temperament might have been learnt by potential rivals at
Mao Tse-tung's side. On his 1967 tour round China, Mao had
been accompanied by, among other notables, the armed forces
Chief of Staff, Yang Cheng-wu, a Cultural Revolution appointee. He drafted an article on the enormous virtues of Mao Tse-
tung and was determined to see it featured by the country's
chief newspaper, the *People's Daily*. Yang Cheng-wu declined
to accept broad hints from others in the Mao entourage that his
declaration of fervent admiration would not be welcome. The
article was printed, and he lost his job. Lin Piao could not
permit the emergence of a new fountain of fulsome appreciation
of Mao's genius and virtues; this privilege belonged to Lin
alone.

As Lin Piao removed a potential rival, he also entertained
hopes that his main chance had come. The Wuhan mutiny in
July 1967 was followed by calls to drag out the anti-Maoists
within the army. The armed forces' dedication to Mao Tse-
tung was under fire. Military uniform seemed about to lose the
power to protect most of those who wore it from the mobs. How
long would it take, the question posed itself, before the downfall
of civilian officials was matched by an extensive overthrow of

military officers? The politicians were adroit enough to realise where demands for inquiries into the army's political morals would lead. In September, Chiang Ching was nominated to defend the boundless fidelity of the troops to her husband Mao, and to launch a campaign to disarm rival factions and to protect state and military property from looters. The politicians also managed to form a united front in dealing with a limited number of explosive parts of the country, including Mao's home province of Hunan, the industrial base of Liaoning Province and the city of Shanghai, a centre of some interest later on.

The politicians were freeing themselves, furthermore, from the embarrassment of unbridled extremists. Many of these extreme leftists were accused of complicity in a plot by the "May 16 Group" to overthrow the Prime Minister; to seize control of the Foreign Ministry; and to establish their own rule. Lin Piao had connections with the group of extreme leftists, and they were invaluable allies. Nonetheless, he probably had no intention of using them for a direct takeover in Peking. Soldiers, after all, would do the job much more effectively. The dismissal of the extremists passed off with almost no opposition, which must have cheered Chou En-lai as an indication of how the country's mood had changed from the first euphoria when all restraints had been relaxed in 1966 to surges of resentment when the rabble took over in 1967.

Many extremists were too naive anyway to survive. Chi Pen-yu is a good illustration. He had won his spurs as an unsympathetic writer of frenzied political essays which sought to review cultural affairs in the terminology and concepts of Maoist ideology. He had a facility for political invective rather than literary talent. The Cultural Revolution gave him the platform his temperament needed, and Chi moved from the realm of ideas to the world of action. He is alleged to have been a driving force behind the "May 16 Group" and its conspiracies. But such criminal activities were not essential for his downfall. That he was tolerated until early 1968 was a miracle in itself. Chi Pen-yu took revolution into every nook and cranny of China that he could find time to visit. Even the inmates of mental hospitals were of major concern to him. He showed great anxiety about individuals who had written to purged notables before 1966 in the abusive or maniac style which marks many of the letters received by public figures. These correspondents had been turned over sometimes to psychiatrists for treatment.

Such decisions had been wrong, Chi believed, for these people had been vanguards of the Cultural Revolution, daring to point a finger at the highest in the land before any other members of the masses. In the Soviet Union, as both China and the Western bloc have noted, the authorities prefer nowadays to incarcerate political dissidents in psychiatric wards. Chi Pen-yu scored no marks with Maoists or anybody else, except the most fanatic of his personal devotees, for unlocking China's mental hospitals on the grounds that inmates were detained for political reasons. His actions were potential ammunition for the Kremlin's anti-Peking propaganda merchants. Chi seems to have been somewhat unbalanced himself. Nevertheless, his desire to liberate patients confined in security mental institutions showed the instinctive horror felt by the Maoist for methods which Soviet communists accept with little fuss. Chi, too, could cite in a defence of unlocking psychiatric wards the precedent of the deliberate dismantling of the Ministry of Public Security's police apparatus by the Maoists, although Chou En-lai, unlike Mao Tse-tung, demanded that the Public Security Departments should be protected against all intrusions by the masses. In any contest between Chi Pen-yu and Chou En-lai for premiership (and this ambition was implied by Chi's alleged "May 16 Group" membership), Chi was not a serious contender for office. The atmosphere was so abnormal in Peking for much of 1967, nonetheless, that juvenile extremists had to be reminded more than once by their Maoist mentors that they lacked the skill and experience to govern China or run a ministry.

Although Lin Piao's chance for a pre-emptive strike was stalemated by Chiang Ching's September speech, he could still believe that power was within his grasp. The chances still appeared high that the civilian leaders would fail to quell disorder, violence and anarchy without the imposition of martial law. Even if the politicians succeeded, the soldiers were being mobilised, after all, to take over administrative and management functions of every sort, a task for which Lin Piao believed the armed forces had been schooled in advance of the Cultural Revolution. New administrative organs were being formed on the "three-in-one" principle. This concept involved using soldiers to act as umpires when technicians or officials were pushed into coalitions with representatives of the masses who had shot to prominence in the Cultural Revolution. Power was to be exercised collectively by the professionals, the rank and file and the soldiers. Whether management by committee functions efficiently depends on many factors. In the last resort, however, the man who musters most votes is boss and eventually can treat the committee as a rubber stamp.

For many reasons, the soldiers were more likely to end up on the side of the professionals rather than the masses despite the Chinese military doctrine that the next war would call for extensive use of guerilla tactics which only work if supported by the ordinary population. The Chinese soldiers should have been better than most at cooperating with the average worker or peasant. Yet between the labour force and the troops lay a wide gulf in 1967 and subsequent years.

First, the soldiers in the People's Liberation Army were subject to the closest supervision. The elaborate foot and rifle drill of the Chinese army, which approaches the ballet in its mixture of vigour, grace and self-control, is the symbol of the discipline imposed on the People's Liberation Army. Parade grounds are where civilian hearts are broken and men are turned into fighters whose greatest virtue is instant obedience to the voice of command. To the soldiers, the idle, demoralised and shiftless elements who set the pace in so many Chinese factories came as a shocking contrast to military life. Secondly, soldiers down to the lowliest rifleman are professionals. The notion that some untrained and inexperienced worker, more devious or loud-mouthed than his mates, could operate a factory sounded suspiciously like mutiny to the troops. Thirdly, the contrast between rural tranquillity and urban uproar was disconcerting. The illegal activities of the peasants to get a little extra cash were tolerable. Soldiers usually run such petty rackets in barracks. The villages stood out as orderly communities where normality prevailed (except on the perimeter of the major urban areas). The peasants were no great problem, which made the strife in the towns even more inexcusable to men sent from drill squads to factory shifts.

The soldiers quickly grew disenchanted with their various jobs: buffers between faction leaders and the former political and factory bosses, general peace-makers and restorers of law and order. They were expected to form "great alliances" out of rival factions, a task which the artful Chou En-lai could not accomplish without days and sometimes months of personal effort. The ordinary soldier often found the factions identical to all intents and purposes, and he was quite unable to distinguish their rival merits. The wisest course often was to support the group likely to provoke the least confusion and whose leaders sounded sanest and most level-headed. An unavoidable result was that the Maoist rebels did not get the soldiers' backing as was their right according to the official directives on army work issued at the start of 1968. The political climate in the towns, however, was totally different from the average barrack-room study group where blunt speech and simple-minded comment were the order of the day. If bored by a political campaign or confused by a new ideological twist, the soldiers said freely and safely what they thought. In the power struggles rending civilian life, honesty was no safeguard. Words became important, as the competition to prove Maoist credentials or loyalty to Mao and the Central Committee intensified.

Many soldiers sent to act as conciliators had never been responsible for a squad, never mind a platoon. In too many cases, ordinary soldiers were sent without weapons into the thick of battles between armed political gangs and asked to restore order. Military units took too many casualties when ordered out to disperse violent mobs for the bulk of the troops to feel much sympathy for the advocates of total trust in the virtue and wisdom of the labouring masses. Some soldiers performed with exemplary efficiency in the crisis, officers such as Sha Feng who became the Minister of Agriculture and Forestry. But here, too, lay a danger. A soldier who shone while on temporary attachment to the civilian administration might be asked to accept his discharge from the armed forces, with a significant loss of pay and privileges for many of the lower ranks. To aggravate matters, the army was short of commanders, platoon and squad leaders and instructors; the period of compulsory military service was slashed in 1967 which resulted in a strain on training facilities. Recruits had to be put through their basic combat and technical courses at an accelerated pace just as the Chinese armed forces were absorbing the lessons of the conflicts in the Middle East and Indochina. The average soldier was soon anxious to resign from his "three-in-one combination" and return to the security of army life where the enemy was easy to identify.

Why had Lin Piao not foreseen these obstacles to using the armed forces as an alternative government? Both he and Mao Tse-tung were too intoxicated by their triumphant experience of the years 1947 to 1949. As the communist forces rolled during those distant years across a country dazed by decades of war, by hunger, by an incredible inflation and the collapse of law and order, the army had proved a gigantic school for reliable officials. The pool of talent within the revolutionary forces was transformed into a bureaucratic structure to rule a population thankful for any form of honest and competent administration and in need of the most basic necessities for survival. Armies can cope automatically with this kind of crisis. The victorious general is the commander who imposes upon the chaos of the battlefield the order and logic of his own plans. Military units unable to forage for substitutes when deprived of regular supplies do not last long. Soldiers are expected, in addition, to know how to deal with captured enemy territory, a facet of military responsibilities much emphasised by Mao Tse-tung in his guerilla days.

But China in the Cultural Revolution was not a battlefield, though torn apart by local conflicts; nor was it conquered territory with a numbed population glad to be delivered from further threats to their lives. The Chinese urban areas were far more complex socially and economically than when Mao Tse-tung was winning his final victories in the civil war. The wartime recollections of Lin Piao and Mao Tse-tung, who was strongly in favour of the people learning from the army, had misled them both catastrophically. The direct involvement of the soldiers in the administration was not a success. Lin Piao's power was illusory. A professional, civilian administration was still needed; and most soldiers were happy to see the return of the old guard to the Party and government machines.

However, while anarchy, armed violence and open combat between factions were still in evidence, Lin Piao's soldiers remained essential, especially as the policy of turning the other cheek was abandoned when military patience eroded and the troops put on displays of force to bring the mobs to their senses. Thus, Chou En-lai was prepared to check the hands of the military bent on using rifle butts to beat sense into hotheads in Kwangtung

Province, and he was able to spend several months on negotiations to form its new administration (a revolutionary committee), finally proclaimed in February 1968. A different approach was unavoidable for the major northern port and manufacturing city of Tientsin. The announcement of the formation of its revolutionary committee in December 1967 was preceded by the deployment of troops in full combat order who established machine-gun posts at the intersection of every key road and around all important buildings. In Kwangtung, the army's freedom to impose a settlement on the province by naked force was curtailed; in Tientsin, no other solution seemed possible. Lin Piao's political life was not yet over, nor was it clear in 1968 how far his importance as commander of the nation's gun barrels had diminished.

Mao Tse-tung could not turn back to Chou En-lai since in 1968 the country was in no condition to switch over to a completely civilian government. Mao could no longer rely on Lin Piao with unreserved confidence because the armed forces had proved both unable and unwilling to carry the burden of ruling a chaotic China. Lin's power had begun to fade as too many civilian leaders had survived the upheavals of 1966 to 1969 to leave the stage clear for Lin and a military takeover. In any case, the same period had seen a perilous gap open between the soldiers and the urban masses. Chou was now the strongest placed of the trio. Such administration as functioned, especially on the economic front, was under the control of his clients. The Prime Minister had also established a basis for a new public image: Chou, the leader on whom the people could most rely for sense, moderation, patience and a return to normality. For a people grown weary of havoc, civil commotion and violent crime, the Prime Minister's new reputation was to prove eventually no less important than Chairman Mao's charisma or Lin Piao's personality cult.

CHAPTER SIX

HEIRS TO THE CULTURAL REVOLUTION

NEW FACES AND names were achieving notoriety in China during 1967. Their emergence was dependent on the secret contest of brains and power groups continuing unabated between Chou En-lai and Lin Piao. For his part, Lin had no grounds for looking on the Prime Minister as an immediate threat. Mao Tse-tung had only one "closest comrade-in-arms," Defence Minister Lin Piao. Chou was steadfast in his invocation of Mao Tse-tung Thought on every public occasion and fulsome in his praise of Lin. The Premier seemed to accept his destiny of never ranking higher than third in the Communist Party hierarchy, after Mao and Lin (just as Chou had been outranked by Mao and former Head of State Liu Shao-chi until mid-1966). If the Premier were discovered to harbour personal ambitions after so many years of playing the ideal bureaucrat without an original ideological thought of his own, Chou could always be removed by Lin. Meanwhile the Prime Minister was a useful Party creature who seemed to lack any ambition to become autocratic. Lin Piao mirrored Mao Tse-tung's attitude towards Chou: reservations and suspicions but a feeling that these hesitations did not justify the inconvenience which would result from the Premier's removal. Lin Piao, therefore, was of positive assistance to Chou En-lai as the pressures for his dismissal intensified during the summer of 1967.

In the peculiar relations between Mao, Chou and Lin, sufficient gaps emerged in the unity of the country's three most prominent rulers for lesser mortals to assume importance. The most colourful of these personalities to take the "helicopter" to the top (as Teng Hsiao-ping caustically expressed it) was Chiang Ching, Mao's wife. This lady has aroused more hatred than any other Chinese since 1949. The venom directed towards her is mostly the product of prejudice and ignorance about her real place in Chinese political life between 1966 and 1976. She got off to a bad start. She was an actress by choice, which did not enhance a reputation for lady-like modesty in old-fashioned China. Her education was superior to the standard she was willing to admit to in later life. She was abducted while still a teenager, although childhood acquaintances felt the lady did not protest too much at being dragged from her mother's protection. In Shanghai, she mixed among well-educated, foreign-influenced and affluent families while still quite young. A film career and a marriage in Shanghai proved no triumphs. She left the city on a journey which was to end in Yenan, the communist guerilla retreat, and a meeting with Mao Tse-tung. Her Shanghai friends included many progressives and Marxists, and she expanded her familiarity with the world of communism. Her theatrical interests had turned into a passion while in Shanghai. She flirted only briefly with film appearances after Shanghai; her interest switched to production and direction, to which her emotional attachments deepened with the years. An important detail of Chiang Ching's personal history is that she was not a native of Shanghai; she was a temporary sojourner in the city whose communist underground had been directed ruthlessly by Chou En-lai.

Mao Tse-tung was captivated by the former actress when she reached his retreat in Yenan. He determined to marry her in 1939. For reasons which have never been clarified satisfactorily, Mao's plan aroused the ire of his Party colleagues who became angry enough to question Mao's fitness to continue his leadership. Part of the wrath was caused by Mao's willingness to sacrifice his current wife, who lay seriously ill. This brave woman had accompanied her husband on the nightmare march across central China in search of the base in Yenan which would be too difficult for his Chinese and Japanese enemies to capture except at inordinate cost. Men such as Chen Yi regarded her with great admiration and felt that Mao's desire to divorce her smacked of betrayal.

Other communist leaders had a succession of wives without the intense debate which Mao's marital ambitions provoked. Chu Teh, for instance, had four wives in all, the same number as Mao. By contrast, Chou En-lai won great respect by his fidelity to his wife and his refusal to accept her proposal to take a second spouse since she was childless. Chou was close to his wife. His refusal to put her away in favour of a more fruitful woman was lauded for the "Confucian" and thus "feudal" virtue it disclosed: control of normal human desires, including the longing for off-spring to perpetuate the family name.

Chou En-lai, strangely, is the reputed match-maker on Mao's behalf, inducing the rest of the communist leaders to agree to the marriage with Chiang Ching on condition she confined her acti-vities strictly to the Mao menage. This restriction could hardly have been produced by fear of her potential power because the Communist Party's chief concern was simply to stay out of reach of enemy armies. More likely, the communist leadership was old-fashioned enough to feel embarrassed about the appear-ance of a person of Chiang Ching's background in respectable society.

Dislike of Chiang Ching lasted after 1949. Occasional news-paper features about the Mao family portrayed her as a typical Chinese housewife. She took a job connected with films. Former members of this department of the Cultural Ministry do not recall her with much fondness. Her sudden emergence in 1966 as midwife to the Cultural Revolution made her a household name overnight. Her part in the Cultural Revolution was not the venge-ful fury which is her usual portrait. Her pressure for the removal of traditional drama, opera and music from the Chinese stage and screen is well-known, for example. That the disappearance of traditional operas would be temporary only is ignored. The most important feature of this period in her career in fact was her return to the stage and her old job of actress.

The stage which saw most of Chiang Ching in 1966 consisted of the streets of Peking; the dramatic role which fascinated her was a part assigned to her by Mao Tse-tung. She suppressed her own personality. This witty, well-groomed woman, with excellent fashion sense and pleasant appearance donned a baggy uniform, used ugly spectacles to remove every trace of glamour from her face. In this Maoist livery, she was able to grasp the microphone at mass rallies with confidence and act out the virago. She ought to have trembled at the vast crowds. The actress's instinct to respond to an audience, whatever its size, asserted itself, and she controlled her listeners effortlessly despite years of semi-seclu-sion. At the start of the Cultural Revolution in 1966, her duty was to set young people on fire with dedication to the Maoist cause. She never escaped from the image she had to create of a ranting, "unisex" fanatic with her face suffused by a half-sneer. She remained the unsullied hope of those who responded to Mao Tse-tung's call to rebel in 1966. The diehard Cultural Revolutionaries maintained their hope for a decade that Chiang Ching would prove a worthy heroine by assisting them to power. To the rest of China, she became the symbol of all the excesses, violence and devastation wrought by the Cultural Revolution. She had played out her script too well for her own comfort in the years to come.

The line she preached veered sharply in 1967. Her husband was not anxious at the start of the year to see almost all his old comrades swept into oblivion. Chiang Ching spoke up on behalf of several major targets of the extremists' virulence. She failed to save them. Her willingness to speak on their behalf shows a courage not usually attributed to her. In early 1967, the mobs could have turned even on Mao's wife. Her success in halting the plan to purge the armed forces in September 1967 has already been mentioned. Extremists got short shrift from her after 1966 in public or in private. Chou En-lai declared that her detractors failed to understand what she was about. With Mao Tse-tung able to move only with some difficulty, Chiang Ching had to act as his eyes and ears, his envoy and spokesman. She was impetuous, over-confident and insensitive to others' views, her husband warned her more than once. He trusted her, however, to represent his interests.

In particular, Mao Tse-tung charged her in 1966 to keep careful watch on Lin Piao. Mao's instruction on this subject was her reason for sticking to Lin like a leech, which had the unfortunate result of making the public see her as a close supporter of Lin. In his 1966 letter to Chiang Ching setting out his fears and instructions on the subject of Lin Piao, Mao forecast that his supporters would be shunted aside, at least temporarily, after his death in all probability. He read the future accurately in the light of the 1976 arrest of the "gang of four." Mao also warned Chiang Ching of serious personal defects. At the same time, examination of Chiang Ching's Cultural Revolution activities does not reveal overweening ambitions lurking in her bosom. She was "Madam," Mao Tse-tung's wife, dutifully doing what she was told. Doubtless, her experiences from 1966 to 1969 gave her a taste for political drama, self-confidence and a sense of self-importance which prevented her from returning to her old status as the self-effacing housewife. By 1972, she refused to be excluded from the political arena any more; and she also refused to confine her dress to the shapeless Maoist uniform, preferring Western fashions on discreet semi-public occasions and adopting a well-tailored severe Soviet-style blouse and skirt at formal receptions unless the prudish masses were to form the bulk of the onlookers. Chiang Ching in politics but without baggy pants and tunic aroused indignant murmurs from those sections of the population who had painful memories of the Cultural Revolution.

In frequent attendance upon Chiang Ching was a youngish man with peculiar eyes which attracted immediate attention. He was well-known in Shanghai and among intellectual circles as a writer of polemical essays. Chinese academic life has its share of bitchiness and of careers made or broken by influential critics. A leading hatchetman in Shanghai was Chiang Ching's protégé, Yao Wen-yuan, rumoured to be her son-in-law. Yao was gifted, and his essays revealed considerable intelligence and genuine commitment to Maoism based on a keen interest in ideology. He functioned best as critic or interpreter of other people's ideas. His occasional attempts at creative thinking were unpolished, woolly and more vehement than lucid. He lacked maturity and direct experience of public affairs on a national scale, defects which marred his efforts to be original. Yao Wen-yuan was widely hated by intellectuals; he seemed to have sold his talents for the privileged status of a Communist Party hack. This verdict was cruel since Yao Wen-yuan usually rose above the shallow tirade, and he wrote with the bite that comes from conviction. Yao Wen-yuan inspired hatred among the bureaucracy through a pamphlet he wrote attacking Tao Chu, an official who had been first elevated and then toppled during the first six months of the Cultural Revolution. Tao Chu represented the cream of the administration, responsible for getting neighbouring provinces to work together. Yao's onslaught against Tao Chou was so callous and vindictive as to suggest personal ambition mixed with spiteful venom. His treatment of Tao Chu was unpardonable in the eyes of many officials.

Yao Wen-yuan did little to enhance his image when acting as Chiang Ching's escort. He toadied shamelessly and echoed her remarks like a schoolboy anxious to stay in the good books of an unpleasant teacher. He seemed a hanger-on, spineless and out to promote his career through his public connection with Chiang Ching. When he spoke for himself, he had a firm personality and a vigorous approach. He suppressed his real qualities in Chiang Ching's company as if frightened of dire retribution should any limelight be diverted from the star of the Cultural Revolution. Mao Tse-tung considered Yao Wen-yuan a gifted young man and felt quite comfortable at having him around. Yao seemed to have more unrestricted access to Mao than any other member of the Politburo. For all the patronage of Mao himself, of Chiang Ching and of their combined prestige, Yao Wen-yuan's hectic activity in the Cultural Revolution raised him aloft but not quite to the summit. He scrambled into the Party Central Committee's Politburo and by 1969 had won responsibility for university reforms. Ministerial supervision of a major sphere of political affairs eluded him. His weaknesses were too obvious to be overcome even by the massive patronage bestowed on him. He was stuck with the academic and literary fields. He retained, however, the image of total commitment to undiluted Maoism and to the ideals of the Cultural Revolution. The zealots of 1966 to 1969 did not abandon their hopes until 1976 that in Yao Wen-yuan they had a vigorous advocate and protector in the highest councils of the land.

Chiang Ching provoked Yao Wen-yuan into servility. Yao had a similar impact upon a much more impressive man, Chang Chun-chiao. He had spent his life in journalism and propaganda and had formed a tenuous connection with Chou En-lai when he worked on an army paper. Chang was a dedicated Maoist from the start and played a prominent role in all ideological campaigns which swept Shanghai. In 1958, he showed a readiness to court unpopularity by pushing Maoist ideals, a trait which almost two decades later was to have disastrous results. Chang Chun-chiao was endowed with considerable political acumen, but his dedication to Mao Tse-tung Thought was misread as extremism. His true outlook was that of the professional politician. Faced with a crisis, Chang Chun-chiao was ready to adopt whatever ideological colours would rally most support to him, so long as he did not have to renounce Maoism. His cynical realism in restoring order to Shanghai in 1967 led to complaints that he was a rightist. A personal threat from Mao to arrest Chang's foes was all that enabled him to escape the disgrace of criticism at a mass rally for his alleged right-wing views. The Shanghai populace was too sophisticated to take Chang Chun-chiao at face value as an extremist firebrand, hence the allegations from the early days of the Cultural Revolution that he was a conservative.

Chang Chun-chiao's intimate relationship with the Mao household began in 1964 as he, Chiang Ching and Yao Wen-yuan involved themselves in the struggle to create revolutionary model operas, an exhausting process because of constant revisions of the libretti. Music was no great problem provided the words spoken and sung on stage struck no false, un-Maoist chords. In Yao Wen-yuan's presence, Chang Chun-chiao seemed to take a back seat. He projected a sense of uneasiness, much as Chou En-lai found Mao Tse-tung a strain even after so many years' joint endeavour. Probably the ideological interests and rigidity of Yao cramped the style of Chang Chun-chiao whose concern was with correct results more than ideological hair-splitting. He seemed almost to defer to Yao Wen-yuan, although from almost every point of view, Chang Chun-chiao was the more able of the pair, and far more impressive intellectually and politically. Yao Wen-yuan's hold over his Shanghai colleague was probably the greater grasp of Maoism which Yao acquired through his concern over ideology, which implied Chang Chun-chiao had to be always on guard in case his speech betrayed a heretical note which Yao's sharp ear might catch. The conclusion must be that the pair were accomplices rather than friends working hand in glove with absolute trust in each other.

Chang Chun-chiao together with Yao Wen-yuan helped Mao Tse-tung to get an article published by the Shanghai press in November 1965 after the Peking papers refused to launch the first open phase of the Cultural Revolution. Both men were thus more than opportunists; they joined Mao's camp when the opposition in the capital was still strong enough to censor an inflammatory Maoist article. At this date, Mao Tse-tung was far from sure of victory. The pair were dispatched in 1966 by the Party Central Committee to sort out Shanghai. The city was in turmoil because its veteran administrators were not prepared to

surrender gracefully. Factory managements, for instance, fought
to retain the workers' loyalty and to maintain production through
lavish bonuses. The radical groups were deeply divided, and disorder engulfed large tracts of the city. The radicals contained
extreme idealists who wanted to imitate the 1871 Paris Commune
and its total control by the masses over all administration.

The formation at the start of 1967 of a "Shanghai Commune"
was the high tide of the Cultural Revolution. If imitated by the
rest of the nation, the "Shanghai Commune" would have led to
the break-up of China into autonomous, semi-autarchic units.
National unity would have been thrown overboard. Mao Tse-
tung was horrified at the prospect. Chang Chung-chiao had
somehow to bring to heel in January and February 1967 the wild
spirits who wanted their Marxism unadulterated by any consideration of practical realities. Chang boasted in a secret speech
made in the same year how he and Yao could have made
Shanghai their personal property during the "Shanghai Commune" movement, and Peking could have done little to restore
central control over the city. Instead, Chang Chun-chiao schem-
ed, dissimulated and manipulated, all of which he unashamedly
confessed, to bring together warring radical cliques in an alliance
—however uneasy—and crush the Commune.

Attempts were made by the opposition to create a split
between Chang and Prime Minister Chou En-lai. Chang
Chun-chiao refused to fall into this trap. His comments testified
to a conviction that Chou was not likely to scheme the downfall
of such men as Chang Chun-chiao who were turning back the tide
of lawlessness. On the contrary, such talent made them candidates
for election to the Chou club.

The "Shanghai Commune" and the refusal of Mao Tse-tung
to bless it and the speed with which the Commune was transformed by Chang Chun-chiao into a conventional city government
were the clearest pointer, hindsight shows, to a ban on further
radical innovations during the Cultural Revolution. Mao himself
suddenly discovered he was not in favour of a fundamental
change in the organisation of China. The communist ruling
class and Chinese political attitudes were what Mao wanted to
transform. But radical administrative experiments which would
split the country into separate units and abolish Peking's authority over the entire nation were anathema. Chang Chun-chiao

established an efficient substitute for the Commune after a protracted struggle. Radical voices complained that Shanghai's new administration, its "revolutionary committee," had recruited too many men from the old city government. Chang Chun-chiao, the extremists charged, restored to office former power-holders which proved Chang's conservative and rightist mentality. Chang could afford to shrug off such criticism as he basked in the approbation of Mao Tse-tung and the goodwill of the Prime Minister. During the summer of 1967, Chang joined Mao on his provincial tour. He was allowed to convey to various groups the comments and instructions of Mao, and as his spokesman, Chang's status rose still further.

Chang Chun-chiao was able to make friends in the highest military circles as well as to obtain direct access to military authority when nominated in mid-1967 to the post of First Political Commissar of the Nanking Military Region (which embraced Shanghai). As Political Commissar, Chang was a senior member of the army establishment. For the Region's armed forces, his military post was a blessing.

One of China's most respected generals was Hsu Shih-yu, Nanking Commander throughout the Cultural Revolution. Hsu aroused enthusiastic applause whenever he appeared in public. Yet he was almost tongue-tied when called on for a political address of any substance. Hsu's attitude towards the Cultural Revolution was a simple soldier's disgust for the rabble which roamed the streets and even tried to halt his car. He was about to use a whiff of grapeshot to disperse idle riff-raff obviously up to no good. Before Hsu ordered his regiments to remove by force political trash from public places, Chang Chun-chiao arrived at Hsu's headquarters. Whether or not Hsu understood why, he was on the verge of branding himself as opposed to Mao Tse-tung Thought; an oppressor of the masses; and an enemy of the people. Hsu would lose his command, Chang Chun-chiao was able to convince the Nanking Commander. The time would come for a punitive expedition against the lawless rabble, and Chang Chun-chiao pledged that Hsu Shih-yu should be among the first to know when to move against the mobs. For the present, Hsu should concentrate on keeping his temper and preserving his troops' loyalty; Chang Chun-chiao would take care of the political action. Chang Chun-chiao won the old soldier over, and Hsu was to repay the favour in kind.

Chang Chun-chiao would probably have enjoyed a career in the central Government without the boost he got from the Cultural Revolution. His chances of making Deputy Premier, however, were very remote until the Cultural Revolution made him a national figure. The Cultural Revolution also gave him an unmerited reputation for extremism and nominated him to membership of Chiang Ching's clique. Chang Chun-chiao performed one valuable service for Mao's wife which fuelled the gossip about their political alliance. During the 1967 disturbances, a senior Shanghai official seized the secret files on Chiang Ching whose contents, apparently, were explosive. Chang rescued the dossier; protected Mao's wife from blackmail; and sent her file intact to Peking. The extremist image stuck although the citizens of Shanghai, who knew his views from personal experience, entertained no illusions that Chang Chun-chiao was on the masses' side during the Cultural Revolution. Once labelled as an ultra-radical, Chang could not free himself from the stigma. Chang Chun-chiao was not widely believed, nonetheless, to hanker for the intoxication of the early months of the Cultural Revolution. The rabid elements looked on him as sympathetic but lacking in fervour.

The inability of Chang Chun-chiao and Chiang Ching to escape from the charges of extremism and disregard for practicality, in the face of all evidence to the contrary, points to a deliberate attempt to ensure the two were tarred by the same brush as a guarantee of their future unpopularity.

Also from Shanghai sprang a photogenic young man, with no political sophistication and hungry for the approval of such personalities as Chang Chun-chiao. The young worker, Wang Hung-wen, came originally from Kirin Province; had lost his parents; and been brought up in Shanghai. The popular account described how he had done his military service and worked on the land before taking a factory job. During the Cultural Revolution, he had organised first the workers in his own textile mill and then elsewhere in the city and thrown them behind Chang Chun-chiao. This sensible deed warranted some reward, and he was brought to Mao Tse-tung's attention. Grand plans were made for his future, based mainly on his physical appearance. The Party Central Committee and the central Government looked its age; photographs of the Chinese leadership suggested the country's rulers were but a step removed from senility. Young faces were conspicuously absent. Wang Hung-wen could freshen up the official group portraits. He could also be used to indicate that China's youth who had cut their teeth in the Cultural Revolution had won the right to tell the decrepit to make room for new blood. Wang Hung-wen's career after 1967 was as calculated an exploitation of an individual for the sake of public relations as could be found in the marketing programme of any capitalist soap-powder corporation.

Chiang Ching, Wang Hung-wen, Chang Chun-chiao and Yao Wen-yuan were believed by ordinary Chinese to be on the closest personal terms, with special access to Mao Tse-tung and with a close sense of unity. They were called the "Shanghai Mafia" outside China. Within the country, they were regarded as a conspiratorial group, based on Shanghai, which wanted to unleash a second Cultural Revolution. Strangely enough, however, apart from a similarity of views which they expressed at top Communist Party forums, examples of their operating together as a quartet in unison are almost impossible to come by. The *Heilungkiang Daily* observed bluntly in January 1977 that the four avoided working together even on their alleged conspiracy to seize power. Outlook rather than deeds seems to have been their common bond.

While Wang Hung-wen was the victim of public relations, a senior official in central China had exploited for years his opportunity for personal exposure. This professional bureaucrat, Hua Kuo-feng, smacked of Mao Tse-tung in appearance, just as Chang Chun-chiao modelled himself on Chou En-lai. Chang kept a rigid public composure, wore neatly-tailored tunics and trousers and presented a dignified, intelligent face to the world. Hua Kuo-feng, who had spent virtually his entire career in Mao's own province of Hunan, possessed a burly figure which made his clothes look somewhat crumpled, off-the-peg efforts, despite his tailor's best endeavours. Hua affected homely manners. He kicked off his shoes and put his feet up on a sofa when receiving foreign visitors with whom he wanted a relaxed chat, for example. He kept his thick provincial accent, and he looked, talked and gesticulated like a man of the people.

Hua Kuo-feng, born in 1921 in northern Shansi, made the

most of his posting as a junior military officer to Mao Tse-tung's native Hunan. His ascent to fame was in part the result of his deliberate and unremitting association with the district which contained Mao's actual birthplace. This devotion brought him early on to Mao's own attention and to the notice of the famous among the hordes of pilgrims to Mao Tse-tung's old home. Hua went further than establishing links with Mao's village. He took great pains to identify himself with Mao's policies. In the 1950s' movements to reform agricultural organisations, for instance, Hua's success record was reportedly the highest in Hunan. Even after Hua had become a member of the regular civilian adminis- tration, he kept up his army connections. During the 1959 debates over the Defence Minister, Peng Teh-huai, and his attacks on the Great Leap Forward for causing misery, Hua helped to keep Hunan on Mao's side. This task was important because Defence Minister Peng's disgrace in 1959 caused much military resentment.

Hua Kuo-feng made several rural forays which resulted in reports Mao is said to have admired. In the provincial govern- ment to which he was appointed in 1957, his first job was in the cultural field and embraced education. By 1965, Hua was in control of a massive irrigation project to transform conditions in Mao's native village. Success with this assignment left Hua poised on the eve of the Cultural Revolution to take over the governorship of Hunan. He had won a good reputation among the peasants, and his rural support was sufficient for Hua to be able to shrug off charges of being a rightist made regularly against him from 1966 till 1974.

Displays of personal devotion to Mao Tse-tung also helped Hua Kuo-feng weather the Cultural Revolution which ruined so many of his colleagues. In 1967, a railway to carry pilgrims to the original Mao homestead came under Hua's stewardship, and its construction was the subject of direct telephone calls to Peking. Hua developed the role almost of adopted son to Mao Tse-tung. During 1968 and 1969, Hua led memorial services in honour of Mao's second wife who had been put to death by anti- communist troops.

Filial piety towards the Mao family was not Hua Kuo-feng's sole source of strength. His careful display of his army ties throughout the years suggests he had a permanent post in the para-military Public Security Ministry, whose master he became in January 1975. The man who spoke for the interests of the various civil and military security organs in the Party Central Committee was Kang Sheng, a shadowy figure who played a vital part in an operation to rescue Hua from his most dangerous crisis in the Cultural Revolution. Attacked by a group of the most ominous radicals to appear in China, Hua Kuo-feng was provided with support by Peking more elaborate than that bestowed on his hard-pressed counterparts in any other province. In part, the reinforcements sent by the capital were a tribute to Hua Kuo-feng's ability to rally the central authorities behind him, though they were also a result of the menace posed to the whole country by the extremists who were determined to seize power in Hunan. The province's extremists were mobilised in a group known as the Sheng-wu-lien. Peking's violent "May 16 Group," later made the scapegoats for such outrages as the destruction of the British Embassy, was said to be linked to other fanatics in China, including the Sheng-wu-lien in Hunan. This latter organisation had followers in other parts of south China and was a direct threat to the Chinese Communist Party in general and to Hua Kuo-feng and other Hunan leaders in particular.

The Sheng-wu-lien came to prominence in the autumn and winter of 1967. Its members were not rabble-rousers and power-hungry demagogues. They realised that their enemy in the last resort was China's Communist Party since the Cultural Revolution was an act of rebellion against the systems, structures and conventions developed during the Communist Party's reign from 1949. The Party might have been led astray by Head of State Liu Shao-chi, Party Secretary-General Teng Hsiao-ping and a mass of other leaders. The removal of these figures in 1966 and 1967 did not imply that the Party would stick to the straight and narrow ideological path for the future. Hunan's radicals saw the Cultural Revolution very much as a charade, with reform and not root-and-branch revolution as its goal. The Sheng-wu-lien wanted a return to uncontaminated Marxism-Leninism and proposed a new communist gospel for China. A revolutionary group with a rival ideology to challenge the official orthodoxy of the Chinese Communist Party was a genuine alternative government. Its analysis of events betrayed a sophistication well above the level of run-of-the-mill faction leaders and men who had profited from

the overthrow of senior officials and colleagues. These beneficia-
ries of 1966 and 1967 expected their ambitions to be satisfied
within the familiar Chinese communist system, however modified
by the Cultural Revolution. The Hunan group wanted an entirely
new system.

Hua Kuo-feng received powerful reinforcements in January
1968. The mightiest in the land, excluding only Mao Tse-tung,
held a forum to denounce the Sheng-wu-lien. The participants,
from Premier Chou En-lai to Chiang Ching and Yao Wen-yuan,
denounced the Sheng-wu-lien in the bitterest terms. Peking had
been concerned earlier that the drive against the Sheng-wu-lien
might be used as a cover to take revenge on genuine Maoists of
a radical persuasion. After the 1968 assembly of notables excom-
municated the Sheng-wu-lien and all its sympathisers, Hua Kuo-
feng and advocates of law and order in the Hunan set-up had
almost a completely free hand.

Mao Tse-tung had shown he could not countenance as drastic
a change as the establishment of the "Shanghai Commune."
Thereafter, radical innovations could not be tolerated which
would cut through to the heart of the Communist Party structure.
The drastic break with the pre-Cultural Revolution China, which
the Hunan revolutionaries wanted, was totally beyond the pale.
The fear that a purified Marxisism-Leninism might seduce sections
of the masses led Chou En-lai to take the closest interest in the
eradication of all support for the Sheng-wu-lien. Hunan remained bedevilled by dissensions and factional disputes. Hua Kuo-
feng could face these challenges more tranquilly than many other
provincial leaders in similar situations. He had to hand scapegoats
under fire from every shade of opinion at the top of the Peking
establishment. Furthermore, Hua had caught the attention of
powerful men who would think well of him if he could dispose
of the threat to the Party's supremacy without a local civil war.
Hua Kuo-feng passed the test.

On the national scene, while Mao Tse-tung was still tied to a
Lin Piao who was being overtaken by 1969 by Chou En-lai, new
faces and fresh voices had made their mark on Peking. The newcomers who did best out of the Cultural Revolution were five in
number. Of this tiny group, Chou was linked to three. Mao's
wife, Chiang Ching, had helped the Prime Minister to defeat the
extremists who attacked him so viciously in 1967 both as Premier

and as patron of Foreign Minister, Chen Yi. The second, Chang Chun-chiao, had made a declaration of trust in Chou En-lai during 1967 despite efforts to poison their relationship. Like Chou, Chang Chun-chiao was concerned with stability. Hua Kuo-feng had been helped by Chou, among others, when Hunan's extremists had fought to destroy the provincial leadership. Mao Tse-tung, however, was even more closely linked to all five. He eventually let Hua Kuo-feng win the highest state and Party offices during 1976. The others became the "gang of four," whom Mao could retain in office only as long as he lived. Once both Mao and Chou were dead, the five who climbed so rapidly during the Cultural Revolution lacked patrons. Their futures depended on the levers of power which they controlled, and on the personal relations they had established between themselves and with their fellow Politburo members.

CHAPTER SEVEN

A TASTE OF FREEDOM AND THE GROWTH OF FACTIONS

FROM 1968 BEGAN the arduous process of reconstructing the national administration. A new government structure was introduced: the "revolutionary committee" used in 1967 to replace the "Shanghai Commune." These new organs were based on a double "three-in-one" principle. They combined soldiers, officials and representatives of the masses; they were also comprised of young, middle-aged and veteran members. Otherwise, they were little different, except in name, from the departments, bureaux and offices which before 1966 had controlled local affairs from the provincial to the factory or village levels. Revolutionary committees had been set up in all provinces and major government units by September 5. China was declared "all red" after the announcement of the last of the 29 major revolutionary committees in 1968.

But cleavages, disputes and brutal quarrels did not end although old professional officials, new revolutionary leaders born of the Cultural Revolution's storms and the armed forces joined together to share power. Alliance and cooperation between the old political masters and the men who had fought to overthrow them were often a transparent sham. The two sides had been forced to sit down round the same table by local army commanders. The stage seemed set for a military take-over. The army, for reasons already explained, was not keen on accepting responsibility for steering the uneasy new coalitions and their unruly supporters for very long. The troops and their commanders were being drawn at the higher administrative levels (such as the provincial revolutionary committees) into a variety of activities which would not endear them to the public. The population at large did not relish a return to the heavy-handed officialdom which prevailed before 1966 and which rapidly reappeared from 1968 onward. By and large, the military mind administering human individuals is the most rigid and least accommodating. The labour force was not enthusiastic about having to obey an inflexible work schedule; yet the troops were in the factories to encourage a return to normal production. The black marketeers, underground factory entrepreneurs and speculators were not universally popular but were regarded by most as useful. The troops formed a new police force, more difficult to corrupt than the pre-1966 Public Security Bureaux. Illegal business activities were under no less a threat than the hated criminal gangs which raped, looted and murdered until the punishment for such crimes became the firing squad For nearly three years, the urban population had been free to thumb its nose at authority, and the peasants had been left largely to their own devices. Now in 1969 bureaucracy and management were about to climb into the saddle, and the army was on hand to help bring the holiday to an end.

The soldiers had no incentive to put up with much popular debate about how life should be conducted. The civilians had come within a hair's breadth of destroying the economy and the whole social fabric. External developments forced the army to expand its control over local civil administrations in the vicinity of disputed international boundaries but distracted the army's concern from civilian problems in other parts of China. On March 2, 1969, border battles between Soviet and Chinese soldiers began on the largest scale since frontier skirmishes started in 1962. The army was not sympathetic to civilian violence when its comrades were being killed in action against the Russians. The possibility of a split between the armed forces and the civilians was more ominous than ever. This trend was alarming because the principle that the soldier was the obedient servant of the civil authorities might crumble beneath the army's contempt for the civilians' inability to keep order in their own parish.

The army had thus to be replaced as far and as fast as possible by conventional administration. In addition, China was supposed to be ruled by a Communist Party. Revolutionary committees in which soldiers, officials and leaders of the masses were combined could not be reconciled with Party control when

Party branches were still suspended. Except to the extent that Peking issued directives in the name of the Party Central Committee, no pretence could be sustained that China was under communist rule. The situation was intolerable. The Party had to be rebuilt and made the supreme source of authority once more. This process set off a fresh round of power struggles. In theory, Lin Piao had been responsible for the organisation of revolutionary committees because of the degree to which their establishment depended on the armed forces. In many instances, individual committees were the creation of other leaders, such as Chou En-lai, even where the revolutionary committee chairman was a soldier.

Lin Piao, through the intervention of the army in civil affairs, was also supposed to put an end to factional fights and the chaos and crime which they created. His prestige as Mao Tse-tung's closest comrade-in-arms should have induced the nation to resolve its differences. Lin Piao was the object of his own personality cult, whic ought to have increased his influence. Although various Lin slogans and directives were introduced into everyday life, Lin Piao made little headway against factionalism. Even the army was unable to go very far towards the elimination of general lawlessness. Shanghai came up with a partial solution adopted in later years by the rest of the country: a militia whose main role was police and civil-defence duties, not military training, and whose motto was "attack with reason and defend by force." (This slogan was attacked, quite unjustifiably, in 1976 as a sly means to intensify disorder.)

Factions became such an integral part of the Chinese scene that they cannot be ignored in an explanation of Mao Tse-tung's lost popularity. Mao Tse-tung issued several appeals and instructions on the need to unite factions, end squabbles and prevent dissensions. The failure to restore order to society and to suppress the interminable factional violence, which became a marked feature of every national political campaign after 1969, revealed the limits of Mao's ability to command the compliance of China's citizens despite the pious verbal response evoked by his name. The public eventually blamed the Cultural Revolution and the group identified as closest to Mao for having unleashed the Red Guards and the intolerable chaos which reigned so long in their wake.

In an important sense, this argument was correct. The Cultural Revolution had bred a crop of individuals with new and valid claims to a voice in the leadership especially at the lower levels. They had obeyed Mao's directives; risked defiance of the old power-holders; and shown their leadership abilities in organising their supporters into coherent groups. An insuperable difficulty, all the same, was that in most places, more than one such leader had emerged. Thus, struggles started between groups of supporters to break their rivals' prestige or to force them to surrender their independence. A secondary problem was that many of these groups were not founded on political considerations which could cut across the normal divisions of society. Instead, young workers tended to take one line; skilled workers a different stance. Various trades, crafts and dialect groups also formed a nucleus of factions. Another basis for a clique was the favours rendered in the past by some minor personality with access to influence (a factory foreman, for instance, who was a Party member). Society was being split, and the new groups being formed often had no common interests on which to build a permanent coalition with other factions except a desire for power and material gain.

The fortunate factions which could make contact with a national leader, such as Chiang Ching, then claimed to be under Peking's direct patronage and acting in obedience to an authority superior to that of the provincial capital. For the most part, members of the central authorities and provincial administrations gave no deliberate personal encouragement to the factions. The followers of individuals within the power elite, however, did sometimes seek to exploit factional support. Thus, indirect connections between top politicians and local factions could be traced. Faction leaders, on the other hand, did not believe they had been deserted by such personalities as Chiang Ching and Wang Hung-wen who were seen as having established and blessed the right to form factions in 1966 and 1967. Professional bureaucrats in both the Government and the Party loathed the factions which had led the mobs to attack officials of every kind in the Cultural Revolution.

With the passage of time, ordinary citizens came to share the attitude of the veteran leaders. What respect did a man deserve who had climbed to power in the chaos of the Cultural Revolu-

tion over the victims of false accusations and physical assaults?
What was a man worth whose career flourished only when
law and order broke down and he could mobilise his bully boys?
A majority of ordinary people came to despise the heirs of the
Cultural Revolution and to resent the scars left on society by
the events of 1966 to 1969.

The most dynamic force behind the continued existence of
factions was their true purpose. These groupings offered their
members substantial benefits. If a faction could capture places
on a municipal, county or provincial revolutionary committee,
its leaders could ensure that decisions were made which
favoured their supporters. (Good examples were the allocation
of work assignments to school graduates or permission to remain in the urban areas instead of being sent to a remote
village.) More vital in many ways, and thus more intractable, was
control over a factory or some other economic enterprise. With
the abolition of all incentive payments based on personal
productivity, the first consideration of a worker was to obtain
a job which called for the minimum physical exertion and the
least unpleasant working conditions. The standard of living of a
worker depended not simply on his wages. Enterprises had
discretion in making special payments for all manner of welfare
purposes.

Enterprises were also entrusted with other powers: making
the preliminary selection, for example, of who should proceed
to some type of post-secondary education. Control over the
management of an enterprise and of the mass organisations, to
which the administrative personnel were supposed to be answer-
able, promised considerable rewards for the faction which came
to the top. Inter-enterprise cooperation, both legal and clandestine, on such issues as mutual exchanges of scarce raw materials
or spare parts or in solving production bottlenecks through
barter of machinery, allowed small cliques to expand their
influnce over a wide area through the establishment of profit-
able economic relations. The more successful the individual
enterprise, the more money it could put aside for its welfare
fund to build houses or pay a family's medical bills, and the
more capital it could save for its investment fund to improve
working conditions through better buildings and more modern
machines.

The factions were concerned with political and administrative power because of the extensive material prizes it brought. Very rationally, when each fresh political campaign temporarily weakened the status of professional management after 1969, the factions regrouped at once. Matters grew more complicated as the tactics of factional politics and division of spoils became familiar to the rural population. Sometimes, the economic power a faction could snatch led to a successful seizure of local political control especially in the 1970s. A prime test of an official's competence became his ability to accomplish the production tasks in the state economic plans. Senior members of the state and Party machines could be ruined when factions slowed down or halted work in a factory or a village. The alternative to possibly suicidal opposition to factions with economic influence was for officials to surrender to the blackmail of a dominant local faction and cooperate with its leaders.

The revolutionary committees established with considerable haste by September 1968 were not effective discussion forums or decision-makers at first, as their memberships reflected fundamental splits among factions from which the masses' representatives were drawn for the most part, and which the soldiers and veteran officials disliked but were powerless to overcome. As the civilian politicians in Peking, and Chou En-lai and his team in particular, steered the nation back towards such concrete problems as industrial and agricultural growth and efficient management, the nature of the revolutionary committees changed gradually. Masses' representatives picked for qualities unrelated to administrative ability eventually counted for less and less at the higher administrative levels. Revolutionary committees lower down frequently managed to develop some cohesion after considerable effort; the impassioned Maoist found himself out in the cold unless he could contribute some genuine talent to the committee's operations. The faction leaders who refused to abandon their overwhelming concern for the narrow interests of their adherents were eased gradually out of power or ignored within the revolutionary committees once the damage inflicted by factional rivalries became apparent.

This bid to exclude their leaders from power intensified the resentment of faction members who justified their demand for power to be surrendered to them on account of their loyalty to

Mao Tse-tung and their instant response to his wishes compared to the record of their rivals. New political campaigns gave them the excuse to resurrect old squabbles over relative ideological merits and defects. From this political position, the battle for power and resources could be resumed. The factions and smaller cliques fought at every opportunity to win back the dramatic power the masses enjoyed in 1966 and 1967 and which the factions believed Mao Tse-tung and his closest allies (his wife, Chang Chun-chiao, Yao Wen-yuan and Wang Hung-wen) wanted them to retain. Until his death in 1971 Lin Piao, too, was thought by the factions to favour their claims.

The drive to establish the Communist Party as the supreme authority in China began on the very heels of the establishment of the 29 provincial or equivalent revolutionary committees. The factions had to start a new round of battles to try to get their representatives into the Party ranks. On October 13, 1968, a Party Plenary session was held, which saw Lin Piao at the pinnacle of his power, just as Mao Tse-tung had appeared at the outset of the Cultural Revolution. Lin, like Mao, was to find the wave which carried him on its crest broke sharply. The Party Plenum discussed a draft Party constitution which formally recognised Lin Piao as second only to Mao Tse-tung and incorporated the 1966 decision that Lin should succeed Mao. The draft constitution excluded from the list of organisations subject to Party control the armed forces, an omission which would put Defence Minister Lin Piao permanently above the Party in his control of the army.

Despite these external symbols of his sweeping authority, Lin Piao suspected about this time that he could be edged aside and that he needed to build up an overwhelming national popularity. What made him wake up to his lack of obvious mass support and the danger which this brought has never been made clear. Perhaps as the selection of candidates for the Ninth National Congress of the Communist Party scheduled for the following spring began to gather momentum, he found a high proportion of nominees were not from backgrounds likely to be much in sympathy with him. He attempted to retrieve his position with delegates to the Congress, it was later alleged, by promises of promotion, by flattery and by various favours.

Lin Piao hoped to solve his popularity problem at the forthcoming National Party Congress with a keynote speech. To the nation as a whole, he wanted to promise a new economic deal. The Cultural Revolution would be announced by Lin Piao as having opened the gates to a new era of prosperity over which Lin would preside. Mao Tse-tung and the rest of the Party leadership found Lin's draft address unacceptable, probably because its intention to buy popular support was too naked. Lin Piao had to redraft his speech without any pledges of prosperity for all. Worse still, the army was put firmly under Party control according to the final version of the Party Constitution approved at the Ninth Congress of the Chinese Communist Party on April 14, 1969. Lin Piao was irate, and he seemed to realise that Chou En-lai had sabotaged him. Nevertheless, Lin Piao's confidence increased rather than wavered. His succession to Mao was approved, and he was untouchable, he thought, unless Mao himself was to be brought into disrepute. Here, Lin was dangerously misled. He had created a situation in which Mao and Chou could develop a common standpoint in opposition to Lin; act in concert for mutual support; and exclude Lin from their councils. The failure to avert this threat to his position reflected Lin's limitations as a political manipulator capable of combining effective power and harmonious personal relations.

Lin Piao's chief tactical error was to have argued with the support of Chen Po-ta (the man who had done much to rescue Chou En-lai in 1967) that the Cultural Revolution had reached its peak. Its political phase was complete, the two men asserted, and the time had come to translate its achievements into concrete developments especially on the economic front. Lin Piao and Chen Po-ta were both accurate in their analysis of the national mood. The country had gulped down as much ideology over the three previous years as any society could hope to stomach. The big menace was cynicism at the constant appearance of more mindless slogans and calls for study of what had been forced down the national throat countless times already.

The cynicism was not moderated by the obvious toll taken by the Cultural Revolution and the costs of giving politics pride of place for three solid years. Crime was rampant. Corruption flourished. Speculation and illegal business were blatant.

Violence was endemic. Traditional practices related to marriages, birthdays and funerals had been given a new lease of life as the Communist Party fell into disrepute. State employees of every rank, from factory managers to school teachers, objected to accepting any responsibility and complained of their ill fortune at being employed in an official capacity. Anyone eager to establish a popular reputation had only to call for a halt to the unending diet of politics and for China's attention to concentrate on practical issues which people could see as important to their daily lives. Lin Piao and Chen Po·ta were not alone in their perception of popular weariness with the Cultural Revolution. Mao Tse-tung made sure by the end of 1970 that his own personality cult was stripped of its extravagances and resumed more human dimensions. He could sense the fatigue with the worship of ideology to the exclusion of such worldly concerns as national prosperity.

Lin Piao and Chen Po-ta wanted an economic upsurge to rally the masses to their side. Although the full details of their programme have never been released by Peking, their general aims can be uncovered. The two men were denounced in the end as "rightists," whose radical image was a sham to deceive the public. The charge had a certain truth since they were not concerned so much with putting Mao Tse-tung's economic theories into practice as with winning a reputation for devotion to the masses' welfare. Such a cynical approach has been a special temptation to many Chinese leaders because Maoism assumes that the Chinese are more eager to sacrifice their private interests for the national good than they have proved in practice. (To be accurate, Mao Tse-tung believed that idealism would evolve slowly from repeated challenges to China's civic conscience.)

Lin Piao and Chen Po-ta wanted modernisation of the industrial sector (defence plants especially); increased labour productivity; better working conditions; and improved discipline in the work force. Wage incentives and bonuses were taboo because of the derision heaped on such "revisionist" and capitalist practices during the Cultural Revolution. Other means had to be adopted to win the workers' cooperation. Lin Piao and Chen Po-ta apparently believed that the solution for the root weaknesses of the Chinese industrial economy lay in the adoption of electronics and automation. Electronics and modernisation would go hand in hand; automated production would reduce the physical strains of factory life. The adoption of electronically-controlled equipment would permit a jump in output per worker. An added gain would be the greater control which electronic equipment and automated techniques would give to management and the reduction in the workers' influence which would follow.

The logic behind this last but crucial point was simple. If a factory depends mainly on brute force to produce goods, the attitude of the labour force determines the volume which can be manufactured. Management's functions become largely an effort to maintain labour force morale. Where the worker is a button-pusher and machinery has replaced human strength as the main productive force, manufacturing turns into a technical process. Labour's role becomes less important than that of machines, and sweat counts for less than skill. The introduction of electronics and automation on a lavish scale was a neat ploy by Lin Piao and Chen Po-ta to deal with a recalcitrant work force in factories where manufacturing techniques were primitive. The armed forces also needed more electronics to create the weapons which the 1969 Sino-Soviet border battles and the lessons of the Middle East and Indochina had shown to be essential even for basically guerilla forces.

The cost of the sort of economic programme which Lin Piao and his advisers had in mind was prohibitive for China, and acceptance of their proposals would be mainly a gesture to the public of the goals to be achieved over one and more five-year plans. Lin does not seem to have struggled very tenaciously for his economic prescriptions. But Mao Tse-tung made a series of remarks on the state of industry which showed how close Lin had come to an open confrontation with Mao, the very trap which Lin previously had determined to avoid. Mao would not agree that the Cultural Revolution had been an economic setback despite all the lost output and the industrial confusion. Before 1966, he insisted, many enterprises had been run by anti-communist elements. The economy had been menaced by a take-over in which the "capitalist-roaders" (imitators of Soviet and other versions of capitalism, according to Maoism) would have destroyed Party control of development. Nor would the argument hold water, Mao asserted, that the Cultural Revolu-

tion had accomplished in full its ideological aims and transformed the national outlook. Quite the contrary, Mao explained. The continued existence of capitalist-minded managements
and the (illicit) use of wage incentives showed how little transformation had occurred since 1949 except of formal ownership.
China was still too close to its capitalist heritage for comfort,
Mao stated, and the ideological revolution could not be
interrupted.

Even at this stage, Lin Piao was still half-blind to the perilous
trend which had emerged. Obsession with his immediate
personal status probably prevented him from seeing clearly
the threat to his future. For Lin, the overwhelming goal to be
achieved at the Ninth Party Congress in 1969 was public
recognition as Mao Tse-tung's successor and as second to Mao
alone in the new Party constitution. Economic plans were worth
sacrificing in the short run for this commitment by Mao and the
Communist Party to Lin Piao as next to Mao Tse-tung himself
in power, wisdom and prospects.

The publication of Lin Piao's new pre-eminence as Mao Tse-
tung's official heir should have rallied a great deal of the
leadership, at the middle and lower levels especially, to his
person. The Party constitution guaranteed that Lin would be
the man of the future. Any sane individual of normal ambitions
should have hurried to make a gesture of homage to the crown
prince. Some such current in Lin's favour appeared to start with
yet more adulation for the sickly-looking Defence Minister of
whom it was joked that Mao Tse-tung would prove to be Lin
Piao's own heir. Almost certainly, Lin Piao was angered by the
failure of Chou En-lai and his technocrats to come forward
with their support for the Lin Piao-Chen Po-ta economic blueprint at the National Party Congress. Chou preferred to back
Mao, an old and tested strategy which had never failed him in
the past. Lin Piao, subsequently and slowly, seemed to
recognise for the first time how large an obstacle Chou En-lai
represented to Lin's total control of China. Henceforward, the
two men would move closer to open hostility. The prize for the
winner would be a China in which power would be shared only
with Mao Tse-tung. Chou En-lai's emergence as the nation's
true genius, to be venerated by his death more than Mao himself, hinged on the destruction of Lin Piao. The split which was

to emerge in the end between Mao and Chou also resulted from the contest between Chou En-lai and Lin Piao to overthrow one another.

The first shots were fired from Lin Piao's side. His tactics for vanquishing Chou En-lai avoided a frontal attack. The Prime Minister had survived too many assaults during the Cultural Revolution to encourage an open bid to oust him. In addition, unity was the official theme of the Ninth Party Congress and the latest Mao directive to China as a whole. Intrigues which would split the central leadership had obviously to be postponed.

Lin preferred to snare Premier Chou En-lai by a flanking operation. The country lacked a head of state. After the Ninth Party Congress in April 1969, Lin pressed hard for the appointment of a successor in this post to Liu Shao-chi, Head of State until disgraced in 1966. How could a self-respecting nation fail to have a constitutional head was Lin's argument. Mao Tse-tung reacted strongly against the idea. To all intents and purposes, he personified China and did not propose to share his supremacy with any lesser mortal, having got rid of Liu Shao-chi in 1966 at some cost. Chou was not in favour of the plan either. He had been solidly behind Mao in the struggles of 1966 and 1967 to remove Liu Shao-chi as Head of State and the rest of the top leadership comparable in status to the Premier. After having become the dominant figure on the central Government side mainly through the downfall of others, Chou was unenthusiastic at having a new "Liu Shao-chi" in the shape of Lin Piao to whom he would be accountable. If the supreme head of the Government also wielded the military and Party strength which Lin Piao had amassed, Chou would be reduced to a mere lackey. Chou En-lai had not risked Red Guard wrath to try to talk them out of toppling all his coterie and wasted hours with factional leaders to keep some form of administration going and defied revolutionaries to preserve his most important economic technocrats and intellectuals simply to finish his career as an exalted messenger boy for a Lin Piao with all the charisma of a dead fish. Mao Tse-tung at least compelled a man's respect, no matter how grudging.

Lin Piao believed himself invincible after his appointment as heir apparent to Mao Tse-tung. Any sins attributed to Lin would damage Mao by whom the Defence Minister had been virtually adopted as far as the average Chinese was concerned. Not even the ruthless Mao would dare take the suicidal step of an open rupture with his official successor; Lin's ruin would accomplish the mortal injury of Mao. Lin's evaluation was borne out by subsequent events. In addition, with virtual open war on the Sino-Soviet borders, who would dare replace the Defence Minister? Such a purge could destroy military morale and hand China's northern provinces and regions on a plate to the Kremlin.

Thus encouraged, Lin ignored Mao's protests and refused to desist from lobbying on behalf of a new head of state. Mao grew weary and reached the conclusion that Lin was deliberately defiant. From 1969, Mao Tse-tung could see that Lin Piao was no longer a real threat. The Defence Minister in the last resort might attempt a military takeover. However, the army was not likely to be thrilled about a permanent involvement in the administration of the nation. The soldiers had not proved very effective (or ambitious) in trying to create replacements for the professional administrative machines of the past, the bulk of whose members at the middle and lower levels had kept their heads down and avoided outright disgrace and hence could now emerge in their old jobs. In the campaign to rebuild the shattered Communist Party, Lin Piao's influence was considerable. Even so, his henchmen did not outnumber the old guard who flocked back to the conduct of official business with open reluctance and secret hopes of revenge. Lin was handicapped during the vital months of late 1969 and 1970 by such poor health that he could not thoroughly mastermind the Party's reconstruction. Chou En-lai took over the administration in the absence of anyone more senior. He assiduously consulted Mao Tse-tung and paid due respect to Lin's status. His conduct as Prime Minister was beyond reproach. But Chou made the vital proposals on appointees to run the country at provincial and lower levels.

The economy remained a key priority. The Lin Piao-Chen Po-ta programme, heavily geared towards electronics, automation and defence, had not won Mao Tse-tung's blessing. Now Chou En-lai had to prove himself superior to Lin. He had to draft an economic blueprint which would satisfy the populace, honour Maoist principles and produce some progress. His preservation of a semblance of economic administration paid off, and September 1969 saw the publication of a new strategy for China's industrial growth, sound enough to remain in force for over a decade. Wage increases could be temporarily ignored; the Soviet threat had worked up patriotic fervour and calmed down the factions. Productivity was bound to rise with the Soviet menace even after actual hostilities halted. The 1969 economic programme's great strength was recognition of the central Government's loss of control over individual enterprises, both industrial and agricultural. Except in the strategic sector, a great number of plants had been taken over (with or without Peking's consent) by local administrations of the areas in which they were situated. Cooperation with economic plans by peasants and urban workers was far from automatic or satisfactory. The trick was to transform this enforced decentralisation into a virtue and to lay the foundations for a gradual reassertion of Peking's direction of every phase of economic activity.

Since individual districts had seized control of enterprises within their boundaries, the answer was to push total responsibility for these enterprises on to the districts. For a variety of reasons—the threat of a Soviet attack, transport economies, specialised local needs and resources—each district was encouraged to become as economically self-sufficient as possible, both as regards existing enterprises and new investments. The state would leave individual districts to raise their own funds; to develop their own raw material sources; and to absorb their production through local market demand. Districts would have to solve their own productivity problems and difficulties with the labour force or face substantial financial losses. The principles spelled out in the blueprint were old favourites of Mao Tse-tung himself, and he could not complain about the new development programme.

Obedience to the state economic plan was in the first and last resort to be a test of ideological probity. For this economic blueprint was produced during the reconstruction of the Communist Party, a campaign which emphasised the duty of every communist to respect Party discipline, particularly Central Committee directives. Peking could impose sanctions, of course,

which operated mainly through the organs most carefully guarded by Chou En-lai from the revolutionaries after 1966 (which
enhanced the influence of the Chou camp). The bank branches
were the linchpin, and they not only supervised financial transactions according to the criteria laid down by the various
planning authorities but trained personnel for general financial
work including tax collection. The state's agreement or refusal
to help a local project off the ground with bank loans and
transfers of skilled workers, equipment and raw materials from
elsewhere plus the provision of a national commercial network
were Peking's weapons. Once an enterprise was past the
cottage-industry stage or had a surplus which its own locality
could not consume, control of a district's economy was back in
the hands of the Government. The central administration's
assistance was essential in disposing of the surplus output.

Furthermore, general agreement existed among both the
Maoist ideologues and the economic technocrats that until
agriculture was revolutionised, peasant cultivation would be a
millstone round the rest of the economy. Hence toleration of a
decentralised economy closely linked to village administrations
made sense to most shades of opinion along the political
spectrum. On this point, Lin Piao and his backers seemed to be
in a minority, as they feared the consequences of such total
priority for farming on output of supplies in desperate demand
by the armed forces. The emergence of a conflict over the division of the national pie between economic development and
national defence helped to build opposition to Lin Piao. Lin
might have a glorious future and be worth cultivating; but local
leaders had constituents crying out for consumer goods or
chemical fertilisers without more ado, and the masses could
still destroy an official who failed to respond promptly to their
legitimate wishes. Lin Piao attempted to crush regional resistance to the demands of the Defence Minister by taking direct
control of factories especially in provinces within reasonable
distance of Shanghai. This seizure of local resources made
enemies for him at the general provincial level, as did the tendency of many factions sabotaging industrial output to invoke
Lin Piao's name.

In 1970, Lin Piao's star waned beyond concealment; real
power had passed to Chou En-lai. The Premier had taken

control of rebuilding the Communist Party. The Party's own authority was being stressed constantly, which meant repeated emphasis on the authority of Party officials endorsed by Chou. Lin Piao's suggestions on economic strategy had been rejected. The economic specialists and technocrats shielded by Chou in 1966 and 1967 were in the saddle. And Lin Piao had intensified Mao Tse-tung's mistrust of his ambitions at the very moment when the capacity or desire of the troops to run the country— Lin's trump card—was very much in doubt.

CHAPTER EIGHT

DEATH OF A CROWN PRINCE

AT THE END of 1970, Mao Tse-tung was determined to revise his plans for the future leadership of China. He had decided that the veterans at the top were too decrepit and out of touch with modern China to be entrusted after his death with the guardianship of the society which he had founded. More practically, the mortality rate among the shrunken band of warriors who had brought Mao to power must accelerate, which implied constant reshuffles of official posts between the survivors and a lack of stability in the highest ranks which could upset the masses. When a country as poor as China is in the middle of a traumatic revolution to modernise every aspect of social, political and economic behaviour, reduction of leadership changes to a bare minimum eases tensions by minimising the strains which every innovation appears to involve. Mao Tse-tung personally decreed that the next generation of Chinese rulers should not be aged over sixty.

Unlike the nation at large, Mao Tse-tung took considerable satisfaction in the rawest recruits to political life thrown up during the Cultural Revolution. They had been pitched into a maelstrom and had won through by learning how to appeal to the masses and how to organise them. They had been forced to accept such considerable sacrifices as "volunteering" for work in primitive villages with no guarantee they would ever be promoted above the rank of peasant. They had been asked to turn their backs on the revered credential for an official career in China, a full university education. The idealism of a whole generation of youth had been tested after the Red Guards had been mobilised in 1966, and the results looked promising to Mao, given time and adequate opportunities to mature. The older members of the new revolutionary elite had not been forced to abandon their families permanently and forsake the cities. They were being tested instead by pressure to refuse the higher salary scales and other benefits allowed to officials and to spend a great part of each year engaged in their old jobs instead of moving permanently to a comfortable office. The Cultural Revolution, furthermore, had pushed to the surface potential leaders who could not be suspected, Mao hoped, of pro-Soviet leanings as they had been schooled in a China whose hostility towards the Kremlin had increased each year. Unlike the veterans, the new blood had never been asked to suspend their criticism of Soviet policies towards China when Stalin had been the undisputed monarch of the world communist movement, and Moscow the school for a high proportion of non-Russian revolutionaries.

The age limit proposed by Mao Tse-tung would prevent Lin Piao from taking over as Party Chairman after Mao's demise, in theory at any rate. Mao had not decided yet what to do about Lin. He had reservations about the Defence Minister which dated back to 1966. Chou En-lai was a perennial headache of course, for who could guarantee his trustworthiness in perpetuity. But the Prime Minister was under reasonable control as he seemed too busy for palace intrigues. Chou had to struggle to get the country functioning normally again under the direction of a rebuilt Communist Party. Chou's tasks had eased in some respects. The 1969 frontier war with the Soviet Union had created a temporary bond of national unity based on patriotism and fear of invasion. The threat of Soviet tanks rolling toward Peking was enough to distract many cliques from local rivalries. The army was becoming less conspicuous in civil affairs, although military commanders still dominated a large number of the new Party Committees. The armed forces had other matters, namely the Soviet divisions, to keep them occupied. Chou En-lai had planned against this day when reconstruction of the administration would be his responsibility.

The Prime Minister had to pay a price for this extension of his power. The stress on orderly rule and respect for authority aroused some resentments. The masses felt a nostalgia for the licence and liberty of the Cultural Revolution and had apprehensions about the reappearance of their pre-1966 bosses. Lin Piao's extensive personality cult also created doubts among the populace (though not the higher ranks of the bureaucracy) about Chou's authority. Lin's carefully-fostered image as Mao's heir overshadowed Chou in this period. The Prime Minister had problems in enforcing his edicts at the grassroots. Officials were still far from confident about their own status, and they were not enthusiastic about Peking's insistence that they earn their salaries by carrying out their duties effectively and demonstrating strong and vigorous leadership. The memories of mass public criticism rallies were too close for the ordinary official to feel free to exert his formal power. He had been left largely unprotected in 1966 and 1967 when attacked for doing what he conceived to be his duty. Who would grant him immunity from similar attacks if the nation went through a second Cultural Revolution? Chou En-lai had enough challenges, with his day filled by the bureaucratic business he adored. The Prime Minister had too many headaches, Mao could feel sure, to dream of letting ambition take control of his cold, calculating functionary's intellect.

Mao Tse-tung's distrust for Lin Piao, the danger that Lin might forfeit the succession on grounds of age and Mao's refusal to heed Lin's pleas on the need for a head of state aroused considerable trepidation in Lin's mind. His clique was even more alarmed. They did not see much chance of a compromise with Chou En-lai who was in a position to run the nation without their assistance. Chou was not vulnerable to charges of disloyalty to Mao, especially once the faction had been exterminated which had accused Chou of being a secret anti-Maoist in 1967. The threat from Chou was displayed nakedly in a dispute over access to the minutes of a closed Communist Party meeting organised by Lin's supporters in the armed forces. This classified record of discussions by senior generals was supposed to remain secret. But Chou, in his capacity as Acting Secretary-General of the Communist Party, insisted that he could not be denied the right to see the minutes of all Communist Party proceedings. The minutes were prised out of a desperate Lin Piao cabal. Chou found their contents sufficiently damaging to Lin's key supporters at the top of the armed forces to be worth passing over to Mao Tse-tung. Self-criticisms by senior military commanders followed. Chou had thrown down the gauntlet; won the first round; and was unlikely to be content with mere words as a guarantee of future exemplary conduct from the Lin clique.

Lin Piao's situation by March 1971 was desperate. His coterie worked out an emergency plan to rid Mao Tse-tung of supporters on whom to lean if he tried to ditch Lin Piao. Chou En-lai would have to go, of course, plus such figures as Chang Chun-chiao, loyal to Mao and with considerable talent. Chou's removal and Chang Chun-chiao's assassination might well prove highly popular. The allegation has been made that Mao Tse-tung, too, was on the short-list for liquidation. The charge is hard to believe because China would have been outraged at his assassination. To give Mao's power to Lin and retain Mao as a puppet, gagged and under constant supervision, would identify Mao with the new Lin administration after it seized power. Mao's inclusion, even unwillingly, in such a set-up would give it a claim to legitimacy, too valuable an asset to throw away in a pointless and dangerous murder.

Thanks to Chou En-lai, the 1971 plot by Lin Piao's coterie was not long a secret. How far Lin was an active party in the conspiracy to seize power and place Lin Piao in command of the Government is unclear. He was foolish enough to put his thoughts of bitter frustration about Mao on paper. Lin's indictment of Mao Tse-tung was incorporated in the "571" dossier, although its style is not typical of Lin Piao. Perhaps the document was rewritten or edited to highlight the more offensive facets of Lin's attitude towards Mao. Whatever the precise parentage of the document, its impact on Mao Tse-tung was horrifying. Mao read how he was a monster who drove family, friends and aides mad. He was possessed of great cunning, unable to tolerate any opposition. He had ruined China through the Cultural Revolution. Worst of all, Mao Tse-tung was described as the creation of a monumental personality cult in a calculated effort to produce national unity. Mao was the reincarnation of the most notorious tyrant in China's history, Chin Shih Huang Ti, the first emperor of the Chin dynasty. This ruler had unified China, its laws and written language two thousand years before Mao. He had also burnt the classics and buried scholars alive. Before the Pacific War, Chin Shih Huang Ti had been compared to Hitler. In 1958, Mao had argued that Chin Shih Huang Ti had been a force for good in Chinese history, contrary to popular belief. He warned, however, that no comparisons should be encouraged of the reign of the first Chin emperor with the Communist Party's rule.

From March 1971, Lin Piao was finished as far as Mao Tse-tung was concerned. Every compromising detail of the plot built up around Lin to seize power and of Lin's loathing for Mao had been conveyed to Mao Tse-tung. Lin's ruin was complete. But as Lin Piao had realised: any criticism of him was an attack on Mao, for Lin was the crown prince, the "closest comrade-in-arms" of Mao Tse-tung. The downfall of Lin was, at the same time, a crippling blow to Mao himself. Even an enraged Mao could grasp how close to political self-destruction he would come through any public revelations of Lin Piao's disloyalty. Chou En-lai must have been able to see with even greater clarity the consequences of making it impossible for Mao to tolerate Lin by his side and yet equally impossible for Mao to disown his official successor. Lin's collapse and Mao's dilemma were Chou's opportunity.

What to do with Lin Piao was Mao Tse-tung's greatest anxiety. Dismissal of the Defence Minister was of no great strategic importance for no significant clashes on the borders with the Soviet Union had occurred for almost two years. Yet Lin's disgrace before the nation as a whole would indict Mao himself. Who would believe that Mao had only allowed Lin to be nominated as his successor in 1966 because of the need to win the armed forces to the Maoist side? Who would sympathise with an explanation that once so nominated, Lin Piao could not be prevented from appearing in the 1969 Party Constitution as Mao's heir, although Mao allegedly had seen through Lin as early as 1966 and made every effort to check his ambitions? Lin Piao also had ample followers as a result of his own personality cult linked to Mao's name, or so it seemed. Who could predict the outcome of any crisis Lin's combined military and civilian admirers might provoke? Finally, who would believe that Lin genuinely had plotted against Mao? The accusation would sound a pure fabrication to a nation whose credulity had been strained to breaking point by the charges made against so many renowned communists from 1966 to 1969. The accusations against them were now being discredited because the veterans had begun slowly to emerge from disgrace as senior officials once more. But Mao could not sit on his hands and wait for Lin to fire his broadside. Lin might not miss the mark.

Mao Tse-tung dragged himself wearily round the provinces from July to September explaining that Lin Piao was a traitor but that his defection from the Maoist camp was to be kept secret from the masses for fear of scandalising them. A vast Peking editorial to mark the fiftieth anniversary of the Communist Party in July contained an account of Mao's military exploits and was a warning that even the most redoubtable military commander was no match for Mao. The provincial administrations, for their part, heeded Mao's instructions. Loyally, they did not leak Lin Piao's crimes until authorised to publicise them by Peking. They were not stunned when the final act in the Lin Piao affair took place. They were uncomfortable about Mao's warning that China would never be free from jackals in the highest seats of power who would jump out regularly to overthrow the legitimate government and bring back the capitalists and imperialists. Mao's gloomy prophecy was a harbinger of unending purges. But intrigue, betrayal and vendetta were the very stuff of which the history of a Chinese dynasty was made; and Mao Tse-tung was visibly coming closer to the end of his reign.

Mao Tse-tung insisted that Lin Piao remain at liberty. If scandal were to be avoided, no point would be served by his arrest. Mao's desire to preserve his reputation from destruction by disclosures about his chosen heir led to a further weakening of Mao's own position. The news media, both national and provincial, continued to grind out a flood of reverent rhetoric about both men, linking their names inseparably. Peking, now controlled by Chou En-lai, gathered a selection of photographs of Mao and Lin in various leadership postures; touched them up to ensure their dignity; and distributed them round the country. Lin's intimates realised that their designs had been uncovered and that they must take desperate steps or face total ruin.

The photographs of Mao with Lin were on their way to the bookshops and news stalls on September 8, when the conspirators tried to begin their coup to save Lin and themselves. The planned assassinations did not take place. Chang Chun-chiao was excellently guarded by Hsu Shih-yu, the Nanking commander whom Chang had kept on the correct Maoist track in the Cultural Revolution. Chang Chun-chiao could not be wiped out.

Chou En-lai had more lives than a cat and went about the capital openly with a heavy though discreet bodyguard. Some members of the regiment which surrounded Mao's person had been seduced from their loyalty but enough members of the praetorian guard stuck to their duty to keep Mao secure and well.

Mao Tse-tung still refused to have Lin Piao and his immediate family and entourage placed in detention. The capital was secure enough. All planes had been grounded to prevent disaffected elements from being flown to rescue or reinforce Lin in Peking. Mao felt he could relax. Lin Piao was entirely at his mercy; fortunes had come full circle since Mao had been a hostage in 1966. Lin would have to cooperate with Mao to stay alive. A voluntary resignation on grounds of ill-health from the post of Mao's crown prince perhaps? Later, a speech on retired soldiers settling in the villages, a new campaign to be led by Lin Piao in person? The Defence Minister could be stripped of all titles and posts discreetly and then pushed into decent obscurity. Mao would be safe.

On September 13, Lin Piao made a fateful decision. He would not lead the life of Mao Tse-tung's puppet. He would not allow himself to be destroyed mentally and emotionally by Mao's colossal psychic energy. Lin took steps to flee from the capital in a British plane, a civilian jet which had first attracted Chinese interest because of its advanced navigational and radar equipment. Chou En-lai's intelligence on Lin's activities was total. The news of the projected plane journey made the Premier hurry to Mao's library where he sought Mao's signature on an authorisation for Lin Piao's arrest. Mao Tse-tung refused to sign the warrant. Since all planes had been grounded, how could Lin Piao take off without the connivance of air force personnel, which was unlikely? When Chou insisted that Lin would soon be in the air, Mao inquired what his destination would be. What other refuge could Lin flee to except the Soviet Union was Chou's reply. The answer satisfied Mao, who argued that Lin in Moscow would be completely discredited in the eyes of the Chinese, and his defection would require condemnation not explanation.

Faced with an intractable Mao, Chou En-lai had to help Lin Piao aloft. Whether the Lin entourage was alive or dead when they boarded the aircraft is unknown. Whether the plane was hit by a missile as it crossed the rocket defences along the northern Chinese border and crashed into a hill in the Mongolian Repubilc (the first inner-Party account) or ran out of fuel and crashed during an emergency landing in Mongolia (as the manufacturers of the plane were given to understand) was a secret the Communist Party's Politburo kept closely to itself. Almost certainly, the plane was induced to fly off its intended course, either to divert it over a rocket battery or into the Mongolian wastelands. Such a diversion was simple electronics. The plane's pilot would have been helpless on this improvised and unscheduled night flight if the ground signal beacons by which the plane was navigated were manipulated deliberately, a perfectly safe stratagem because the sky was empty of all other craft.

Even now, with Lin Piao dead on the Mongolian steppes, Mao Tse-tung could have been saved from dishonour. Some announcement was possible about the Defence Minister on a tour of the country's northern defences and falling victim to engine failure in his imported aircraft. Lin would have been given a martyr's funeral, with anti-Soviet sentiment whipped up to new heights. Instead, at astonishing speed for China, a detailed account of the Lin plot was passed to the Communist Party's grassroot branches and then to the ordinary population. The haste with which such a complex and traumatic event was made known through the Party apparatus was without parallel. Simultaneously, the pictures of China's two hero's, Mao Tse-tung together with Lin Piao, were put on sale. After some delay, publications which portrayed the two men photographed together were distributed. For three weeks after Lin's death, provincial radio stations and newspapers continued to heap praise on Lin Piao whom nearly everyone knew to be a charred corpse. The provincial administrations were obedient to the instructions Mao had issued during the summer on maintaining the fiction of Mao's love for Lin until Peking ordered otherwise. Chou En-lai could have asked for nothing better since the Mao-Lin relationship was now a macabre propaganda stunt turned into parody for all to see.

Of course, the nation could not be expected to hear the news of Lin Piao's alleged treachery and demise with total impassivity. One poor teacher reading to the class the official (but unpublished) version of Lin's death met with blank disbelief and then indignation. The first news about Lin's death seemed to the students a plot to discredit the man closest to Mao Tse-tung, and they dragged the teacher off to the security authorities to be charged with sedition. The police eventually convinced the students that the teacher was not blaspheming and that the account of Lin's plot had been issued by Peking. For many others, Lin's alleged conspiracy against Mao Tse-tung took a massive effort to digest. Lin had been hailed for too long as the model Maoist to be accepted overnight as the arch-traitor.

Not until August 1973 did the Communist Party dare publicly to denounce Lin by name. Even after constant invective against the dead man under various caricatures, Chou En-lai refused to give any detailed public account of Lin's misdeeds. The mystery and the confusion over the last hours of Lin added to the public's interest in the affair. Mao Tse-tung maintained a lengthy silence on the topic except in conversation with privileged foreign visitors. The men closest to Chou En-lai met enquiries from Chinese citizens about the plot with a shrug of the shoulders, a smile and a suggestion that everyone should seek his own answer as to how Mao's closest comrade-in-arms turned traitor. The winks and nods were far more incriminating of Mao than any overt attack on his infallibility would have been. Somewhat tardily, a national campaign was launched by Mao to reject Lin Piao's claims that Mao was a genius.

Mao Tse-tung found it difficult to face the Chinese people after the Lin Piao scandal. What explanation would convince any citizen of average intelligence that the sickly, fawning Lin Piao had deceived Mao Tse-tung, with his vast experience of political intrigue, of men driven by ambition, and of politicians hungry for power at any price? Mao had caused the expulsion of so many notables from the Communist Party for lack of ideological integrity that his tolerance of Lin Piao over so many years seemed incomprehensible unless Mao were no longer fit for office. Mao Tse-tung graced Party formalities until 1973. The Chinese population thereafter had to seek increasingly for clues about Mao's health and state of mind from photographs and television films of his receptions of foreign delegations. But the stream of foreign governments on pilgrimage to Peking after so many years during which China had been isolated from the outside world could not rescue Mao's reputation or self-esteem. Even the conversion of President Richard Nixon into a friend of China who came in search of reconciliation in February 1972 was not testimony to Mao's worldwide influence. The limelight was hogged by Chou En-lai, who, as always during his career, took the credit for the charm and realism of Chinese diplomacy. Mao's talks with Nixon, Dr Henry Kissinger or the Japanese Prime Minister were exercises in courtesy by men awed to be in the presence of a living legend whose historical importance they hoped would rub off on his guests. Chou belonged to a different category. He was filmed at the airport, at the banquets, at the negotiating table, escorting the world's most distinguished notables for the benefit of a vast Chinese audience. The homage was being paid to Chou En-lai, the average citizen might conclude, rather than to Mao Tse-tung. For his part, Mao received his visitors in his library like a retired professor still bent on making a last contribution to knowledge which would earn him the Nobel Prize.

CHAPTER NINE

ECONOMIC CRISIS AND A RETURN TO THE PAST

MAO TSE-TUNG WAS not the man to tamely permit Chou En-lai to take over China when Mao died. The manner of Lin Piao's death and the rush to expose Lin's sins to the nation also gave Mao good grounds to mistrust Chou En-lai. The Premier profited too obviously from Lin's removal. Chou alone should shoulder most of the blame for the failure to shield Mao from discredit. The press and radio could have been ordered to cease speaking of Mao and Lin in the same breath. Some plausible fiction could have been invented to cover Lin's death. Instead, the Mao-Lin comradeship was being highlighted by the propaganda departments while the Chinese population was being informed at closed conclaves of how Lin had perished while fleeing after his failure to seize power. This contradiction between what was being blared forth about Lin's devotion to Mao in public and revealed about Lin's betrayal of Mao in private came close to satire. Further, how hard had Chou En-lai tried to obey Mao's instructions that Lin should be left to his own devices and not subject to interference, Mao could well inquire? The basis for confidence in Chou as Mao's loyal Premier had received a violent jolt.

Mao Tse-tung tried to fight back on two fronts, the ideological and the economic. The public had not yet been told of Lin Piao's 1969 plans to stress economic progress at the expense of political revolution. Lin thus remained for the average citizen a symbol of Cultural Revolution extremism. The country identified him with ultra-leftist policies, which the population believed must be abandoned or modified drastically after Lin's death and denunciation. If Lin were totally discredited, so must his extremist policies be flung aside, the public reckoned. Few suspected that Lin could be accused of sham leftism but genuine rightism. Hence, a large proportion of the population believed after Lin's death that radical extremism, or ultra-leftism, was permanently out of favour. Factory wages went up in 1972 by ten per cent, and officials received backdated salary increases. The pay rises were a sign that living standards were of greater concern than Maoist slogans. Threats to deprive peasants of their private plots, heard while Lin still lived, were silenced. This change was also a pointer to a new concern with economics rather than ideology. Morale improved, and the economy took on a new thrust. In education, which had once been a hotbed of radicalism, teachers exerted their authority once more, and examinations were reintroduced. These changes were supposed to herald a new status for professionals. The theatre had been captured for the revolution by Chiang Ching in 1966, working under Lin Piao's orders. New plays appeared in 1972 which did not conform to the criteria laid down as the tests of Maoist drama in 1966. (In 1976, Mao Tse-tung was posthumously depicted as a cultural liberal, a peculiar interpretation of his record.)

The man who could be accused of starting the trend to undo the radical triumphs of the Cultural Revolution was Chou En-lai, now alone at the top with Mao Tse-tung. A year after Lin Piao's death, Mao Tse-tung struck back with a campaign designed to defend the Cultural Revolution and to embarrass Chou En-lai for the reversals of radical policies since September 1971. The Prime Minister and the rest of the leadership were forced by Mao to make a backward somersault. The whole nation at the end of 1972 was directed to cease attacks on Lin Piao as an ultra-leftist and to condemn him for rightism. Criticism of radical leftists was to stop as well. This abrupt ideological about-turn was hard for the population to fathom and made large numbers of officials appear out of step with the correct Maoist line preached by Peking. Chou En-lai was too light-footed to stub his toe and stumble ideologically.

The next thrusts the Premier had to parry were aimed at the economy and professionalism. A crackdown started against all incentive payments to workers, no matter how trivial. By the end of 1973, the urban labour force was back on a standard wage packet for each grade of worker, unrelated to individual performance at the factory work bench. The attack on professionalism was indirect but no less real for the trained managerial and technical personnel purged in 1966 and 1967 and reinstated with Chou's blessing. The 1971 decision by an unpublicised National Education Conference to recall for refresher courses all college students whose studies had been interrupted by the Cultural Revolution was discarded even though the decision had been endorsed by the Party Central Committee. Educational policy veered sharply back to the radical path, with a new disregard for academic standards and professionalism. Chou En-lai had no choice but to go along with this chillier ideological and economic climate, although the atmosphere inside the Party and government ranks grew tenser and the factions revived.

The condemnation of those who had accused Lin Piao of ultra-leftism was a very effective weapon for the Maoist camp. Every time a political movement harped back to the Cultural Revolution and the need to defend its gains, officials felt endangered. Every such campaign lauded the vast changes wrought by the Cultural Revolution and the masses who had led it to victory. Such declarations gave the factions an excuse to reassert themselves and claim the rewards due to their Maoist zeal. When officials felt threatened, they stopped all activity which called for personal decisions. When factions hoisted their banners again, law and order began to crumble once more. Each upsurge of factional activity and each retreat by officialdom enlarged the scope for illicit and criminal activities of every sort. For the Prime Minister anxious to organise a machine to run the country with maximum efficiency, the state of affairs produced by every new Maoist directive and campaign was a harebrained exercise in barely-controlled anarchy.

Whether they liked it or not, officials were being forced to adopt ominous remedies to stay in business. The general public could see few signs that prosperity was round the corner or that docile response to Party injunctions would produce any material benefits for their children, let alone themselves. The ordinary official had to satisfy two sides, his superiors and his constituents. His superiors wanted a variety of plans and targets to be accomplished. The most important were economic goals as a rule, because results could be measured at once in dollars and cents. When short of machinery, spare parts, raw materials or transport, the management of an enterprise often found it hard to resist the temptation of unlawful trade or barter deals to maintain output. Illegal transactions on the grey, if not the black market, were less perilous than criticism sessions conducted by senior Party personnel. The national and provincial administrations grew stronger; their demands for results became more strident; and their ability to investigate plan defaulters increased as well. An official could win a reputation for being a manager versed in both political revolution and economic production if he had the resources to buy the cooperation of workers who would otherwise take time off, on full pay, to engage in factional disputes. Money would also win popularity for an official if he could purchase immunity for those in his care when threatened by criminal gangs which invoked key political figures as their patrons, claims it was safest not to investigate. Gangs openly used such titles as "Chiang Ching Red Guards." After the Cultural Revolution and the Lin Piao plot, anything was credible. Officials preferred to help influential constituents to pay extortion money rather than risk a political vendetta on top of physical assault.

During 1973, the atmosphere worsened steadily. The chief reason for the deterioration was, paradoxically, the improvement in China's international situation. The Soviet threat had receded. President Richard Nixon had flown to Peking to pay political tribute to China. These developments induced a relaxed mood among Chinese toward the outside world. Events on the home front could thus absorb the energies of both functionaries and factions after a period of external pressures resulting in a measure of internal unity in which local and personal interests had to take second place to national priorities. In addition, the ban on wage incentives did not mollify the masses or increase the administration's popularity. The factions were not slow to seize their opportunity to mount a renewed drive to recapture the power their leaders had enjoyed from 1966 to 1968. Political quarrels would have been unavoidable, anyway, because the Tenth National Congress of the Communist Party was to meet in August 1973. This event provoked battles first to dominate the selection of delegates to the Congress and then to win control of the Congress itself.

Chou En-lai was being strained to breaking point in this period. Mao Tse-tung remained Chairman of the Communist

Party, and his signature was essential on top-level directives. Mao no longer saw Chou regularly, even to attend to state affairs. Mao's reluctance to receive frequent visits from the Prime Minister was no great surprise after the way in which Lin Piao's death had been exploited to Chou's benefit and Mao's discredit. Chou En-lai had to depend on a variety of subterfuges to visit Mao and obtain the Chairman's endorsement of major Party decisions: when accompanying foreign guests to Mao's residence, for example. Chou had also been warned he had cancer, which failed to respond satisfactorily to treatment. The Prime Minister needed reinforcements. He could not look to his own brains trust, for he had conditioned his coterie into placid acceptance of all Chou's initiatives and wrung their natural toughness out of them. He needed a hard man, who would stop at nothing to do his duty, a man ready to snap his fingers at Mao Tse-tung and the whole of China, if his conscience or common sense so dictated.

The matter was urgent because Mao Tse-tung had started to bypass the Communist Party apparatus. He had encouraged his wife, Chiang Ching, to establish direct links with a number of subordinate organisations. Party rules did not permit members to obey instructions handed down from the top through such covert and irregular channels. Enough individuals were to be found, however, who believed that they would get accelerated promotion by assiduous cultivation of Mao Tse-tung or of the next best thing, his wife. Most Party members were indignant at this transparent scheme to avoid the correct Party procedures of open communication to members of directives from Peking and active discussion of their contents at Party branch meetings. Many Party members suspected that Mao was indicating his lack of confidence in the Party rank and file, in the majority of the Party officials and in Chou En-lai. They were prepared to believe that the clique within the Party which Chiang Ching was exploiting would be used eventually to advance her own interests and those of the Maoist cabal, especially the "Shanghai Mafia" later christened the "gang of four." But denunciation of Chiang Ching was out of the question. The time was not ripe for criticism which came so close to Mao himself.

This duplicate Party structure along which orders passed in

opposition to the directives issued by the regular Communist Party and government machines increased Chou En-lai's burdens. For the first time in his life, he had to face a direct clash with Mao Tse-tung on a matter of principle. The Premier wanted a stand-in and the right to select his own assistant. Chou's preference was for an individual, Teng Hsiao-ping, whom Mao resented because of years of refusal to perform the usual gestures of obeisance in his direction. Teng had been one of the first and most important victims of the Cultural Revolution. The latest self-criticism had been dragged out of him in 1972. He confessed his anti-Mao sins with the greatest reluctance and after considerable persuasion. He looked for all the world like a plough-share being hammered into shape on the anvil, red-hot sparks still flying in every direction as he yielded slowly under the blacksmith's hammer. He was stunted in stature with a head that grew directly out of stocky shoulders, which Chinese regard as a sign of durability and obstinacy. He was offhand with officials but could not resist children whom he adored. He was gifted with considerable intelligence; was a talented administrator; and he had a keen interest in ideology. His tongue was like a whiplash, and he was indifferent to the resentments of the mighty and humble alike provided his caustic comments improved their performance.

This dedicated individual, perpetually doomed to pay bitterly for his inability to show fear or favour, Teng Hsiao-ping, was the Premier's remedy for the pressures on him: some created by Mao Tse-tung; some by the Maoist coterie; and some by incurable cancer. From Chou En-lai's point of view, Teng was too valuable to waste any longer in the wildernesses of Inner Mongolia. Teng was held in high esteem by the army as a commander who had prised open the gateway for the communist forces to pour into southern China as they swept to national victory and the establishment of the People's Republic in 1949. The way in which, as Party Secretary-General, he had sacrificed himself in 1966 to prevent civil war and give Mao Tse-tung a fair opportunity to participate in the key Party Central Committee meeting at the outbreak of the Cultural Revolution had earned him the reputation of an honest official. He knew the Communist Party personnel from one end of the country to the other. When Party Secretary-General before 1966, he had not grumbled at Mao's neglect of his files. Teng had been happy to review Party

appointments and promotions. His clients and protégés dotted
the country. He also had a good nose for the men who had
curried favour with Cultural Revolution leaders hostile to Chou
En-lai and who would need to be shunted aside.

Teng Hsiao-ping had a personal acquaintance with national
agricultural and economic problems. In addition, he could be
entrusted with the task of presenting a bleak face to foreigners
in diplomatic negotiations. He had helped rid China of Soviet
troops and commercial enterprises in 1954; he had been a Peking
spokesman in 1961 when China gave notice to the Soviet Union
that the Kremlin had forfeited China's respect. Teng was the
truculent technocrat whom Chou needed to lash out at the idio-
cies, inefficiencies and illegalities which were flowering profusely
and threatening to choke Chinese society.

A first hurdle was Teng Hsiao-ping's utter rejection of Chou
En-lai's insistence on his return to office. Teng had been humiliated once for his honesty; history would honour him. He had no
desire to have any further relations with Mao Tse-tung on whom
he had always refused to fawn. Mao had complained of Teng's
pointed habit of ignoring the existence of Mao Tse-tung at the
start of the Cultural Revolution. Teng felt constitutionally incapable of Chou's miraculous self-discipline in appearing to
comply with Mao's every wish and still getting his own way.
Teng was unprepared, too, for any sacrifice of his good repute
for selfish considerations, career or public esteem. Chou En-lai
spent hours talking Teng round. In the end, Teng agreed to join
the Government on one condition. Mao Tse-tung had to write a
letter asking Teng to come home on the grounds that all was for-
given. Mao Tse-tung would have to invite Teng back to prove
that he had not been tempted to resume high office by the power
and privileges it brought. The Mao summons to Teng was discreetly advertised, so that the population was left in no doubt
about Teng's new-found respectability.

Teng Hsiao-ping demanded a price from Chou En-lai for help-
ing to bail out the hard-pressed administration. Mao Tse-tung
was not to be content without his pound of flesh for accepting
the reinstatement of the impertinent Teng. Mao wanted to have
a strong voice in the nominations to the Party Central
Mommittee's Politburo which the Tenth National Party Congress
Could be called upon to endorse with loud applause in August

1973. Mao was particularly keen to see a hitherto unknown Shanghai worker, Wang Hung-wen, appointed Vice Chairman of the Communist Party and asked to deliver one of the keynote speeches. The step, Mao believed, would emphasise his preference for a new generation of leaders and reduce the odds in favour of Chou En-lai, Teng Hsiao-ping and company taking over by default on Mao's death. Wang's appointment as Party Vice Chairman also strengthened the popular suspicion that the "gang of four" was a power to be reckoned with and favoured by Mao himself. Wang would rally the younger officials and the Cultural Revolution profiteers, like Wang himself, to the Maoist camp. Whenever he came under pressure, Mao preferred to mobilise radical elements whose strident views, shrilly expressed, gave the impression of greater force and influence than the less extreme and calmer voices of the more balanced groups in Chinese political life. And Wang Hung-wen, with his image of youth able to rise to the top in Peking, was useful even to the aging Chou En-lai band of veterans.

The contents of the Tenth National Congress speeches were of great interest to Mao Tse-tung. The addresses delivered to the Tenth Party Congress by Premier Chou En-lai and Vice Chairman Wang Hung-wen were studded with quotations from various Mao documents which had been circulated among Party members but never published for general consumption. The impression the 1973 Party Congress was supposed to make on the Party rank and file was that Mao was still on top and that the Party was run by him. Chou had no objection to the Party being given this version of life at the summit. The Government was not at any peak of popularity. The bad weather must make matters worse by hitting the harvest. Fresh political storms were on the horizon. The Prime Minister was far from upset by Mao's desire to be seen at the helm. Any opprobrium would go to his account rather than hurt Chou.

While preparations were underway for the Tenth Party Congress, with the inevitable fights to control the nomination of delegates, Chou En-lai was strengthening his own position against an attack about to be launched on him from a peculiar quarter. Chou, with Teng Hsiao-ping's aid, scrutinised the delegates to the Party Congress and excluded most potential dissidents and opponents of the Prime Minister. Hopes were dashed for the

extremists of a return to the influence they had enjoyed during
the Cultural Revolution and the period immediately after the
establishment of the revolutionary committees.

Chou En-lai had also uncovered a means of creating confusion
in Mao's own camp. Chiang Ching's appetite for political life had
been whetted by the power she had wielded through the formation on Mao's behalf of her own network within the Party. The
suggestion that she be kept in the Politburo was received with
horror by the grassroots Party organisation. They wanted her to
stay close to Mao's bedside as he was looking far from strong
and obviously in need of a wife's constant care. The last place
she belonged, according to majority sentiment, was in a sensitive
Party position. Chou insisted in the face of strident opposition
that the lady stay in the leading ranks of the Communist Party.
No one would be able to accuse him of seeking to exclude Mao's
nearest and dearest from Party deliberations. Her participation
would make it hard for Mao to denounce Politburo decisions.
Chiang Ching's admirers, who saw her as the last hope of the
genuine adherents of the Cultural Revolution and its attack on
the old political establishment, would be less able to discredit
respectable Party leaders so long as their heroine was admitted
to the most secret Party conclaves. All in all, Chou En-lai had
paid a small price for having made possible the return to the
Peking social round of Teng Hsiao-ping on the arm of one of
Mao's nieces at a state reception in April 1973. Mao was happy
enough with the Tenth Party Congress in August. Chiang Ching
was in Chou's debt. The extremists and factions had been out-
manoeuvred. The possible bonus for the future was a separation
of Mao from his wife, since Mao was sufficiently sincere in his
ideals not to tolerate the idea of a dowager empress ruling the
country in his stead. The busier Chiang Ching went about palace
intrigues as age confined her husband more and more to his
library, so must his suspicions swell about personal ambitions
lurking in Chiang Ching's bosom.

Against this background, the fiercest attack began on Chou
En-lai which he had ever faced. The campaign was led by an
academic, a member of the very class Chou had sought consistently to protect. True, Professor Yang Jung-kuo was not a very
distinguished intellectual outside Canton circles; yet he was a
professional philosopher educated in the old school. In August

1973, Yang published two articles in the Peking press which opened the gates for a veritable flood of verbiage on Confucius' place in Chinese history. The word soon went round that Mao Tse-tung had read Yang's opening shots in the campaign to attack Confucius and recommended their publication. The movement began with considerable excitement among literate Chinese. For the first time since 1949, they were urged to read as extensively as possible the masterpieces of the national literary heritage. The familiar renditions of Confucius into modern Chinese were altered subtly, to some extent in the light of modern research, and by political considerations as well. The enthusiasm with which Confucius and other sages were pored over and the new glosses on their meaning weighed and analysed, was a tribute to the unbroken emotional bonds between the oldest Chinese literature and those capable of reading such treasures.

The campaign had a number of objectives, as political movements in China invariably had during Mao's epoch. The indictment of Chou En-lai was an aim difficult to perceive with any certainty at the outset of the new ideological drive. Chou En-lai could not be revealed as the movement's true victim until his position had been sufficiently undermined by the mass drive. The open attack on Chou was to come as the dramatic but delayed climax of the anti-Confucius campaign. The immediate goal was to discredit Confucius for two very different reasons, one supported by Mao Tse-tung and the other very much to Chou's taste.

Confucius was accused in 1973 of being the protector of an elite ruling class, a privileged order of rulers; and of framing a philosophy to suppress the masses. Confucius was the root from which all mandarins had sprung. Mao Tse-tung wanted to eradicate the concept of a class of wise or educated individuals whose brainpower entitled them to government offices. The philosophy of Confucius would perpetuate class differences in China, he believed. The fortunate few would pass their educational advantages on from one generation to the next; the semi-literate or even more disadvantaged workers and peasants could merely beget sons and grandsons bound perpetually to the same wheel of physical labour. The anti-Confucius movement aimed at promoting Mao's dream of equality for the future. But the present was affected also. The condemnation of Confucius' ideas in fact denied officials any right to exercise their authority on the basis of personal merit. The only credentials left to them were: service to the masses; unity with the masses; and approval by the masses. These criteria were entirely to Mao's own taste. Every Chinese official was at risk in this campaign. The better his education, the more polished his manners and the more courteous and refined his behaviour, the greater the grounds for accusing him of being a secret worshipper of Confucius; for this sage advocated learning, manners and propriety. Needless to say, Chou En-lai was everybody's image of what the Confucian official should look like at his best.

For Chou En-lai, the campaign was worth a gamble. The opposite of Confucianism is "Legalism," a school of thought whose ideas have never achieved the fame outside China which Confucius has enjoyed. The follower of Confucius believes that men are essentially good. Properly instructed, given sound example and guidance by the elite and treated leniently for their errors, the common folk voluntarily and gladly comply with the state's edicts. Mao Tse-tung himself took such an approach in his advice on how to deal with political offenders, insisting on the right of all but the most heinous sinners to repent their errors and make reparation. The Legalists took a less romantic view of human nature. A code of laws embodying harsh punishments should be rigidly enforced to suppress evil-doers. The Legalists had found their most important follower in Chin Shih Huang Ti, the unifier of China but synonymous with cruel despotism for over two thousand years.

The anti-Confucian campaign became like a game of musical chairs, with Mao Tse-tung ending up on Chou En-lai's lap before being pushed on to the floor. Chou favoured strict laws to replace the vague and unpredictable edicts issued by Mao which overthrew all normal rules and regulations and left government policies and programmes in a state of turmoil. Tough penalties would mean the extremists, factions and other opponents of law and order could be suppressed. Stable, established authority backed by harsh sanctions would increase official power and lead towards the evolution of a Leninist (or, in practice, Stalinist) state, which Chou favoured.

Mao Tse-tung's grasp of Chinese culture and its impact on ordinary lives went deeper. On the surface, the disciples of Confucius seemed to be liberals. But Confucius' followers advocated social and ethical controls over the individual. A man's behaviour was to be governed by obedience to conventions, traditions and the conservative canons which usually make up a society's moral norms. When a society is to be ruled by a mixture of social conventions and ethics, men can never be free from rules and can never escape the scrutiny of those who impose their administration on the populace by an all-embracing code of morals. No distinction can be made between the private and public domains when moral standards replace laws, and no limits can be set to the power of rulers to interfere with citizens' lives.

Legalism was in fact the more liberal regime. Whatever the law did not condemn was assumed in advance to be tolerated. The individual's freedom was supposed to be unlimited except by formal laws. The Confucian system thus came to resemble in its effects the system of harsh restrictions on human freedom for the benefit of society advocated in theory by the Legalists. Legalism, by contrast, represented a degree of freedom to act in accordance with personal conscience and social pressures as the individual chose except when the law specifically decreed otherwise. Confucianism and Legalism, when put into practice, simply swopped roles, a point well understood by Mao Tse-tung anxious to prevent unnecessary repression of individual liberty. But most Chinese thought of the simple meaning of Legalism: tyrannical officialdom backed by oppresssive punishments. The subtleties which worried Mao passed over the heads of most Chinese. For public consumption, Chou had no views. However, he actually favoured Legalism because of the support its popular interpretation lent to his views on tough and effective government. Mao advocated Legalism because he saw the reality underlying the theories. Both were temporarily on the same chair.

Chou En-lai now had to push Mao Tse-tung off his lap and bury him in his own campaign. This feat was achieved by a simple trick. Lin Piao was described as a follower of Confucius, and the campaign quickly developed the urgent theme that Lin Piao could be identified with Confucius. The two were bracketed together by the Maoist group to link the ancient philosopher with a contemporary traitor; otherwise the campaign would

become merely academic and irrelevant to the country's present
needs. But if Lin Piao were Confucius and if Legalism stood
opposed to Confucianism, the next step was short but fatal.
Mao Tse-tung was the mortal enemy of Lin Piao; Chin Shih
Huang Ti was the greatest opponent of the Confucians and the
outstanding Legalist. Lin Piao was the modern personification
of Confucius; therefore Mao Tse-tung must be the reincarnation of Chin Shih Huang Ti. Lin Piao had made this very
allegation according to the "571" dossier. Out of a stubborn
pride, it seemed, Mao clutched Lin's charge to his breast and
sought to refute it by transforming Chin Shih Huang Ti into a
heroic but misunderstood progressive monarch calumniated by
centuries of feudalistic scholars.

Millions of words were devoted to the theme. Mao's identification with Chin Shih Huang Ti grew firmer as the essays
poured off the presses "proving" that the tyrant's innovations
in his own era foreshadowed, albeit imperfectly, the vast
changes introduced by Mao in this century. However, the image
of Chin Shih Huang Ti as a monstrous tyrant could not be
altered. Centuries of indoctrination about his wickedness could
not be eradicated from Chinese emotions whatever their intellects believed or their mouths uttered. Mao Tse-tung was finally
branded as the willing pupil and latter-day heir of the most evil
force in Chinese history. The monstrous and inaccurate accusation had been made possible by Mao's direct backing for the
anti-Confucius movement and its praise of the Legalists. Mao
was at last in the mire, though still by innuendo and historical
analogy and not by overt allegation. No one yet dared to
challenge openly the Mao legend and his right to rule like the
Oracle of Delphi: by inspired but cryptic slogans.

Mao Tse-tung might have resisted the introduction of Lin
Piao into the anti-Confucius campaign. He was in no position,
however, to protest at the stress given to Lin Piao in the movement for important reasons related to the kind of individual
who would rule China after his death. Lin had taught that
Mao Tse-tung was a genius; his works, the product of an
immense intelligence; his instructions, the essence of wisdom.
Mao disliked this elevation although the aura created around
him by such veneration was useful in putting his authority
beyond question at the start of the Cultural Revolution. But

promotion to the ranks of wondrous and unearthly sage implied that Mao was separated from the rest of the Chinese population and could lead to the sentiment that he was too celestial to be comprehended by mere mortals.

Furthermore, from the charges levelled at Lin Piao, his purpose was clearly not just flattery of Mao Tse-tung on a gross scale. Lin had entered the realm of ideology. The dilemma for Lin Piao was exceptional. Mao had taught that the masses possessed the various correct ideas and genuine principles needed to organise and administer the nation properly. The masses' ideas were, unfortunately, in a state of disorder, Mao went on. Therefore, the Communist Party had to go among the masses to collect these unordered ideas and give them a logical and coherent format. This way of explaining the Party's relationship with the population was fine, provided the bulk of the Party, the leadership in particular, was above suspicion. But in 1962, Mao openly warned that the Party had been penetrated by persons ready to betray its principles. He explained the following year how the truth is only understood by hard struggle and practical experience. He added that those who discovered truth by their ardent labours might well be a mere minority inside the Communist Party. Since Party arguments were supposed to be decided by the votes of the majority, truth might never get a hearing within the Communist Party. Yet Party discipline was not to be thrown overboard and replaced by battles among its members.

The conclusion reached by Mao Tse-tung was frightening since the Party was supposed to be the infallible guide for the nation's conduct and even its daily thoughts. In 1963, Mao was prepared to accept that the minority, however correct, would fail to carry the rest of the Party. Never mind, he advised; wrong ideas will be put into practice and fail to produce satisfactory results. In the end, the false or incorrect notion would be discarded for it would have failed its practical test. Mao's solution to this dilemma was acceptable up to a point. In some cases, the failure of an idea would be so dramatic that its rejection would be automatic, especially in the economic sphere where results could be measured in objective financial or other material terms. Ideological and social goals were a different matter. Who was to judge that China had advanced over a given period towards greater enthusiasm for the Marxist Utopia?

The Party leadership in theory should perform such a function since Party discipline, as preached by Mao, made the lower levels subordinate to the higher organs of the Party. After the 1966 denunciation of Liu Shao-chi and Teng Hsiao-ping and of Lin Piao in 1971, who could happily trust the judgment of the Party leadership?

The test of truth and correctness during the Cultural Revolution had become what Mao Tse-tung thought of a particular individual, situation or plan. China was prepared until 1969 to accept Mao as its inspired judge; it did not defy his verdicts through overt and vocal protests until April 1976. Even during the post-1969 era, when Mao's credibility as unerring helmsman of the ship of state declined, he could still have the last word in any debate. Although less and less could he compel enthusiastic compliance with his decrees in these later years, his veto was absolute and beyond all challenge until April 1976.

Any successor to Mao Tse-tung would want to have a similar power to decide what was acceptable truth and what heresy was to be rejected, particularly as Mao would no longer be available to interpret his often contradictory essays and directives. Lin Piao found a solution to the problem by justifying Mao Tse-tung's right to decide for the nation what was true and practical on the grounds of exceptional wisdom. The same superior intellect would have to be attributed to Mao's heirs to justify their claims to an unerring wisdom. For Mao, the idea of such intellectual superiority had to be rejected because it isolated the leader from the masses in much the same way that Confucius' followers had taught that the mandarins were a race set apart with an innate right to govern China. In addition, if Mao's heir had to have a superior intellect after Mao's death, he must possess it while Mao still lived. This made the heir equal to the ruler. Hence, Lin Piao put himself on the same level as Mao Tse-tung. Whether Lin had seen this implication of his elevation of Mao to the status of genius is doubtful. His intention was of no importance. Others were able to read into his praise for Mao a plain desire to succeed Mao while he still lived. Mao himself shared this suspicion of Lin Piao's bestowal on him of the title of genius.

The shift from an offensive against Confucius with Lin Piao as a lesser villain into a full-blown denunciation of both simultaneously meant that Chou En-lai was virtually certain of survival. With Mao Tse-tung's unwitting consent, Confucius had been equated with Lin Piao not Chou; and Mao, not Chou, was to come out of the movement as the victim, equated with the imperial monster of history, Chin Shih Huang Ti.

Even without the superb reversal of the campaign into the first major criticism of Mao Tse-tung since the pre-1966 period when Mao had been satirised occasionally, Chou En-lai was well poised to emerge victorious. In the first place, the campaign to criticise Confucius depended heavily on intellectuals, the class which had obtained more protection and sympathy from Chou than from any other leader over the years. The intellectuals had no great love for Mao and plenty to lose if Chou fell. Secondly, the diverse themes of the campaign were so numerous that to lead the campaign to a pinnacle from which Chou could be thrown down into disgrace was a difficult task.

The criticism of Confucius was supposed, for example, to emphasise the Chinese cultural background to the Maoist version of communism and to remove the belief that Marxism was an alien creed first imported via Japanese translations and later from the Soviet Union and based on the distant world of nineteenth century Europe. The ordinary citizen was to be encouraged to overcome his feeling of awe when confronted by the great sages of the Chinese past. By reading and criticising the classics, workers were expected to kill off the mystery and reverence which surrounded scholarship. The actual result was a dramatic rise in the numbers of ordinary people who had first-hand contact with the magnificence of China's cultural heritage and who were deeply inspired by its munificent treasures. This trend was by no means a waste. The academic and cultural levels of hundreds of thousands of ill-educated individuals were raised to new heights by wrestling with Chinese literature, history and philosophy. The ordinary worker or peasant, it was hoped, would be infected with a self-confidence from acquaintance with the classics which would make him capable of controlling schools, colleges and research institutions and of tackling complex technical problems in the factory or on the collective farm. After all, the mental effort required to learn sufficient archaic Chinese to follow a classical text is not much different from the energy needed to employ a strange technical formula in assessing, say, the right composition of chemical fertiliser to apply to a piece of land.

Chou En-lai was supposed to be drawn into the anti-Confucius campaign by an oblique process of association. The scorn heaped on the Confucian image of the scholar-official, which Chou represented more and more as he aged, has been mentioned. A second facet was denunciation of his desire to bring back to favour personages who from 1966 to 1969 had fallen into obscurity. Chou was acknowledged as responsible for the political resurrection of an army of officials disgraced in the Cultural Revolution. The attempt to find parallels between Chou's style and policies and various anti-Marxist features of Confucius was quite imaginative. The most obvious parallel of all proved a failure. References were made to Confucius' respect for the Duke of Chou. For Confucius, the public was supposed to read Lin Piao; and for the Duke of Chou, the Prime Minister of the same name. This interpretation would make Chou En-lai the inspiration of Lin Piao and his plot against Mao Tse-tung. However, the words for Duke of Chou had too many meanings in Chinese: "Uncle Chou," endearingly; "Chou Esquire," the most formal title of address and inscribed on a man's tomb. To "visit the Duke of Chou" means to sleep. Premier Chou En-lai was not the first thought, therefore, that flashed through the mind on seeing a remark about the Duke of Chou. An additional difficulty was the refusal to believe that Confucius the Sage was really meant to be ridiculed, an attitude especially prevalent in rural districts.

The plot misfired to transform the 1973 movement to criticise Confucius and Lin Piao into a campaign to topple Chou En-lai in 1974. A large number of officials realised that the target of the movement was supposed to be the Prime Minister. They were terrified as they watched the switch from a cultural to a political campaign. These officials lacked the sophistication to perceive that Chou had far more effective control over the direction of the "Anti-Lin, Anti-Confucius Campaign" than the Maoist group which was supposed to orchestrate it. These less politically-aware bureaucrats mistook Mao Tse-tung's original endorsement and encouragement of the campaign as proof that he and his associates remained its sole directors. The notion of a showdown between Mao and Chou spread panic among the less astute functionaries in the first few months of 1974. The factions came to the fore once again. The economy started to stagnate and then to decline. Drastic steps had to be taken to convince the bureaucracy that it could abandon its timidity and start to manage the economy again without risk to its members' careers. The "Anti-Lin, Anti-Confucius Campaign" had to be toned down rapidly in mid-1974. The truth was that no groups in the Politburo and the Party Central Committee in 1974 were prepared to let the nation slide back towards penury, even to overthrow the Prime Minister.

Another factor was the response of the armed forces to commands to denounce Lin Piao. He was to be damned by the soldiers because he had refused to engage the enemy in battle unless the odds were overwhelmingly on his side. He had rejected Mao's instructions in the belief that proximity to actual hostilities in 1947-49 gave him, Lin, an insight superior to any intuition the Party Chairman could have about what tactics were most appropriate. Lin had reservations about the trust which could be placed in civilians who had recently come under the rule of the communist armies and of the enthusiasm and real support of such people for the communist cause. The prudence and caution Lin displayed in his drive through Manchuria to Peking was to be explained in 1973 and 1974 by his cowardice and insubordination. Such a portrayal showed an astonishing ignorance of the military mind. Commanders from platoon to division level who had been humble infantrymen in Lin Piao's great sweep through the north were being told why they were still alive: their commander was reluctant to waste their lives. Soldiers value such consideration on the part of generals.

The army displayed no fervour for the attacks on Lin Piao either as a disciple of Confucius or as a military commander. This silent insubordination did not imply any great affection. His conduct during the Cultural Revolution had not done the armed forces any good. Lin had proved that soldiers should leave politics to the civilians. Yet again, although the anti-Lin drive fell flat with the troops, the movement was put to some good. China's armed forces preserve carefully the separate identity of individual units. During the anti-Lin campaign, units recited their epics and how they had won their battle honours, a valuable means of instilling a sense of group pride into soldiers. However, the distaste for the movement evinced by the armed forces meant that Chou En-lai could only be toppled by pushing on with the campaign at the risk of alienating the army.

Revenge was taken on the armed forces. The first few weeks of 1974 saw a host of scandals publicised in the local and national press. These sensational reports involved corruption and string-pulling to get into university. The proportion of military commanders' offspring who confessed that they had got into college "through the back door" was significantly large. The revelations did not enhance the armed forces' prestige. Another hostile move had come by January 1974 and seemed to be a case of waving a big stick on Mao's behalf at the High Command as a warning that they should find some means to fill their subordinates with enthusiasm for the "Anti-Lin, Anti-Confucius Campaign." A number of eminent generals were switched from commands they had occupied for long enough to regard them as their private estates. These transfers deprived them of the political posts they held at the top of provincial Party and revolutionary committees. The commanders affected were professionals who took the inconveniences inflicted by civilians in their stride, but the officer corps did not accept these insults without protest. By March, Mao Tse-tung found it prudent to direct that the army should no longer be attacked.

When Wang Hung-wen made the obviously inspired suggestion in January 1974 during a secret speech as Party Vice Chairman that some bright lad of similarly tender years to himself should take over as a major military commander, the armed forces started to growl. Wang Hung-wen was also a Vice Chairman of the Party's Military Commission. By mid-summer, the High Command felt the young Shanghai worker was taking his military responsibilities too seriously for everybody's peace of mind. A delegation so informed Mao Tse-tung in blunt terms. Mao had a healthy respect for his generals when of a single mind on an issue of importance to the armed forces. The anti-Wang representations were much talked of in both military and official circles. Mao's prestige gained nothing from Wang Hung-wen's simple-mindedness. He was, everyone understood, Mao's personal appointee to his lofty office. Wang Hung-wen eventually got the message and felt that he was not treated with the respect his eminence merited and blamed Chou En-lai for his growing obscurity. A complaint to Mao in late 1974 on the issue got Wang nowhere. Mao had just come off second best himself in a tussle with Chou.

By the middle of 1974, Mao Tse-tung was close to complete ruin as China's charismatic figure who could make or break any man, no matter how senior. His faculties were failing although his mind was generally clear. He was unable to control Chou En-lai who had lost all his old timidity. The public had been led to examine the history of China's most terrible despot, Chin Shih Huang Ti, in terms of his similarity to the reign of Mao Tse-tung. But 1974 had seen two other tragedies. The first was personal: a complete loss of confidence in his wife, Chiang Ching, who had enjoyed a short burst of acclamation and influence in early 1974 but was soon to fade from the scene and from Mao's household. The second was the desertion to Chou En-lai of officials who were gambling that Mao Tse-tung would not outlive the Premier and that they should take steps to be seen early as Chou supporters. The crowning blow was Chou's decision to go ahead with a national conference of the highest importance in the face of Mao's personal opposition to what Chou planned to do at the meeting.

CHAPTER TEN

THE ISOLATION OF MAO TSE-TUNG

DESPITE THE PLOT to use the "Anti-Lin, Anti-Confucius Campaign" to unseat Chou En-lai, despite the slump in the economy, and despite the resentment of the bureaucracy (and the military establishment in particular) at attacks on their moral integrity, the remarkable feature about China in 1974 was the ability of the central authorities to go on working together as a team. Personal differences had not been poisoned by insoluble political dissentions; and the clash of ambitions had not led to intractable antagonisms. On any normal logic, the Politburo and the Party Central Committee should have fallen apart in 1974. An enormous temptation was being offered to any man with his eyes on the very summit of power. Underway was the campaign against Lin and Confucius whose climax was supposed to be the eclipse of Chou En-lai. The campaign was an invitation to would-be premiers to help to dispose of the current Prime Minister with the minimum delay. The temptation was resisted, and Chou was not stabbed in the back. This unity at the top, albeit frail, was the result of the character of Teng Hsiao-ping, who now ranked third in the Communist Party after Mao and Chou. His post was that of acting prime miniser for all practical purposes. The trust which Chou knew he could place in Teng to keep the Government working efficiently allowed Chou En-lai to concentrate his ebbing energies on holding together the leadership group he had formed in 1973. The Politburo and the most senior ministers needed time to establish solid working relations with each other. They also needed a man of Chou's moderating instincts to smooth down ruffled feathers and encourage division of responsibilities and coordination of personal efforts.

Teng Hsiao-ping, now basking in the glory of his appointment as Deputy Premier and Party Vice Chairman, was a solid Chou En-lai supporter not so much out of gratitude but more out of a general integrity. As Mao Tse-tung once remarked of Teng when the Red Guards were about to savage him, Teng never conspired in dark corners. In 1974, Teng was in no position to betray Chou, even if the thought had occurred to him. Mao Tse-tung had taken the precaution in 1973 of circulating right down to the most insignificant Party member Teng Hsiao-ping's self-criticism dossier, the last addition to which had been made in 1972. This step emphasised that Teng's position in the Government must in Mao's view be limited severely and probably remain of an only temporary nature. Mao had blocked by this act an alliance between his coterie and Teng.

Other members of the top Party elite, such as Li Hsien-nien, were so much part of the Chou club that disloyalty to him was inconceivable. Yet Mao had calculated that Li Hsien-nien, for example, was so faithful and subordinate by nature that Mao did not have to worry about him. Military figures such as Wei Kuo-ching, now a key political figure in southern China, were indebted to Chou for his efforts to solve the crises which had almost paralysed life in Kwantung and Kwangsi during the Cultural Revolution. Other men, Peking Military Commander Chen Hsi-lien, for instance, saw their duty as an obligation to defend the Party Central Committee, which precluded ganging up with any particular personality.

Wang Hung-wen whose dizzy rise to fame was the result of Mao Tse-tung's own affection for his youthfulness seemed to be conscripted for the Mao camp. In January 1974, he gave a secret Party speech. He picked on a theme close to Mao's heart: the danger of "capitalist-roaders" in the top communist echelons. The reference to these capitalist types did not signify a precise sort of heresy. A "capitalist-roader" had come to mean anyone whose opposition to Maoism was too dreadful to be tolerated. The Communist Party's theoretical journal, *Red Flag*, had tried in 1973 to arouse some interest in the continued presence of capitalist-roaders in the Party. Its words fell on obstinately deaf ears. Wang Hung-wen was inspired to chase the same quarry. He bluntly asserted that persons previously denounced as capitalist-roaders and since returned to grace after formal recantation of their errors could not be assumed to have mended their ways. Wang Hung-wen was alleging that the men disgraced in the Cultural Revolution and since rehabilitated (mostly by Chou's intervention) were still untrustworthy and to be kept perpetually on probation. This slander was too much to bear. The Party leaders shuddered with disgust and wrote Wang Hung-wen off as a young man not worthy of being advanced any further. He should have known better. Wang admitted in his speech that the public had resisted in the strongest possible manner during the preparations for the August 1973 Tenth National Party Congress any more inquests on who was or was not to be classified as a capitalist-roader. Society was weary of constant attacks on elderly officials with long records of devoted service to Mao's revolution. Teng Hsiao-ping was later on to voice a popular reaction to witch hunts for hidden capitalist-roaders: such purges were the work of individuals drooling for their bosses' jobs.

Mao Tse-tung discovered that his personal backing in the Party Central Committee and even the Politburo was for less solid than the support for Chou En-lai. Furthermore, Mao's personal entourage showed a disturbing tendency to seek closer links with the Chou club. Mao's most trusted allies drifted or were driven in Chou's direction. In July, November and December 1974, Mao expressed his misgivings about the behaviour of Chiang Ching, Wang Hung-wen, Chang Chun-chiao and Yao Wen-yuan. Their relations, he asserted, looked like those of a secret clique. He harried them again in May the following year on the same grounds. Mao felt that because of his failing health and faculties, the "gang of four" was not totally under his supervision anymore. He suspected them of plotting to form a rival politburo of their own, a project he himself had first encouraged.

Wang Hung-wen, for all his Maoist sentiments, soon found he had little hope of regaining Mao Tse-tung's blessing. Yao Wen-yuan in 1975 tried to return to Mao's favour with an article on the way in which the Communist Party was led astray by anti-Maoist elements. Mao approved the article but remained dubious about its author. Chang Chun-chiao published an article on the same topic a month later in 1975 which showed no inclination on his part to cultivate the Mao ego. Wang Hung-wen's final reaction was that of any idealistic and inexperienced man. He attached himself in 1975 to the Chou club even though he was blackballed as a member.

Chiang Ching's case was peculiar in the extreme: she could no longer side with her husband whatever her sentiments. Teng Hsiao-ping had ruined her and led Mao Tse-tung to class her as worse than a woman found in adultery. She had given hours of interview in August 1972 on her life, on the Mao household and on her feelings for her husband. The trusted recipient of these confidences was an American, Professor Roxane Witke. Chiang Ching took extraordinary precautions with the tapes made of the interviews. But copies of a draft for publication based on Chiang Ching's revelations had been obtained by the Chinese Mission in the United States and forwarded to the Prime Minister's Office. Chiang Ching was presented as narrating a gloomy picture of an unfeeling husband and of a wife who had never felt much excited by him. Chou En-lai foresaw that Mao's reaction would be brutal insistence on a divorce on the spot. Chou had no objection to Mao through the "Anti-Lin, Anti-Confucius Campaign" making himself appear to China to possess a malevolent and despotic disposition. But for Mao to be ridiculed and classed as next best thing to a cuckold did not suit Chou.

If Mao lost his dignity in front of the nation through a divorce at the age of eighty, with all the suggestiveness such a break-up of his thirty-year-old marriage would bring, Mao would be an embarrassment to the Government. How could Mao be disposed of under such circumstances? What alternative ideology to Maoism could China be offered? Chou En-lai ordered the four copies of the American Professor's work to be suppressed. Teng Hsiao-ping saw no harm in letting Chiang Ching explain away to Mao the statements attributed to her as she had forced so many to account between 1966 and 1969 for comments and sentences dragged out of context, distorted or deliberately misinterpreted. A translation of the choicer portions of Roxane Witke's prose was delivered to Mao Tse-tung by Teng. Chou was barely able to restrain Mao's demands for a divorce. A compromise was reached by which Chiang Ching kept her husband's name but was denied entry, except at his express invitation, to his library in particular and to his quarters in general. She was also forbidden to have her speeches published. Her presence at public meetings was to be subject to the closest scrutiny. Finally, Chiang Ching was no longer to be allowed access to foreign guests unless the national interest dictated otherwise.

Some foreign heads of state or government insisted on an undertaking to be received by an official Chinese delegation which included Chiang Ching in case her husband was indisposed and unable to be photographed with the foreign visitor. Chiang Ching was still permitted to represent her husband to this extent. The only man to whom Chiang Ching could turn for protection now was Chou, who had arranged the pact which made her wedding with Mao possible in the first place and prevented its legal dissolution in its final crisis.

Chiang Ching did not fall gracefully into Chou En-lai's arms. She had decided to promote her own rival to the famous Tachai Production Brigade, the model farming community in Shansi province, central China. The village had been the epitome of China's poverty and blankness when Mao Tse-tung had come to power. By its own efforts, guided of course by Mao Tse-tung Thought, Tachai had worked wonders in conquering nature and turning barren hills into fertile fields. In 1964, Mao had proclaimed to the whole country that, in agriculture, Tachai must be the model. Chiang Ching in September 1974 took Madam Imelda Marcos, wife of the Philippines President, around parts of China. The pair of first ladies had travelled to the major northern port of Tientsin, in whose suburbs lay a village called Hsiaochin-chuang. Chiang Ching probably hoped to prove to her husband that she was still the standard-bearer of his ideals. The Tientsin village was remarkable for its political evening schools and its equally political folk verses and ditties inspired by current events. The whole set-up was typically Maoist. The average reaction, however, was summed up as usual by Teng Hsiao-ping who dismissed the subsequent drive to learn from Hsiaochinchuang as a stunt to push Tachai off its rightful pedestal. Teng had no love for Chiang Ching, and the populace was cynical about her motives to a similar degree.

Nevertheless, political evening schools became all the rage, thanks to Chiang Ching's endorsement of their value. Although not credited with sponsorship of this movement, its success was some compensation for the disappointments she was forced to suffer on account of her first love, the stage. Madam Marcos' visit was marred by a public indication that Chiang Ching was not in command of cultural affairs. This demotion followed an attempt earlier in the year to act as both wife and a faithful member of Mao's revolutionary vanguard. Peking in January 1974 saw a gathering of dramatic talent from northern China for a theatre festival. Among the companies of players was a Shansi troupe which put on a play called *Three Visits to Peach Mountain*. The production was much applauded and got a favourable notice from the official New China News Agency. The Agency was appalled shortly afterwards to find that the play was in reality "a poisonous weed" concocted to spread anti-Maoist views. A wave of denunciation followed of this play and dramas of a similar ilk. The attention devoted to theatrical works in the first half of 1974 was incredible. The country's fate seemed to swing in the balance so long as seditious cultural works went on flourishing as they had since Lin Piao's death in 1971.

In the sea of words on dramatic problems, Chiang Ching received her meed of praise as the original reformer of China's degenerate, feudalistic, theatrical repertoire, as the Maoists expressed their aesthetic opinions. The news media were charitable enough not to mention how Chiang Ching's formal duties in reforming the stage and screen had been conferred on her by the traitor Lin Piao, under whose instructions she was stated in 1966 to be working. Chiang Ching was still alive and a force to be reckoned with in the Politburo as far as the ordinary citizen could tell. In retrospect, the wave of indignation whipped up against the play *Three Visits to Peach Mountain* was Chiang Ching's last spectacular appearance on the political stage. Thereafter, she found even supporting parts difficult to come by. Since relations with her husband were non-existent, maritally speaking, and once the drama campaign got bogged down in an exposition of Maoist cultural theories without leading to public castigation of any notables, Chiang Ching could sense that her teeth had been drawn. In May 1975, she spoke respectfully of Chou En-lai in addressing a closed meeting of Peking Foreign Ministry staff. Her speech was on olive branch offered before a distinguished audience. She was henceforth on Chou En-lai's side from 1975 for better or worse, mostly worse as matters turned out.

Throughout the power establishment and its three main branches, the Party, the state bureaucracy and the armed forces, a morbid interest was being displayed in the health of both Mao Tse-tung and Chou En-lai as 1974 wore on. The speculation was considerable about who would outlast the other. Given a free choice, the bulk of the men who counted would have simply sworn allegiance to whichever was pronounced by his doctor to be in better shape. The situation, however, no longer permitted a rational choice of which bandwaggon to climb on before the funeral of one or other started a stampede among the minor minions. The difficulties arose from several conflicting forces.

The first was the way in which the government structure at the provincial and central levels was changing. The new pattern was highlighted as every major state function brought back to public life some man who had been ejected from high office by the Red Guards and cursed and reviled before mass audiences. The implications of this trend were more obvious in the provinces, however, where the effect of such resurrections could be measured in terms of who actually wielded power.

The army's role in civil administration was reduced substantially by Lin Piao's death in 1971 and the transfer by 1974 of senior military commanders. The armed forces were not shedding any tears at leaving the civilians to their own devices. The representatives of the masses had acquired of late somewhat better representation in the major Party committees and hence more access to the levers of power. They remained a definite minority, but the increase in their numbers was an incentive to factions to push harder to strengthen their voice in government affairs. Nevertheless, the shift back to tried and trusted administrators, a large proportion of whom had suffered a run of bad luck in the Cultural Revolution, was the most striking feature of provincial affairs. The further promotion of young cadres who had done nicely out of the Cultural Revolution was checked by the rehabilitation of the old guard. But the veterans had earned their positions by achieving results demanded by Peking before 1966, and they had learnt how to reconcile Peking's demands with the reluctance of a province's inhabitants to lift a finger to help the rest of the nation or assist the central authorities in any way.

The charge was heard discreetly in the period up to 1975, and boldly thereafter, that the rehabilitation of veteran officials was a form of revenge for their Cultural Revolution humiliations.

They blocked the prospects of younger men, now subject to their wills, who had been recruited to fill the vacancies caused by the overthrow of officials accused of implementing anti-Maoist policies in the years 1962 to 1965. The recall to office of the senior generation of administrators had little to do with the Cultural Revolution directly. Their reinstatement was dictated by Peking's necessities and not even by provincial loyalties or popular opinion.

The men who had come to the fore during the Cultural Revolution had their merits, despite wide distaste for youthful faction leaders who had spread violence and vendettas in 1966, social evils which still festered throughout China a decade later. Their Maoist credentials were indisputable, which gave them an essential self-confidence as political campaigns seemed to demand a fresh weeding out of the bureaucracy. These new officials had a degree of mass support locally which meant they could mobilise peasants and workers to back Peking's programmes. They were familiar with nuances of the provincial political scenes and could achieve a fair degree of local consensus. Their defects were linked closely to their virtues. Because they were products of local turmoil from 1966 to 1969, their commitment to a larger interest was limited. They had no reason to feel obligations to promoting the national welfare since their political horizons did not stretch beyond their own parishes. They did not have the training or the inclination for understanding how to balance Peking's directives against local realities and how to act as honest brokers between their provincial constituents and the central administration.

The new cadres were moulded by Peking's stress on local self-sufficiency in both agricultural and industrial products and its emphasis on self-reliance in finding capital and raw materials for industrial development. The Government had not abandoned these principles, and decentralisation of economic responsibility remained the rule. But Peking's grip on the national economy was tightening. Ministries were much less tolerant of local administrations which went their own way without respect for Peking's plans and policies. The anti-Confucius campaign, which tried to enshrine the strict rules and regulations advocated by the Legalists, reinforced the moral authority of the central Government. The men capable of striking the right balance

between central orders and local resources were men who had
been bred for the job in the years before 1966.

Peking's dependence on the veterans was brought home by
the way in which the capital had to intervene in mid-1974 to call
a halt to the political strife which had terrified rank-and-file
officials and caused agricultural and industrial growth to falter.
Instructions went out from the centre, couched in broad terms,
ordering a return to political and economic sanity. Translation
of this sort of directive into practical results was not a task for
which new bureaucrats had been trained. Politics they could
handle. Politics mixed with economics and couched in sweeping
imperatives needed an instinct they lacked about what Peking
really thought but did not want to put into words for fear of
giving scandal to idealists, revolutionaries and Mao Tse-tung
himself.

Another important reason prevented a straightforward choice
in terms of their relative life expectancies between Mao Tse-tung
and Chou En-lai. Wang Hung-wen's secret Party speech in
January 1974 and the "Anti-Lin, Anti-Confucius Campaign"
were ample evidence that Mao had strong reservations about anyone who had been dismissed in the Cultural Revolution. The
repeated calls for officials to prove their mettle by performing
manual labour with the masses was aimed at the professional
administrators not the new officials. The latter had often kept
their old jobs and were only part-time officials. The constant
transfer to farm work of administrative personnel was another
indication of a lack of respect for the bureaucracy. Any intelligent official could see that the policy made sense to some extent
in theory but not in practice. The removal of trained and
experienced officials to the villages might strengthen village
administration and improve control over the peasants, provided
the rural population could be induced to trust the newcomers.
Yet a gap was left between the top echelons of the provincial
administration and the villages themselves. The downward
transfer, either on a long-term basis or for periodic stints of
collective physical labour, meant that provincial bureaucracies
were split in half: generals and rank and file. The middle
management needed for day-to-day decisions and supervision
was weakened.

Instinct and experience were enough to convince large numbers of bureaucrats that the mistrust in which they were held as a class and the reduction of administrative efficiency were not to be laid at Chou's door. Mao Tse-tung was the culprit, which meant that officials had no reason to think that pledges from them of support for Mao against Chou would be either welcomed or believed. The bureaucracy had the further difficulty that a free choice by the masses of China would show a vigorous desire to retain Chou's services for as long as possible. The Prime Minister was widely regarded as the only hope of ending the constant talk about ideology and of resuming the mustering of every resource for economic development. As will be shown, the average citizen was feeling a financial stringency and wanted to see some progress towards prosperity even if the holiday atmosphere of the Cultural Revolution had to be sacrificed. Officials who swung against Chou faced a dwindling of popular confidence in them.

The final reason why the choice between Mao Tse-tung and Chou En-lai could not be made with any comfort involved the succession to both men. By the end of 1974, the pattern for the future of China's leadership had been made quite clear by both the Mao and Chou clubs. If Chou died first, Teng Hsiao-ping was due to be axed fairly promptly partly on grounds of age but more because of Mao's dislike of the man whom he had been forced to recall to office in 1973. Mao had said the next generation of leaders should be aged under 60, which sharply restricted the candidates to take over from Chou. Since the Premier was not only head of the government machine but also ran the Party when Mao was unable to attend Politburo meetings, two successors were needed. The first had to be a relatively young man to take over Chou's power. The second ought to be an elder statesman to ensure that the accumulated wisdom of the Prime Minister's Office was not buried with him. Chou's twin roles made possible the combination of young and old quite neatly. The lucky youngster who had caught Mao's eye was a secret. The veteran favoured by Mao was widely identified as Li Hsien-nien, Chou's confidant and economic specialist. Li Hsien-nien was so close to the Premier, although Mao also trusted Li completely, that to side with Mao who had Li Hsien-nien in the wings was almost the same things as backing Chou En-lai.

If Mao Tse-tung died first, questions of age would not arise.

Chou would take over Mao's role by popular acclamation, while relying on Teng Hsiao-ping to play the part of premier. Since Teng and Li Hsien-nien were believed to be horses of an identical colour, an official showed himself to be a Chou supporter in reality whether he tried to attach himself to Mao and declared a preference for Li Hsien-nien or whether he chose Chou and backed Teng Hsiao-ping.

An edge was given to the Mao Tse-tung and Chou En-lai split in the eyes of the power elite by the decision to hold a National People's Congress in January 1975. This body, the equivalent of China's parliament, had last been convened in 1964. The provincial authorities had several times forecast in the 1970s that the Congress was on the point of being called into session. Each effort to mount a Fourth Congress fell by the wayside, however, because unsuitable delegates won a majority of the representation. Unlike the Party, which numbered a mere 28 million when the Tenth National Party Congress was held in 1973, the Chinese citizens with a right to be consulted on a choice of delegates to a National People's Congress were both numerous and not subject to strict Party discipline. Extremists and factions were able to pick up spokesmen among the delegates with a success the Party machine was able to deny them when it came to a National Party Congress.

The factions were forced to pin their hopes of a comeback on extremists and anti-Chou En-lai elements since the middle-of-the-road Party or government official was a firm believer in law and order. The factions and the extremists alike made much of their Maoist credentials, which put them in the camp opposed to Chou and the existing leadership, local and national. The extremists lacked support in the Politburo. Their heroes, the "gang of four" (Chiang Ching, Chang Chun-chiao, Yao Wen-yuan and Wang Hung-wen), were no longer Mao Tse-tung's favourites. The anti-Chou minority had come unstuck when the anti-Confucius campaign rebounded against Mao himself. The fervent Maoists were being left high and dry by a tide which was flowing full-flood in favour of Chou.

The latter half of 1974 saw the economy paramount in the minds of the people, officials and politicians. News of a definite date for the National People's Congress aroused the avid interest of the factions. They were to find themselves finally outbid by

the opposition, in spite of strong efforts to capture a large proportion of the delegates. The factions were undermined by an
appeal over their heads to a mixture of selfishness and patriotism. The Congress would lay the groundwork, the population
was led to believe, for a steady rise in living standards to start at
once. More important, a strategy would be mapped out for a
rational approach to agricultural and industrial growth and
social progress which would give the current generation's grand-
children a richness of life to be financed by a national affluence
equal to that of any other state in the world. A land fit for
heroes today and paradise the day after tomorrow was the basic
slogan. Since Chou En-lai and his colleagues had a good record
for rebuilding the economy successfully every time some natural
or man-made disaster brought it to the verge of collapse, no
faction could offer more than the central Government to the
public. Workers and peasants expected the National People's
Congress to announce plans for wage increases and a host of programmes to reform every aspect of life and give the place of
honour to practical rather than ideological criteria. A combination of Chou En-lai and the National People's Congress in
January 1975 was predicted to be a foretaste of miracles.

Mao Tse-tung heard reports of what was afoot and could
pretend no great joy at what lay in store. He would have liked
to denounce the whole affair. Chou En-lai was canny enough to
invoke Mao as the inspiration of the national development
strategy he unveiled: commitment to the "four modernisations",
the modernisation of agriculture, industry, national defence, and
science and technology so that by the end of the century, China
would have joined the league of the world's most advanced
nations. Chou dug out a 1964 quotation from Mao which put the
proposal beyond argument unless Mao wanted to disown his
previous edict. Chou's speech to the Congress was optimistic in
tone though concrete policies, other than the "four modernisations," were conspicuously absent. Mao had succeeded in
slashing from the Premier's draft address specific pledges on a
better deal for the masses. Mao's deletions from Chou's speech
were explained officially in January 1977 as a demonstration of
concern for Chou's failing health and the strain of a lengthy
formal address. Chou's paragraphs that Mao judged of least
importance were the parts of the speech the public most wanted

to hear. Mao was concerned over Chou's political health as well.

A new constitution was promulgated at the Congress. This basic law incorporated Mao's own promises to the peasants of private plots to be exploited for personal profit; to the workers of the right to strike; and of freedom for workers to use their leisure on a limited scale for personal gain. The legal guarantee of these rights was good for peasant morale in particular.

The most important feature of the new constitution did not dawn on China immediately. In the first place, the new basic law was described as a continuation of the 1954 constitution. This declaration meant that the 1954 constitution had been valid since its promulgation and that the total disregard during the Cultural Revolution of its provisions, ranging from the manner in which ministers were to be appointed and removed to individual human rights, had been totally unconstitutional. The attack on the unlawful behaviour of Mao's supporters in the Cultural Revolution was implied but not spelled out. After the anti-Confucius campaign, nevertheless, and the praise heaped on the Legalists for their devotion to the law of the land, no profound analysis was needed to decipher the message. Laws are opposed to Confucianism. The Cultural Revolution, heavily influenced (despite official assertions to the contrary) by Lin Piao, was a display of defiance of every form of law. The Cultural Revolution's supporters could find themselves accused of being opposed to legality and thus in the same category as Lin Piao, condemned as worshippers of Confucius.

So much for the past and the threat to use it as an excuse to transform Cultural Revolutionaries into anti-Maoist disciples of Confucius. The future was even bleaker. Any criticism of the new 1975 constitution or the acts performed under its authority would be an attack on proper Legalist respect for law and hence indirect proof of a veneration for the precepts of Confucius. The message was made all the clearer by the choice of speaker to explain the new constitution and its provisions. The fortunate individual was Chang Chun-chiao who got a major chance to disassociate himself from the extremists even though he was inflicting an intolerable wound on Mao's stature as creator of the Cultural Revolution and arbiter of good and bad in China. Chang had broken with the Mao group by agreeing to deliver this speech. At the local levels, his address was well received but his conversion from extremism came too late to convince the populace that he was permanently on the side of the angels.

The importance for the future economic and political climate of the 1975 constitution concerned most of all the appointment of ministers. A lawful process for the appointment and dismissal of heads of government departments, deputy premiers and the prime minister had been laid down. No longer could the state tolerate failures to observe the constitutional provisions or a return to the casual style in vogue from 1966 onwards by which men came and went according to the personal whims of the Communist Party Chairman, Mao Tse-tung, and any members of the Politburo he chose to consult. The men appointed as deputy premiers and ministers, taken as a group, were a slap in the face for all those who had answered Mao's call to clean out the Government from 1966 to 1969. Key positions were in the hands of men savaged, abused and disgraced by Red Guards and extremists. The Government represented a collection of talent and experience not ideological expertise or Maoist zeal. The direction the Government would take was clear from its composition. Its practical cast of mind and its willingness to leave political campaigns to others while the administrative team ran the country and reshaped agriculture and industry were only too apparent. Small wonder that Mao Tse-tung was unable to play any part in the proceedings and that he ignored the National People's Congress completely. His ability to receive foreign visitors while the Congress was in session merely highlighted the belief that Mao could find no place at the National People's Congress and that ill-health had not kept him away. Not given much to hypocrisy, he simply boycotted the affair.

The ordinary citizen was not aware of the depths of Mao Tse-tung's displeasure. For one thing, Chou En-lai's policy objectives had not been revealed to the world at large. They were still the private property of the inner cabal which made up the real Peking power-holders. In addition, Mao's wife had been prominently present. She received no official appointment. She nevertheless represented the Mao family, and thus her husband's implied approval, throughout the Congress. Wang Hung-wen and Yao Wen-yuan were given no government prizes, which was a token of the Chou club's refusal to accept their membership

applications. The "gang of four" no longer looked like the
power behind the throne. Chang Chun-chiao was made a Deputy
Premier. He took charge of political work in the entire armed
forces shortly afterwards when Deputy Premier Teng Hsiao-
ping became Chief of Staff. Chang Chun-chiao's elevation to a
deputy premiership and the influential post allotted to him in
the military sphere were rewards for his speech on the constitution at the Congress. Chou appreciated his talents; trusted his
political good sense; and felt no anxiety that Chang Chun-chiao
would try to suborn the troops.

The factions had failed to dominate the National People's
Congress. They did their best to sabotage its proceedings. In
some places, inflammatory posters appeared in the streets.
Trouble broke out among small groups of workers, and, in some
instances, troops had to be called out. Violent agitation during
a national forum of such prestige was without precedent and
betrayed the resentment and frustration of the factions and other
minorities who had hoped to see their influence extended
through the National People's Congress. The disturbances also
marked the despair of the most idealistic revolutionaries at what
seemed a renunciation of all they had set out to accomplish in
1966.

CHAPTER ELEVEN

THE POLITICAL PRICE OF A
WAGE PACKET

MAO TSE-TUNG'S RIPOSTE was not long in hitting the headlines. He took advantage of a campaign planned in advance of the National People's Congress to dispel the euphoria the occasion had aroused on account of Chou En-lai's offer of material gratification rather than still further sacrifices to build a strong, purified and moral society. The campaign was designed to promote the study of Lenin and was constructed around a series of quotations from the communist classics. On almost every topic on which they were cited, Mao himself had expounded in the past; yet Mao's writings were not quoted once. The substitution of Lenin for Mao had a significance which was immediately obvious. Yet the move was orthodox enough since Mao had voiced his fears that, by neglect of the earlier Marxist masters, China might not see the tree from which the Maoist branch had grown. He regarded the new ideological drive very favourably.

For Mao Tse-tung, the campaign was a confirmation of his direct descent from the founders of Marxism. For Chou En-lai and his coterie, Lenin served a different purpose. The exclusive reliance on Maoism as China's ideology would be ended gradually through getting the population to widen the number of Marxist classics to which they looked for enlightenment and guidance. The problem as to who would interpret Maoism and unravel its contradictions after Mao Tse-tung's death would be less crucial if Maoism were not the only source of communist doctrine with which the nation was familiar. The references to Lenin where Mao would have been equally relevant served to dramatise the inability of Mao to claim any monopoly of truth or wisdom. Not that he ever had; he simply refrained from violent objections when his adherents gave such an impression.

More important was the symbolism of Lenin. The Russian
stood for a tightly-knit Party out of which Stalin, never repudiated by Mao's China, had built a monolithic, implacable and
omnipotent Party machine to serve his will. Leninism is what
well-organised, dedicated communist parties with totally obedient
members are all about. The Lenin campaign was to be a first
step towards much firmer control by the Communist Party over
national life. On one side, the population would be offered progress and eventual plenty by the National People's Congress. On
the other side of the coin would be the acceptance of greater
control by the state through the Communist Party. The bargain,
however, was not a matter of ideology or conscious preference
for the Soviet style of arranging affairs.

The practical consideration was the need to find additional
resources in a still very poor country to meet the mounting pressure for better living standards. Any surplus ought to be devoted
to investment so that new factories would be built to produce
more tractors and fertilisers; more steel and machine tools; more
plastics and electronics; and the host of other goods needed to
modernise farming and manufacturing. Funds taken away from
new investment to raise living standards would delay China's
progress. Chou En-lai had promised a speed-up of modernisation. Close scrutiny of the economy discovered the answer to how
to give more away to consumers without reducing vital investment. Slackness, inefficiency and indiscipline created considerable waste in China. Valuable equipment and raw materials piled
up in warehouses instead of being repossessed by the state for
use in new plants. The low prestige attached to technicians ever
since 1966 and the fall in educational standards had resulted in a
misuse of valuable machinery. The indulgence shown towards the
peasants allowed them to waste land, machinery and chemicals on
activities which enriched the individual family or the village but
ignored the state's needs as expressed in economic plans. Such
waste could be eliminated, very largely, by a genuine Leninist
Communist Party, or so felt the group who saw Mao as foolishly
obsessed with mass wisdom and mass liberty. The masses would
cheerfully forego their Maoist freedoms if discipline produced
tangible material benefits.

This outlook was the essence of what Mao Tse-tung regarded
as Russian revisionism. His communist colleagues often failed to

see his point since he himself called for better Party organisation and discipline and had ordered due regard for regular improvements in living standards. The difference between the Maoist viewpoint and its critics was one of degree and came down to the time factor. As far as Mao was concerned, a century was as nothing in the vast expanse of recorded Chinese history. A decade earlier or later in arriving at some goal was not of great consequence. The urgent need for economic progress, nevertheless, could be illustrated in a host of ways. Agricultural advance was pitifully slow when measured by the goals set for the peasants. China is split up into 2,200 counties. These were supposed to have achieved the targets under a National Agricultural Development Programme to be completed by 1967. Yet by 1975, 1,400 had failed to do so. In 1964, Mao Tse-tung had called on the villages to learn from his model of Tachai and become self-reliant, politically-advanced, grain-surplus communities. The North China Agricultural Conference of 1970 made this goal a national measure of rural progress. By the end of 1975, only 300 counties had reached the Tachai standard. The official figures suggested that a bare 200 counties sold grain to the state to feed the urban population (apart from the agricultural tax paid in kind and the compulsory grain levies). Steel was still a semi-precious metal, with total output in 1975 below 30 million tons and an increase in production over the previous five years of only 24 per cent. National income per head was a mere US $320 according to the best available estimates. The nation had moved forward quite creditably during the 1970s, but the peasant world, 80 per cent of the population, was very sluggish; while the rest of the economy had no massive surpluses to finance dramatic breakthroughs in the race for prosperity.

For Mao Tse-tung, people's attitudes and commitments mattered most. Their progress towards a prosperous society was supposed to be educational as well as materially rewarding. Furthermore, Mao did not believe that more money in a man's pocket equalled the sum total of his measure of human happiness. Hence a society in which inequality still existed was unjust; the removal of this blemish was far more important to Mao than the eradication of its poverty once people no longer starved or froze to death. Mao Tse-tung summed up his moral view of society in terms of perpetual class struggle, with the old exploiting classes fighting, by fair means or foul, to poison the nation's soul. Once the Communist Party ceased to concentrate on class struggle and the conquest of influences derived from the former exploiters of society, the Party would have abandoned its true purpose: the liberation of the mass of the people from whatever made them slaves hired and hypnotised by wages. By 1975, Chou En-lai, Teng Hsiao-ping and the rest of the club felt they had a better idea of what the masses really wanted than Mao who had been confined to his library for too long.

By itself, the campaign to study Lenin might have been quite popular as its first stage could well have removed the corrupt and the petty deposts in officialdom. The campaign, however, took a totally different twist and left the public cynical, dispirited and resentful after the optimism generated by the National People's Congress. The campaign turned into a drive to freeze wages more or less permanently, except for the very lowest grades, and to introduce a system of voluntary overtime. The move to make a habit out of working additional hours for nothing was greeted with astonishment. The number of model factories and other enterprises which boasted of having introduced such an innovation was far from high. Wage increases were an even more delicate point. The sensitivity over pay packets was connected to the debate as to whether or not China suffers from inflation.

Wage rises taken as an average for urban industrial employees had been very slow over the years. The official statistics claim these pay packets rose from RMB 650 in 1971 to RMB 720 (US \$360) by 1975. Compared with 1952, industrial wages showed an increase of over 50 per cent by 1975; the last big rise, Peking declared, had been a 10 per cent jump in 1972. If the real purchasing power of wages went up steadily because official prices were lowered, as the Government asserted, the workers had nothing to complain about. For the most part, the Government reduced prices as supplies rose and manufacturing productivity improved. The grain ration was also heavily subsidised and its price strictly controlled. On the whole, therefore, the Chinese family could afford to buy more each year even on a fairly fixed income. The crunch was food bought in the free market or in state shops but whose prices rose and fell with the seasons. The items in question were often produced by peasants in their free time and sold for a profit or grown by villages which specialised in food production other than grain. A decent Chinese meal needs not only rice but some of the following: meat (pork, chicken, duck, and, less popularly, beef), fish, eggs and, always, large amounts of vegetables. As the weather worsened through the 1970s, the peasants had less time to spend on non-grain food production. The weather affected the output of peasants' private plots. The supplies of these foodstuffs delivered to the towns and cities became uneven, and prices went up.

Faced with a higher food bill, the normally steady improvement in living standards seemed to halt for a large proportion of the urban work force. Food prices are a sensitive issue in a poor country because meals still account for the greatest outlay from the family budget. The workers needed higher pay packets to compensate for the adverse effects on their real incomes of the cycle of bad weather and more expensive food items. The peasants were not much better off. The additional earnings they planned to get from the urban markets were not forthcoming as quantities dropped but such costs as transport and time spent first in cultivation and then in marketing remained at the same level. The inflationary spiral was slight, almost insignificant by world standards. Yet the higher prices were enough to antagonise the labour force.

When in February 1975, the good news was announced that the Chinese were above such small-minded considerations as working only in accordance with the wages earned, factory managements found output slumping again. Bribery, profiteering and peculation reached new heights in the countryside. Factions were described by two provinces as being worse than during the Cultural Revolution. Little doubt can exist that the turn taken by the movement to study Lenin was not designed to make life easier for the Government.

The irate nation needed a scapegoat and found one quite easily. Chang Chun-chiao had advocated equality of wages and voluntary overtime in 1958. This long-forgotten article was identified as the inspiration of the 1975 campaign. Chang Chun-chiao had few friends left among the workers as a result. They needed the extra cash; they felt that a work shift plus political study sessions left them little enough leisure without more pressure to stay still longer at the factory bench during a wage freeze. The ironical point is that Chang Chun-chiao probably brought this animosity on his own head. By February 1975, Chou En-lai's health was obviously worse than Mao Tse-tung's physical condition. Chang Chun-chiao, in retrospect, seems to have felt he had been rash in pushing the Chou line and wanted to move closer to Mao. In shifting his political balance, he needed to show how he had always been close to Mao, even long before the Cultural Revolution. He permitted himself to be identified as Mao's partner in the bid to keep down wages. His move was political suicide. Within weeks, Chang realised his peril and tried to retreat by claiming that the campaign was not aimed at wages and material rewards but at individuals in the Party and the Government who believed they could live on their past experiences and neglect political study. Chang's ploy failed to convince.

Chang Chun-chiao tried again to recover lost ground in April with a long article which promised that peasants could keep their private plots for years and which condemned extremists who wanted to abolish overnight rights to conduct legitimate household business for profit in the family's leisure hours, rights guaranteed in the constitution. He also rejected the extremist views that once a capitalist-roader always a capitalist-roader and that those who had been disgraced in the Cultural Revolution and returned to office were still the biggest threat to China. He argued instead that because of the powerful influence of the past, new representatives of the old exploiting classes emerged constantly on the scene. These new, would-be exploiters were his real concern. In this way, he sought to protect the veteran officials and win their goodwill. However, he had changed sides once too often.

Yao Wen-yuan had written an article in March on the same topic. He had submitted it to Mao who had approved it. Yao Wen-yuan's piece suffered from an unwonted woolliness. He tried to balance every shade of opinion. He found himself identified with opposition to better living standards, which did him no good. Almost in despair, he seems to have cast in his lot with the Chou coterie and Teng Hsiao-ping, even though snubbed. Yao Wen-yuan was responsible for the overall editorship of the national press. His job was to see that only the correct line appeared in print. By mid-1975, the national press was publishng regularly proposals and slogans later denounced as the anti-Mao fabrications of Teng Hsiao-ping. Yao was clearly a willing servant of Teng in getting his ideas into print. Teng did not want allies like Yao Wen-yuan but could not prevent Yao from enlisting in his service.

Teng Hsiao-ping refused to bow to the campaign to halt Chou En-lai's plans without a struggle. The speech full of detailed proposals Chou had been expected to give to the National People's Congress in January 1975, Teng made for him. As Chou lay dying of cancer, Teng Hsiao-ping attended one conference after another, speaking with seething irony of the ideological clichés which hamstrung, so he insisted, China's progress. Who cared, he asked, if a scientist was an "all-red" Maoist as long as his discoveries worked? Who in his right mind, he inquired, could talk of class struggle every day? If China had a massive oil surplus, swop it for foreign plants and technology, he thundered. The peasants needed a close eye kept on their activities and lots more modernisation. Even the army was in no great shape, with poor commanders and a failure to appreciate that modern wars consume vast amounts of steel. He declined to shake hands with representatives of industrial managements he considered to be too cowardly to organise the factories. He lambasted officials promoted without adequate experience and training. Schools and universities were a disgrace. The list of complaints rolled on. He did not hesitate to voice his firm conviction that wages must not be frozen. His caustic tongue and his contempt for the incompetent won him new enemies in the official world.

Teng Hsiao-ping was quite unperturbed. He had been kicked out once before and would happily accept the same fate a second time, he proudly declared. The Maoists loathed Teng's talk; the officials were often terrified; but the masses lapped up every word. Teng Hsiao-ping was on their side, and they on his. Other deputy premiers, key generals and a large number of the top provincial leaders also took the Teng line. This line was summed up by the so-called "Three Directives" attributed to Mao but repudiated by him in January 1976. The Mao instructions pushed by Teng and eagerly grasped by the cream of national leadership and the bulk of the provincial elite were "Chairman Mao's directives concerning the study of theory, combating and preventing revisionism, promoting stability and unity and pushing the national economy forward."

Through the "Three Directives," Teng Hsiao-ping was able to appeal to the most basic aspirations of the people. The first part of the Mao Tse-tung instruction related to ideology. The nation had seen enough political disputes in the century up to 1949 and was quite happy to settle for a single party in power and to foreswear allegiance to any but the Chinese Communist Party. The people had a great yearning for "stability," for an end to the violent upsurges in political life which caused acute mental contortions for any reasonably intelligent person hoping to keep abreast of official policy. Life lacked the security for which a people reared on war, revolutions and disasters longed. More "unity" would mean an end to the criminal and political gangs which fought for power as if the civil war were still in progress. Finally, the people wanted some indication that penury, deprivation and unremitting toil and sacrifice would not last indefinitely. Indeed, prosperity was their keenest concern, for poverty was too close for ease of mind.

As a matter of interest, the first formulation of the "Three Directives" in roughly this form was uttered by Mao in 1957. Chou En-lai spoke in similar terms in 1974. Yao Wen-yuan and Chang Chun-chiao employed a similar formula in their famous 1975 articles. The one man who scrupulously avoided anything like the "Three Directives," although happy to steal the basic concepts, was Hua Kuo-feng. Hunan, his own parish, was however the last province to publicly use the "Three Directives" in a favourable context even after they had been repudiated in Mao's name. Cautious Hua was a discreet fan of Teng Hsiao-ping and, occasionally, his courageous supporter. The "Three Directives" returned to the officially approved vocabulary of China only in January 1977 when, very appropriately, the army used them publicly in a favourable context without apology, just as the armed forces had done exactly 12 months earlier.

Teng Hsiao-ping's struggle took time to pacify unrest. In the meantime, labour agitation provided exactly the breeding ground on which the factions waxed fat. The factions had been given renewed hope that they could force their way back into positions of influence with the aid of the political extremists. National conferences were scheduled for the trade union movement, the Young Communist League and Women's Congresses. The trade unions were depicted by Maoists as an ideal recruiting ground for new Party members. The ploy deceived no one. The unions accepted all and sundry into their ranks, especially representatives of the masses from which faction leaders and their allies were heavily drawn. The idea of opening the Communist Party to such recalcitrants evoked an immediate protest from Teng Hsiao-ping who insisted the unions stick to the advancement of their members' welfare. Rather than face the dangers of mass organisations trooping to the capital where they might try to relive the heady days of the summer of 1966 or assault the Foreign Ministry as in 1967, throwing top-secret files into the streets for all to read, Teng Hsiao-ping caused these national conventions to be postponed indefinitely.

The factions and their allies were stubborn too. Their dream was of an enlarged Party Central Committee meeting to which they might be invited as happened in the Cultural Revolution. Chairman Mao Tse-tung would declare the National People's Congress of January an act of treason from start to finish; demand the resignation of all ministers it had appointed; and instal in power the ardent spirits on whom he had relied during the Cultural Revolution. Mao was out of Peking at the time these plans began to take concrete form. He was in Hangchow, a beautiful lakeside town with a population of 700,000 people in Chekiang Province, a place to rest, drink wine and write poetry shaded by its 300 million trees. A man of civilised habits, Mao spent a great deal of time out of the capital in his Hangchow retreat. His wife was close by. The city's 200,000 industrial workers manufacture silk as well as a range of factory products. Its workers had been in an ugly mood in 1974. An attempt was made to quell brutal fights among the workers by recruiting them into the militia. This act gave them access to armouries; rifles and sub-machine guns passed into the factions' hands. The setting was ideal for an upsurge of revolutionary violence to topple the municipal administration and put the masses into power. Wang Hung-wen was sent by the central authorities to tame Hangchow; he had won his spurs as an organiser of agitated factory workers. The job was right up his street. Unhappily, he failed to pacify the masses.

Teng Hsiao-ping then showed what a veteran revolutionary was worth. Trains from Shanghai no longer made the run in spring 1975 through Hangchow because their drivers were too terrified of what the mobs might do to them. The breakdown in communications between Hangchow and the outside world was the basis of the strategy employed by Teng Hsiao-ping for taming the dissidents. The city was encircled by the army. Entry to and from Hangchow was made virtually impossible. The plot to hold a meeting with Mao Tse-tung to overthrow the decisions of the National People's Congress was now hopeless; the anti-Congress elements could not get near the city. The next step was to disarm the factions and put an end to their street battles in which they hoped to bring things to such a pass that the municipal authorities would be discredited completely or otherwise disposed of. Indeed, some members of the city's ruling body were wounded by the extremists. Teng arrived in person escorted by Public Security regiments generously loaned to him by their Minister, Hua Kuo-feng. These para-military security forces disarmed the militia; restored the weapons to the armouries; and exerted a pacifying, not to say, glacial influence on the city.

Once peace was restored and law and order reimposed, the troops were moved into the city. In July, members of the armed forces were ordered into factories to work alongside the labour force and set an example of strict obedience and hard work to the rebellious elements in Hangchow. The workers were to be reminded of the power of the bayonet by flooding the city with troops. Hangchow returned to normal. The same tactics were employed with considerable success elsewhere, including coal mines. One facet of the Hangchow incident was the heavy reliance on the "Three Directives" by the provincial authorities, who took over responsibility from Teng once the worst was over. The repetition of this slogan in Chekiang, the province where Hangchow is situated, and other areas of the nation hit by factional violence testified to its popular appeal. The "Three Directives" appeared to destroy the main plank of the platform from which factions sought mass support, namely the failures of the Government to deliver orderly administration, a measure of prosperity and orthodox Maoism. The "Three Directives" became spontaneously and astonishingly a slogan more popular in its invocation and impact than almost any other since 1966 despite the general cynicism about political catch-phrases and directives engendered by the non-stop ideological campaigns.

The final abolition in 1976 of all material inducements for the individual worker to respect factory regulations and raise output to the maximum appears utter foolishness to many Chinese and most outsiders. The labour force had no reason, once incentives were banned, to exert itself except to avoid boredom. The notion of constant rises in labour productivity and respect for self-imposed discipline through the influence of Maoist precepts seems wishful thinking divorced from the coarse selfishness of human life. Furthermore, the approach is out of tune with what Marxists believe about social progress. Marx, Lenin and Mao Tse-tung himself had emphasised that men only very slowly, after a long transition, could become paragons of virtue who needed no governments to regulate their vices and no money to control their appetites. Mao insisted repeatedly that China was still contaminated by its capitalist and imperialist past, hence his refusal to drop class war. Yet the abolition of incentives for workers (and moves to treat peasants likewise which, sensibly, were checked) implied that the social morality of the masses had reached an extraordinarily high plane of human virtue. No effort, needless to say, was made to substitute Soviet-style coercion for bonuses and piece rates. Every effort, it goes without saying, was made by managements to find new ways around the ban on incentives. Often they entered into conspiracies of silence with their workers by which bonuses were paid on a basis of individual performance with a pact to conceal this grave violation of industrial regulations from the higher authorities.

But Mao Tse-tung was not being hopelessly naive in advocating that the Chinese worker could be deprived of all hope of personal reward for his contributions to improved industrial performance without damage to the economy. While personal rewards for above-average performance were prohibited, workers knew that the greater their productivity, the larger the funds which would be allocated for welfare purposes. The incentives were not abolished, therefore, but changed from a personal to a group basis. The shift from concern with personal to group welfare was supposed to be hastened in this manner. Such a shift is an essential part of the ideal process for building the Marxist Utopia. A factory in which labour discontent resulted in a failure by the enterprise to meet its targets under the state plan was penalised. The cash to build housing (in chronic short supply), creches, schools and other physical amenties for employees and their families would not be available. The potential rewards for improved performance by the entire, plant were generous. However, these collective inducements did not spark the individual's determination to produce the maximum possible at the least cost to the enterprise. The work force did not welcome the loss of personal rewards even though these were not appropriated by the Government but converted into benefits for the whole factory.

The explanation for this reaction against a switch from individual to group incentives was confused. In part, the typical worker saw the policy as a threat to his personal freedom of action. In the assessment of who should get new houses, for instance, priority was usually offered (though not invariably accepted) to the senior personnel, members of the Party branch committee, management organs and political activists. The hardest worker was by no means sure of receiving favourable consideration. A new set of privileges was created for the chosen few. The allocation of such benefits also represented power over the worker unrelated to his performance at the factory bench. He could not afford to quarrel with faction leaders, Party members, trade union officers and political activists for fear of being penalised in the allotment of the factory's physical facilities and amenities. The contrast was too large and too sudden between the freedom of the Cultural Revolution when those with power bowed low to the masses and the new situation when the masses had to mind their manners.

Another factor was the general attitude towards work. A high proportion of the labour force was new to factory life. The tyranny of the factory bell was repugnant to them. The Cultural Revolution had shown them that a worker was under no compulsion to struggle to maintain the same rate of output as his machine's capacity with only a single meal break, eight hours a day and six days a week. If political study justified stopping a production line for an afternoon (as it had between 1966 and 1969), fatigue was an equally valid reason for switching off a machine while its minder took a break. The pressure to halt machines was especially high since so much equipment was manufactured under primitive conditions and required constant attention to prevent the materials it processed from being spoilt. Crude machines raised the strain on the labour force to a point where only direct rewards or modernisation could induce an employee to give his unremitting attention to production.

This defect in the country's industrial organisation was recognised in 1975 by a discreet campaign to do the maximum to reduce the physical strains of industrial life and to cut back labour intensity in every sort of work by greater exploitation of more sophisticated machines. Until the equipment problem was overcome, it was doubtful whether material incentives for the individual, except at excessive levels, could have pushed up output very much further, and some merit existed in the change to group rewards. Incentives did affect productivity in other ways all the same. No bonuses or piece rates meant that labour discipline would not be enforced by automatic losses in earnings for the unruly; absenteeism could not be discouraged through the wage packet; and improved quality of output could not be encouraged by rewards. Nonetheless, the authorities could assume that in the long run, the workers responsible for a factory's failure to reach its targets and, hence, to build up its welfare funds would become unpopular with their workmates and subject to strong social pressures to improve their performance.

Mixed up with the lack of enthusiasm for group rewards was suspicion of the privileges which the various functionaries and political activists and faction bosses would acquire. Part of the 1975 drive to study Lenin was aimed at the restriction of "bourgeois rights," the advantages which an individual could obtain, legally or by string-pulling, because of his status or his connections with the official machine. The move to get people to read Lenin, as with all ideological campaigns in China, had its practical, hard-headed side; and clean government was a major 1975 objective. But an improvement in the bureaucracy's performance was hard to achieve. The average official was still shell-shocked by the Cultural Revolution, and any return to its public criticisms provoked nightmares. The factions were a threat to officials, especially managerial personnel. Law and order was shaky because of the association between gang violence and political ambitions. What frightened officials was not the ordinary citizen but the prospect of crowds shouting political slogans and witch-hunts conducted by large groups. The threat to the Party or government bureaucrat was the masses transformed into a mob. No one could be sure, even after the publicity given to Hangchow, that mobs would be dispersed as a threat to the country's stability. Such assurance did not come till April 1976. The safest course was to accept passively the wishes of the masses and avoid any incitement which would arouse mob passions.

On his own, the ordinary citizen was in a totally different position. In the villages and, to a lesser extent, the factories, officials were supposed to be kept in line by annual evaluations of their work and behaviour by the masses, and the unpopular functionary could be removed. But the individual needed the official's help for all manner of purposes throughout the year. As the Party was rebuilt and its authority stressed, so the power of Party functionaries grew. As the administration was decentralised by sending middle-level bureaucrats to the front line of production (mostly the villages), so the supervision of lower-level administrators weakened and the ease with which appeals could be made over the head of the local power-holder was reduced. The staff to check up on conduct at the grass-roots also dropped. The ordinary citizen was at the mercy more and more of a bureaucracy which could injure the personal interests of the bulk of the workers and peasants taken as single individuals. Local bureaucrats had a growing monopoly of power and control over the individual. One consequence was offical arrogance: petty perquisites such as free theatre tickets; better food and clothing than the average; and refusal to queue and to suffer delays in getting semi-luxuries such as consumer durables. Another and more serious result was outright corruption.

An official took a risk in remaining within the bureaucracy. He invested far more time and effort in keeping his post when new ideological campaigns swept dangerously close after 1969 to even the highest in the land. The efforts needed to win promotion were huge. An official had to be prepared to sacrifice such legitimate benefits as car travel to and from official functions to maintain an image of not standing aloof from the masses who walked, cycled or caught buses. An official's family also had to to be sacrificed. His children had to be seen to be eager to work in distant villages after finishing secondary school. A middle-rank official's offspring suffered discrimination in the allocation of jobs and college places. The official's family might findi tself forced to move to inferior accommodation to prove how proletarian and revolutionary it had remained despite the father's profession. The chances of a transfer away from wife and children were also higher. The rewards in cash terms were in no way adequate compensation for such sacrifices. Only when an official joined the elites, which ran provincial or central government bureaux and departments, did the benefits become substantial. The children could go to special schools. Houses, cars, personal staff and the right to the best on the retail market could be taken for granted. Crowds parted in deference to such dignitaries or were elbowed roughly aside by aides and bodyguards. But the majority could not hope to reach such elevated heights.

The official could not be blamed for seeing his career as an investment. He resembled in some ways (as references to capitalist-roaders or bourgeoisie in the Party and administration indicated) a capitalist corporate executive. He risked a great deal to perform his job satisfactorily. His future was unpredictable. His fate depended on his subordinates' collective response to his efforts to enlist their cooperation and on his superiors' appreciation of his delivery of concrete results—and his political flair in running his little kingdom. His one advantage was that, in a bureaucratic state such as China, his power over the individual and his welfare was enormous. He could intervene to obtain a favour from the administration for some humble petitioner. He could negotiate changes in state economic plans which would benefit a particular group of individuals. He could veto all manner of applications: to study; for leave to travel to a sick relative; for financial assistance in the event of illness. The official's business was administration and many treated their offices as commercial undertakings, so complained the news media almost daily. Households had to wine and dine venal officials; provide women for their entertainment; pay cash; give presents; and flatter and fawn. Official posts could be made to yield dividends over and above the legal pay scales, provided the bureaucrat were unscrupulous enough.

An individual could complain; often his allegations were dealt with by friends of the official. In any event, the masses had done little since 1966 to endear themselves to officialdom. An individual being squeezed by a bureaucrat had little chance of being backed in a fight for justice by his workmates or neighbours

unless the functionary's appetites had grown to such intolerable limits as to scandalise the generous humanism which characterises Chinese attitudes to an individual's weaknesses. A man in trouble with the local Party or government boss would find too often that most of his friends and acquaintances were more fearful of the official's vengeance than outraged enough to defend their humble comrade. Officials could charge what the traffic would bear for exercising their power in favour of a client. Popular demands for "nationalisation," to coin a phrase, of an official post through direct action by the higher echelons would only follow an official's rejection of a reasonable price in return for doing his duty or for showing favour towards individuals in the execution of his functions. The analogy with the landlord or the semi-monopolist in a Western capitalist state is striking.

Again, the dire prophecies of the fate which awaited the Chinese should they permit the spread of capitalist and bourgeois ideas, stressed so interminably in 1975, had a basis in fact. Few provincial authorities failed to demonstrate their concern over their corrupt subordinates. Public Security Minister Hua Kuo-feng made plenty of friends by his commitment in October 1975 to hound corrupt officials. Hua was echoing a complaint which Teng Hsiao-ping had made with some force as a result of his feel for society's most pressing grievances.

The difficulty lay largely in the desire to avoid fresh purges or coercion because of the need to restore officialdom's self-respect after its treatment as the nation's lepers in 1966 and 1967. But an equal obstacle was the way in which entire groups of citizens conspired with officials to defy the upper levels of the Government either by paying piece rates illegally, for example, or by falsifying agricultural returns to allow the village to make an illicit profit. The official and the public were too often in a mutual plot to obtain some personal gain or advantage at the public's expense for Peking or the provincial administrations to repose much confidence in the ordinary citizen's willingness to act as a watchdog over the bureaucracy. Of couse, when public opinion in some area was outraged brutally by bureaucratic grossness, resentment against the oppressive behaviour of officials boiled over into violence, and the factions had a field day in their struggle to buttress their influence and win support for their role as an alternative administration.

Teng Hsiao-ping also took the line that far too many officials had not been appointed on their merits. Men had been admitted into the bureaucracy for reasons of political convenience or the patronage of some politician who had profited personally from the Cultural Revolution and was not averse to giving friends and hangers-on a leg up the official ladder. Clean Government is linked to open competition for official appointments and promotions based on merit, efficiency, qualifications and industrious integrity. Teng recognised this truth and was unrestrained in his condemnation of the deterioration evident in the administrative machines built up by Chou En-lai and which Teng Hsiao-ping had helped to operate. Teng wanted to comb out the ranks of officialdom and get rid of useless bodies especially the novices whose coarse voices had carried them to high offices in the Cultural Revolution. As Minister of Public Security, Hua Kuo-feng, in addressing a 1975 national agricultural conference convened and opened by Teng, insisted that the criminal law be used against worthless officials. Hua was even tougher in his outlook than Teng. One complication, again supposed to be resolved by the 1975 drive to study Lenin, was that a less corrupt bureaucracy would require more vigorous vetting and supervision. These duties would mean a more efficient, dedicated and disciplined Communist Party. Clean Government in China thus implied a Leninist or Soviet rather than a Maoist approach to the Party.

CHAPTER TWELVE

THE MASSES' HERO AND DEFIANCE OF MAO TSE-TUNG

IN DECEMBER 1975, Chou En-lai lay in hospital beyond all hope of recovery. A macabre stor y was spread abroad to conceal his impending death. A Shanghai surgeon was reported to have been flown to Peking in November to operate on a patient wheel-ed into the theatre with his face completely masked. Chou's friends were fearful that the responsibility of performing despe-rate surgery to save the Prime Minister's life might overawe the Shanghai specialist if he knew his patient's identity before the Premier had been sown up again. The operation was said to have been highly successful. The ruse was not a total failure. The storm clouds which Teng Hsiao-ping had attracted to him-self were dispersed without difficulty while Chou still lingered on with reports of recovery very widespread.

Mao Tse-tung was an angry old man. A campaign to denounce a famous novel, *Water Margin*, in August 1975 was started with a longish quotation from Mao on the book's sins. The campaign proved a total failure. The Mao magic no longer worked. The campaign was ill-conceived anyway. The novel had been given a thorough criticism in university circles the previous year with no publicity, and it was under study by the general public in mid-1975. The campaign was going over old ground therefore. Since *Water Margin* was about the adventures of popular heroes rather like Robin Hood, the chances of convincing the community that the novel was a "poisonous weed" were pretty slim. Robin Hood and his Chinese counterparts are not so easily defamed. Mao's prestige was fading visibly.

Mao Tse-tung had a good idea whom he should blame for the sorry pass to which he had been brought: Teng Hsiao-ping brought back from the disgrace to which he had been consigned in 1966 to buttress Chou En-lai and his technocrats in 1973. In November 1975, Mao was given documents which showed that attempts were being made to reverse the reforms introduced into university life by the Cultural Revolution. He blessed a criticism movement on the subject among undergraduates. Teng Hsiao-ping was unruffled. The undergraduates could be handled with no great effort. The two Peking universities which were to be loudest in their attacks on Teng in the following months quoted approvingly his "Three Directives" in mid-December while their defence of the Cultural Revolution's dilution of academic standards was in full spate. Teng was being hailed and hated at the same time (but with no public mention of his name). Maoist fervour at the two most prestigious Peking colleges waxed strong. The students suddenly found themselves outwitted with a call for them to volunteer for work assignments on graduation in the most far-flung and inhospitable parts of the nation. They had no choice but to prove their Maoism was genuine by making appeals for permission to leave civilisation and migrate to the wildernesses of mountains and steppes.

This fate was exactly what had alarmed the undergraduates most when Teng Hsiao-ping's associates had come forward with plans to implement the spirit of the 1971 educational conference endorsed by the Party Central Committee and to return the universities to a state of academic respectability. Any student whose personal file revealed that he had graduated between 1966 and 1976 was marked for life as a semi-literate, pushed through secondary school and into college regardless of his academic ability. This particular decade had seen the education of most students seriously disturbed by the Cultural Revolution and the closure of the country's educational establishments. New college entrants in the autumn of 1975 were the first intake of young men and women since 1966 who had been given a reasonable grounding in secondary school and who could cope with college work up to a satisfactory level. The 1975 graduatng class, on the other hand, realised that they were destined forever to work in backwaters, with advancement blocked and with every chance of being exiled to the border regions and the most barren parts of China where any sort of education was welcome. Such a destiny seemed unfair; the students hoped to reverse this verdict on themselves by sustained and bitter protests. Instead, they found themselves tricked into the very jobs they least wanted. When allowed to accuse Teng openly of being the backstage manipulator of the improvement of academic standards and the consequent downgrading of Cultural Revolution students, the undergraduates' venom knew no bounds. They vented their spleen on Teng on a scale which the rest of society steadfastly declined to imitate.

Teng Hsiao-ping had a hint of trouble with the Central Committee of the Communist Party in December 1975. Some voices were raised in alarm about the path on which his economic policies would lead the nation. Teng had the backing of the men who counted most in the armed forces, in the central Government and in the provinces. He silenced the minority with no loss of the Party's confidence in him. Before the end of 1975, Mao Tse-tung tried to put pressure on Teng by an outright condemnation of the "Three Directives." The Mao invective was published in a truncated form on January 1, 1976, with no damage to Teng's standing. Yao Wen-yuan showed no desire to serve Mao in running the national press at this point, and Yao's sympathies were obviously with Teng.

Mao Tse-tung by early November had heard enough of Teng Hsiao-ping's plans to reform the legacy of the Cultural Revolution and Maoist principles born in its storms. But the Central Committee as a whole (not just the quartet which formed the "gang of four"—as was to be claimed in 1976) refused to pay any attention to the aged and lonely figure, so Mao told European guests. Mao was still able to encourage his most faithful adherents to attack his foes, thanks to the special Maoist network his wife had established within the Party. Hence, both the Peking universities which led the assault on Teng and a famous Shanghai army unit admitted subsequently that their criticisms were not authorised in advance by the Party Central Committee. But the universities, instead, had access to Mao. Most significant in the light of later developments was the revelation by the Shanghai soldiers that neither Chang Chun-chiao nor the rest of the "gang of four" had known in advance of their criticisms of Teng or given the army unit any inducement to attack Teng. (Chang Chun-chiao only sought to move against Teng in February 1976 when a nation-wide campaign had been launched against him inspired by Mao himself.)

The situation was too good to last for Teng Hsiao-ping. In January 1976, Chou En-lai died. The Premier's disappearance from the scene provoked a collossal crisis. His choice for the next premier was Teng Hsiao-ping, in which a majority of the Politburo concurred. Mao Tse-tung declined to agree. An attempt was made to persuade him to abide by the rule of the Communist Party that a decision is validly made if it wins a majority of the votes cast. Mao threatened to have a new meeting convened in his presence but was told bluntly that his single vote would make no difference. Teng commanded a plurality of the Politburo members. Mao conveyed his intention to overturn the Politburo decision on his own authority and defied the Party leadership to challenge his right to do so. The Politburo was so accustomed to Mao's ability to make or break even the loftiest since 1966 with a mere nod, so to speak, that its habit of obedience to his enactments still chained them to his will. The anger of individual members knew no limits. Deputy Premier Li Hsien-nien, regarded by Mao as incapable of questioning an order, reportedly pounded the table in his indignant frustration till he smashed his spectacles. Chen Yung-kuei, the peasant from Mao's model Tachai farm, threatened to go back to his native hills if Teng were ousted and kept his word. Mao was not to be baulked of his personal veto on Teng's elevation to the post of premier by this display of solid outrage. However, even Mao dared go no further for the moment than order a search to commence for a prime minister whom he would find acceptable. He could not hope to win the Politburo's endorsement of Teng's dismissal.

Chou En-lai's funeral caused a similar furore. Mao Tse-tung refused to attend. Since he was not too sick to receive foreign guests during this period, Mao's absence was a conscious decision. To be fair, he could no longer walk and was barely able to totter a few, unaided steps. He declined to reappear before the Chinese nation in a wheelchair. But he could still have graced Chou's obsequies. Mao could have directed, for instance, that the funeral cortege pass by his residence on its way to the Premier's old office in accordance with Chinese funeral traditions. This route would have allowed Mao to appear at his front door to pay his respects in person to the late Prime Minister, his comrade who had served China for so long and so well and without whose aid Mao would not have survived. Mao preferred to ignore the funeral, and not without reason. The greater the tributes paid to the late Premier, the greater would be Chou's prestige after his death and cremation. The higher Chou's posthumous prestige with the masses, it was a safe assumption, the more difficult it would be to disregard his political will and testament: the appointment of Teng Hsiao-ping as premier and China's commitment to economic and social progress at all costs.

The eulogy to Chou En-lai was itself a cause of controversy. The proper man to read it on behalf of the Communist Party was Chou's heir, Teng Hsiao-ping. To grant Teng this privilege would be inconvenient since Mao Tse-tung had plans for Teng's second dismissal from office in disgrace. The old soldier, Chu Teh, settled the matter and insisted in a quavering voice, whose Szechwan accent betrayed that he came from the same province as Teng, that he was the most senior and would read the eulogy himself. This insistence was a Szechwanese ruse. Shortly before the official memorial service for Chou En-lai began, Chu Teh thrust the speech into Teng's hands and complained that old age would prevent him, Chu Teh, paying this last tribute to his old commander, the late Premier. Teng Hsiao-ping was presented to China as Chou's heir.

The depths of national anguish for Chou En-lai took most bureaucrats by surprise. They had seen him as a hard man who wanted a smooth machine to run the country and could treat officials like dirt when angered. They did not realise the hopes which the public had placed in Chou to lead them out from a turbulent society never quite free from the threat of economic breakdown into a tidy, friendly world of comparative plenty where politics would not be the staple diet. The shudders of grief and anxiety at Chou's death reached even Mao Tse-tung who found them alarming. In death, Chou had become the focal point for public veneration to which he had not aspired at Mao's expense during half a century of collaboration. In deference to Mao, the various mourning ceremonies arranged by people all round the country were ordered cancelled without explanation. The name of Chou En-lai disappeared almost totally from the national and local press. He might never have existed. Even ordinary people dared not whisper his name. A claim was made that forged versions of Chou En-lai's last will and testament were in circulation, giving rise to subversive rumours which the masses must

track down to their sources and unmask them. No ore wanted
to risk a reference to the late Premier which might be denounced
as a rumour.

But Chou's will was reported widely in illegal posters and
stated that the country's two outstanding officials were Teng
Hsiao-ping and Chang Chun-chiao; that China should get on
with economic development; further upheavals like the Cultural
Revolution should be shunned; and that every state, including
the Soviet Union, should be offered a chance to establish cordial
diplomatic ties with China.

By the start of February 1976, an open campagin had mounted in ferocity against Teng Hsiao-ping to ensure that even though
Chou En-lai's heir, he did not become prime minister. The
vituperation heaped on him (still not by name) seemed an act of
desperation. In late January, the Party's Military Commission
had given its overwhelming support to Teng, including a vote in
his favour by Party Vice Chairman Wang Hung-wen. In a public
announcement on January 21, the highest military body in the
land had the impertinence to quote the "Three Directives"
approvingly, which showed whose side they were on. Provincial
leaders, generals and deputy premiers who had quoted the
"Three Directives" in 1975 as a slogan to sum up the national
aspirations refused to recant, even though the slogan was denounced in Mao's name as a distortion of his instructions. Mao
Tse-tung could no longer comand a majority of the Party Central
Committee; the votes were in Teng's pocket.

The affair was like a rerun of 1966. Teng Hsiao-ping could
have challenged Mao Tse-tung to a showdown but preferred not
to split the country by removing the man who had been
established over the years as the sole voice of ideological orthodoxy. Who could replace him and maintain national political
unity? Teng was offered troops to silence his opponents by force.
He was no more willing in 1976 to start a civil war than he had
been a decade earlier. His main concern was to prevent the disintegration of the Government which Chou En-lai had fought so
hard to weld into a balanced team since the Tenth National
Congress of the Communist Party in August 1973. His colleagues
wanted to quit with him. Deputy Premier Li Hsien-nien, for
instance, regarded any criticism of Teng on the grounds of his
economic policies as an insult; Li Hsien-nien was vehement in

his assertions that he alone ran the economy and that responsibility for economic policy was his alone. Teng had to persuade
Li Hsien-nien not to let his principles and personal loyalty get
the better of him. Teng had been prepared from the outset to be
disgraced as an honest official for the second time. He had unashamedly forecast this fate the previous year. He had every
expectation that the future and history would prove him right
and Mao wrong.

With reluctance, Teng's comrades assented to him acting as
scapegoat and taking on his prominent and very square shoulders
the blame for any heresies which Mao and his minions might
uncover. Teng voluntarily surrendered his claims to the premiership. As a result, his integrity became widely admired, and his
influence increased. Teng Hsiao-ping. in terms of power behind
the scenes, ended up not much inferior to Mao Tse-tung himself.

No volunteers could be found to take over as premier who
would command Mao Tse-tung's acceptance and the respect of
the Party and the Government until February 2. Chu Teh was
doddering in his gait and not very coherent in his speech but he
knew all about crises and had never treated Mao as much more
than a wayward but bright young recruit. Chu Teh felt Hua
Kuo-feng would be a sound man to take over as premier. He had
come up the hard way in the Hunan provincial apparatus and
should not be suspected of having prostituted himself for high
office. Hua knew Mao, who liked him. He had managed to get
such different figures as Chou En-lai and Mao's wife, Chiang
Ching, to come to his aid in 1968 when the extremists were about
to snatch control of Hunan. He had been denounced so often
as a rightist that he must be a man of common sense with an
instinct for popular responses or he would never have mustered
the support from the masses to survive such charges. He was a
protégé of Li Hsien-nien which meant Chou would have approved of him. He had not tarred himself as a Teng man by using
the "Three Directives." Yet Teng Hsiao-ping and he had seen
eye to eye on such key issues as an agricultural revolution,
economic development, administrative reforms and the introduction of tougher discipline. Since his province was the last overt
local example of support in January 1976 for the "Three Directives," he could not be accused of having sold Teng for Mao's
golden opinions. He had worked well with Teng as Minister of

Public Security in tackling local violence and factionalism. In 1971 and 1972, he had been discreet and moderate in running the investigations into the ramifications of the Lin Piao affair, which suggested he was not a vengeful man.

Hua Kuo-feng was particularly acceptable because he had no personal power base apart from a single province, Hunan, of which he was not a native. He belonged to no group in the power establishment and stood neutral between the Party, the central and provincial administrations and the armed forces. Hua would be very reliant, therefore, on the old guard who commanded the loyalties of the Party rank and file, the soldiers and the state functionaries. He was under the 60-year age limit Mao had laid down. He also had a toughness of mind and character, both Chu Teh and Teng Hsiao-ping agreed. Teng would fall in with Chu Teh's choice. Chu Teh had himself driven to Mao's residence and dared to barge in, unlike everyone else in China who sought permission in advance before venturing into the presence. Chu Teh said Hua Kuo-feng would not do badly as premier, upon which Mao clapped his hands to signify his agreement since normal conversation was now beyond him. On February 7, Hua Kuo-feng was revealed to the world in his new capacity of "Acting Premier." The "acting" was a deliberate courtesy to both Teng and to the Party Central Committee.

Mao Tse-tung gave instructions that the veteran leaders were not to interfere but were to give Hua Kuo-feng his head and let the spotlight shine on him alone. The bulk of the leadership took a similar view for reasons of their own: they wanted to stay out of sight to indicate their displeasure at the turn of events without undermining Hua Kuo-feng in any way. General agreement was also reached that no one should be permitted to suffer for his open support of Teng Hsiao-ping's proposals. The policy was adopted of letting the waves of hatred wash over Teng personally, as he wished, thus exposing the chief sources of extremism and anti-Chou En-lai sentiment and gauging, at the same time, public reaction to the attacks on Teng and the practical reforms he had advocated the previous year. The press and radio had a field day at Teng's expense from then on. They were encouraged by a series of quotations allegedly from Mao Tse-tung sneering at Teng as a man who never understood Marxism; an enemy within the Communist Party whom most people were too stupid to recognise; a renegade bent on restoring the old order. Since specific admission was made that Mao's own decision had returned Teng to his eminence in 1973, Mao's credibility was diminished still further. Mao's Head of State, Liu Shao-chi, had proved a viper; Mao's official heir, Lin Piao, was accused of having plotted to kill Mao and seize power; now the disgraced Teng, resurrected on Mao's written authority, was said to have been a dangerous turncoat all along.

In truth, Teng Hsiao.ping, like Chou En-lai, was on the opposite side of the ideological fence to Mao Tse-tung after 1966—but not deliberately. Teng, however, had throughout 1975 insisted that close attention should be given to making sure that draft programmes were in harmony with Mao's edicts and reflected Mao Tse-tung Thought with copious quotations from the *Selected Works*. Teng was, almost certainly, sub-conscious in his doubts about the validity of Maoism in China's current situation. Teng's attitude was a marked contrast to Chou En-lai, whose opposition was deliberate as he fought to protect himself and an administrative nucleus from Mao's Red Guards in 1966 and 1967. Chou's opposition had hardened as he wrestled with Mao's official heir Lin Piao and then had to divert the "Anti-Lin, Anti-Confucius Campaign" away from himself as Prime Minister. Of course Teng Hsiao-ping treated Mao Tse-tung in an intolerably offhand manner; in 1975 and 1976 Teng was the totally honest official incapable of servility even to appease an irritable Mao. To the public, talk of Teng's "anti-Maoism" was meaningless. The record showed that three times men chosen by Mao Tse-tung for the highest offices in China had suffered his displeasure and their dismissal. Mao seemed too easily misled about those closest to the throne to be trusted with the nomination of the national leadership. Mao's personal power was nearly at an end.

Teng Hsiao-ping's voluntary abdication, as the *People's Daily* obliquely summed up in July 1976 the post-Chou En-lai drama, had a curious effect. Unlike his plea of guilt in the Cultural Revolution, Teng now chose to follow the example of fellow-Szechwanese and late Foreign Minister Chen Yi. Teng would not criticise himself and beg forgiveness. He stood his ground. The more the criticisms poured off the presses, especially from Shanghai, narrating his proposals and policies, the more convinced the ordinary people became that Teng had been a worthy heir to Chou En-lai. The publicity given to Teng's condemnations of everything which held back the economy and his calls for better incomes and proper regulation of society aroused a ground-swell of national indignation at the abuse heaped on Teng. Support gathered for what he represented. Senior Peking officials admitted that Teng was under serious attack but could not be ousted.

In late March, the final act in the drama began. Students in Nanking were prevented by a sentry from laying a wreath in memory of Chou En-lai. The soldier was acting on orders which were countermanded too late to prevent a wave of protest at the apparent insult to the late Premier. The news spread like wildfire. The central administration had ample warning that the first week of April would be marked by large demonstrations over the failure to observe all the mourning rites due to Chou. The authorities made no effort to prevent such protests although they took precautions to prevent the situation from getting out of hand. In most major cities in the first few days of April, posters appeared, crowds gathered and pro-Chou and indirect anti-Mao views were heard. The authorities turned a blind eye to these blasphemies.

The explosion occurred on April 5 in Peking (and almost every large city in China). The ostensible explanation was the secret removal the previous night of wreathes in honour of Chou En-lai. All over China, nevertheless, the crowds struck up basically the same chorus as they defied the police, militia and troops to have their say. They wanted Teng Hsiao-ping to take charge of the administration. They demanded implementation of the "four modernisations." They expressed their distaste for Mao Tse-tung's wife, Chiang Ching. They identified Mao with the infamous tyrant of Chinese history, Chin Shih Huang Ti, and indicated their desire that his reign end forthwith. Sedition ruled supreme, as it had for several days. Inflammatory speeches were made. Party members and militia who were foolhardy enough to remonstrate with the masses were attacked. A few were killed. The troops showed no desire to enforce the law and scatter the rioters. In Peking, some of the demonstrators stuck it out till the very end and were captured or killed.

Arrests on the days which followed showed that participants were often quite nonchalant in discussing the demonstrations. The impression was that the participants had given vent to long-pent-up feelings and were indifferent as to who came to know which leaders they loved and which they loathed. The determination shown by 100,000 in gathering in the capital's main square ("The Gate of Heavenly Peace") was shattering. The authorities were defied with the utmost provocation by the crowds. An army barracks was set on fire. A strenuous bid to break into major buildings was mounted. Yet this square was the forum where till 1971, Mao Tse-tung had been wont to survey with more complacency than dignified composure a million or so men, women and children march or dance by on major festivals wishing him a life ten thousand years long. In the same square, he had seen the mass rallies of his young warriors, the Red Guards, who forced the mighty in 1966 to bow to Mao's will. In this very square, Mao had proclaimed in 1949 the birth of the People's Republic. In April 1976, the same square witnessed Mao's rejection by his own people and his political fall after a carefully-engineered decline in his power.

For Teng Hsiao-ping, the announcement two days later that he had been dismissed from all official posts including that of Chief of General Staff of the armed forces could not touch him. Mao Tse-tung was named in the official statement intended to disgrace Teng as the prime mover for Teng's ejection from all Party and government posts. The leadership knew that Teng had to go. Riots could not be tolerated when the nation was already close to conflagration. Mao needed to be retained as a symbol. But Teng was in no way dishonoured. Mao had been unable to get a majority to back Teng's dismissal from Party membership, which showed the Central Committee to be still faithful to Teng. The riots were not alleged to have been engineered by Teng. He was left with the satisfaction of being the only man since 1949 for whom people had risked liberty and sometimes their very lives to express for him their support at mass rallies in defiance of Mao's personal condemnation of him. Teng was the only man whom large numbers of the populace had called on to replace Mao Tse-tung and his appointees at the head of the administration. Mao Tse-tung had been rebuked in public by so many hundreds of thousands that the era of unquestioned authority vanished for ever. Teng Hsiao-ping was now for the second time the honest official exiled from the court because he would not stoop to intrigue or fawn or exploit his official power to save his own career. No matter what the future held, he could never climb higher than the pinnacle of the days in April 1976 when the people had gathered to insist on his return to office.

Mao Tse-tung did not deserve such a political death. He had served his country to the best of his ability. Compared with the rulers not only of the Soviet Union since 1917 and the rest of Eastern Europe since 1945 but also with leaders of Third World nations in general and Chinese rulers of the past, Mao was sensible and moderate in his policies. He exhibited the strongest distaste for the use of terror and bloodshed as instruments of Government. His comments on the organisation of political and social reforms for a poor country had much to commend them. His economic precepts based on a realistic appraisal of the dominant position of the peasants and their world could hardly be improved on as a theoretical guide. Teng Hsiao-ping deserved his triumph but not at the expense of Mao's reputation.

The significance of the April riots went deeper than the personalities involved. First, the demonstrations showed that the Chinese were not a gullible society. After years of a massive personality cult and constant adulation for Mao Tse-tung, the people retained an independence of mind which showed China's underlying maturity and sound sense whatever the froth on the surface whipped up by political campaigns. The Russians took three years to summon up the courage after Stalin's death to have a secret conference to disclaim his meticulously-cultivated greatness. Mao's achievements were far grander than Stalin's record; yet enough Chinese people were concerned with the realities and harsh facts of life to dare to go against the Maoist tide even before Mao's death. The Chinese possess a special immunity to brain-washing, it appears.

The second important feature of the riots was the political aim of the demonstrators. They did not adopt the impractical stand of calling for the overthrow of communism. They did not demand that China be turned into a land in which the consumer would be sovereign. Their attitudes were as realistic as the pressures which had taken them on to the streets. The rioters wanted no radically new administration; they wanted Teng to continue to run affairs. Their prime concern was the implementation of Chou En-lai's promise that through the "four modernisations," by the end of the century, China should have joined the ranks of the world's advanced nations. The popular cry was for modernisation of the economy so that an unborn generation should live a life without material worries. It would be hard to find a similar example of rioters in an underdeveloped economy showing such a sound appreciation of the national economy and such long-range ambitions. Their hard-headedness and comprehension of how development is achieved were also fruits of Mao's efforts to educate China.

Vituperation of Teng Hsiao-ping got worse in the news media. But in the provinces, the anti-Teng campaign was the merest excuse for the authorities to start to crack down on the unruly and lawless elements who had been disturbing the peace, disrupting political and economic life and fomenting crime for a decade. Teng's supporters were the provincial authorities. The cry went up universally that violence, looting and sabotage must be suppressed. The criticism of Teng and the claim that precautions against further disturbances were essential allowed the first moves to be made against gangs which had been virtually free to thumb their noses at the authorities for years.

Inevitably, the task of wiping out years of anarchy in as large and complex a society as China was not a simple one. The local administrations made slow progress, but for the first time, they, refused to allow the public's attention to wander from the lawless elements in their midst. The press suggested that factions were the result of Teng's wicked policies, an assertion devoid of any factual basis; the accusation merely made the political excommunication of factions far easier. Once politically isolated, the intimidation of local police bureaux and municipal or county authorities would be far more difficult. Previously, criminal elements had been intermingled with factions which were linked to individuals with some political muscle. All such groups were described henceforth as associated with Teng Hsiao-ping and, therefore, beyond the pale. The factions, however, retaliated instead of beating a retreat; and many localities were in a state of almost open civil war from May to the end of August 1976.

A pattern was now established which the Government followed zealously. Mao Tse-tung the autocrat was finished; his personal power need no longer be feared. Mao Tse-tung the ideologist was important because for Maoism, no substitute existed. The nation had been so bathed in the rhetoric of Mao Tse-tung Thought that his slogans and key concepts formed the only common language of Chinese political life by 1976. This aspect of Mao's cult could not be ignored without a split in the Communist Party over what ideological truths to cling to and a veritable babel of conflicting jargons and Marxisms. Since Mao the personal ruler was being rejected, the key members of the Party who knew themselves to be identified with the Mao coterie should have started to look for shelter. The desire to preserve Maoism made the struggle for survival all the more important. Chang Chun-chiao seems to have been the one to have realised most clearly among the "gang of four" how isolated he and the rest of the quartet had become from the community and from the rest of the leadership. He tried to win Mao's blessing by attacks aimed at Teng Hsiao-ping in January and February. But he now seemed a born turncoat even to Mao. Those closest in the public's view to Mao over the years would offer the most authoritative interpretation of the true meaning of his teachings. The group believed popularly to be nearest and dearest to Mao were his wife, Chiang Ching; the young man nominated by Mao as Party Vice Chairman, Wang Hung-wen; and the two men constantly received by Mao in the Cultural Revolution, Chang Chun-chiao and Yao Wen-yuan. Yet the quartet—the "gang of four",—were the odd men out in the Politburo, barely tolerated during Chou En-lai's life and no longer the darlings of the general public.

Since all four had close ties with Shanghai, the natural assumption was that they would use the city as their base and let the rest of the leadership try to lay siege to them there. The quartet was no longer on good terms with Mao Tse-tung, a fact obscured from the average citizen. The four had been forced across the Politburo to Chou En-lai's side, despite last minute efforts to return to Mao's good books. The late Premier displayed great tolerance of them since they kept the Maoists under control. The quartet had started their careers in Shanghai; yet the city was not their loyal bastion. Chang Chun-chiao, as he had declared, had fought to keep Shanghai out of the hands of the extremists and under the central authorities. For this feat, Shanghai had attacked him as a rightist. Thereafter, Shanghai showed a caution and moderation in its political commitments, having been bitten badly by Chang Chun-chiao when the Shanghai masses thought they were on the true Maoist road.

The city had moved over to Teng Hsiao-ping's side at an early stage. In December 1974, even the leading Shanghai political monthly, *Study and Criticism* (condemned in late 1976 as a mouthpiece for the "gang of four"), drew attention to Teng's excellent combat record, thus building him up for his appointment as Chief of Staff of the armed forces in the following month. The day before the attack on *Water Margin* was launched in Peking during August 1975, Shanghai published a totally different view of the novel. This act could hardly have been an accident because preparations for major campaigns are made well in advance across the country. Since *Water Margin* was condemned in Mao's name, the moral was obvious enough. The city had gone into an uproar in March 1976 when a local paper ran an unflattering article about the late Chou En-lai. Shanghai had published in such detail Teng Hsiao-ping's economic programmes that the city seemed bent on ramming home to the country what a splendid leader had been lost by his ouster. The way in which Teng's various policies had been presented for public consumption by Shanghai hinted strongly at satire on the anti-Teng campaign and a covert desire to protect his position. Shanghai promised no sanctuary to the "gang of four"; they were left to make out as best they might in Peking.

On July 28, an earthquake struck northern China and damaged the capital and the coastal city of Tientsin. The epicentre of the earthquake was Tangshan, a city of over a million inhabitants with a further six million in the surrounding prefecture. China's biggest mine with an annual output of 25 million tons of coal was at the heart of the earthquake. Communications between Manchuria's industrial wealth and the rest of the country were severed. Mao Tse-tung was moved from the capital as fresh tremors were expected. The Government strengthened its hand by using the rescue operations as a cover for the transfer of front-line combat units from the Sino-Soviet frontier to the environs of Peking. These troops had fought under Deputy Premier Chen Hsi-lien, the Peking Military Commander, during the fiercest battles of the 1969 border confrontation with the Russians. These soldiers' instant response to his orders could be taken for granted.

At the same time, a debate started in the Politburo which indicated the need to prevent any small clique presenting itself to China as the infallible heirs to the wisdom of Mao Tse-tung. This role must be safeguarded for the legitimate Party leaders. The argument was started by plans for reconstruction after the earthquake which was described as the worst calamity to hit China since 1949. Condemnations were published of any return to the sort of emergency measures which Teng Hsiao-ping had been associated with during the three years of near-famine which followed the collapse of the 1958 Great Leap Forward. Such condemnations pointed to the existence of advocates of every possible expedient to rebuild the shattered areas of north China, especially as earthquakes in 1976 had affected other parts of the nation and the weather had been atrocious once more. The spirit of self-reliance was hailed, just when doctors, technical staff, skilled workers and supplies were brought in from every part of the country to relieve the distress of northern China. Hua Kuo-feng, who had been appointed substantively to the post of Premier and promoted to the rank of First Party Vice Chairman as a result of Teng's dismissal in April, took charge of relief and reconstruction work. This venture was the first national test of his abilities. The speed with which key services and industrial plant were restored to normal, and the attempts to safeguard the welfare of the population in the affected area were conducted, won him extensive applause. He seemed to be the stuff of which prime ministers in China need to be made.

On September 9, Mao Tse-tung died. Even his mourning rites showed how his personal identity had been buried in the April riots. His wife did not stand in the place of honour at the memorial services. Of the country's 29 major administrative units, only six bothered to mention their sympathy with Chiang Ching on the loss of her husband; the rest overlooked her existence. At only one provincial memorial service for Mao was the widow's name mentioned. The silence of the country was an obvious denunciation of Chiang Ching, just as the provinces' silence when asked to retract their support for Teng Hsiao-ping at the start of the year had testified to their support for him. Chiang Ching was on notice that her husband's name could not buy her the normal courtesies extended assiduously by Chinese to bereaved families. Could his name bring her anything but danger now that he was dead? No widow stood at one side of the catafalque, as custom demanded, to receive the condolences of the mourners and to return their bows after they had bowed to the corpse and then to the family. Instead, Chiang Ching sacrificed her place as Mao's widow and the margin of immunity it might have brought. She agreed to stand in line as a mere Politburo member on the understanding that this gesture of solidarity as Mao's wife with the rest of the leadership would be repaid with protection for her life and dignity.

Chiang Ching helped to create an image of solidarity at the top in Peking; the gesture forfeited her whatever sympathy she might have enjoyed from the masses. She seemed heartless in her refusal to act as widows were expected to behave to pay their final respects to their husbands. She could not have been prevented forcibly from her widow's rights to be the principal mourner, for lavish tears and some dramatic collapse or attempt to throw herself on the bier would have been enough to display her widow's grief. Such behaviour is the normal reaction of women in China whose relatives try to restrain them from emotional excesses over their bereavement.

Almost to the month after Mao's death while still in the deepest period of mourning, Peking let the news trickle through to the outside world that Chiang Ching, Chang Chun-chiao, Wang Hung-wen and Yao Wen-yuan had been detained for plotting to seize power. The news was then announced to the country, with Hua Kuo-feng proclaimed as Party Chairman in succession to Mao Tse-tung. Their arrest had been planned well in advance. Deputy Premier Ku Mu, an economic specialist and a Chou protégé, had been so confident that the onslaught against Teng Hsiao-ping's economic policies was only temporary that he had said so to foreign visitors in March and May. The first attack on the "gang of four" appeared in the press as early as August. The disgrace of the "gang of four," was simply a matter of waiting for Mao Tse-tung to breathe his last and be laid to rest. The members of the Chou club would then face few obstacles in restoring the late Prime Minister and his policies to their rightful place of honour.

CHAPTER THIRTEEN

VENGEANCE ON THE MAOISTS

THE EASE WITH which the "gang of four" were removed from the scene so abruptly after Mao Tse-tung's death came as a shock to many inside China and even more observers abroad. The smooth military arrangements were an important factor. The presence of troops whom the Peking Commander, Chen Hsi-lien, had led in combat against the Russians as recently as 1969 helped. The authority of Defence Minister Yeh Chien-ying ensured that the armed forces as a whole would support the arrests. The refusal of Wang Tung-hsing to regard himself or his praetorian guards as the personal retainers of the Mao household removed the chances of physical opposition.

The actual operation to detain the quartet is easy enough to follow. More difficult to explain is the apparent lack of support for any of the quartet. Why did they seem so deserted? The answer lies in their failure to build any far-flung and popular power bases. Only Chang Chun-chiao was a member of the central administration and in a position to use civil service patronage to buy followers. The bureaucracy had no love for Deputy Premier Chang. The officials' loyalty was reserved for Chou En-lai and his associates to whom they had looked for protection during the Cultural Revolution. The bureaucracy also identified with Teng Hsiao-ping who had shared their public disgraces and vilification. Chang was also head of the armed forces' General Political Department. His grip on the troops was so weak, nevertheless, that he could not prevent an army magazine from publishing the script of a film denounced by Chiang Ching. The army had shown in January 1975 that it backed Teng. The officer corps preferred men such as Chou and Teng. The officers and soldiers would also obey such favourites as Yeh Chien-ying who happened to be a founder-member of the Chou club. The various speeches of Wang Hung-wen in 1974 on the subject of the army's defects and his dismal showing in the face of civil disorders in Hangchow also ensured that the army would not seek to rescue the "gang of four."

To both the public at large and to officialdom, Chiang Ching and Yao Wen-yuan symbolised the worst excesses of the Cultural Revolution. Mao's widow was held personally responsible for the violence which had swept the country ever since 1966. The invocation of her name by so many extremist groups, which far too often degenerated into criminal gangs, made her universally reviled. The masses in the urban areas were also disenchanted with the "gang of four" for simple financial reasons. The 1975 campaign to start voluntary overtime and to freeze wages was linked to a 1958 article by Chang Chun-chiao on this subject. The masses thus had no reason to look upon Chang and the rest of the "gang" as potential benefactors. Quite the reverse. The ordinary factory employee could foresee a Spartan future if the "gang of four" ruled China. Much the same attitude prevailed among the peasants who regarded the "gang of four" as responsible for the radical voices which had insisted on severe controls on the countryside's free markets.

As for the Communist Party apparatus, Chou En-lai had taken over the task of the Party's reconstruction from Lin Piao. Teng Hsiao-ping had been returned to office in 1973 at Chou's request because of his intimate knowledge of the Party at all levels. The refusal of provincial Party bosses in 1975 to recant their support for Teng Hsiao-ping's "Three Directives" after these had been condemned in Mao's name showed a stubborn fidelity to Teng. The silence of most provincial Party Committees about Mao's widow when transmitting their formal condolences to Peking indicated what the Party apparatus felt about Chiang Ching and the "gang of four."

The "gang" had no base in the army, the bureaucracy or the Communist Party. They had no popular support. Even Shanghai could not be relied upon as a refuge. The quartet could look to only three restricted groups for support. The first was those college students whose education had been interrupted by the Cultural Revolution and who would suffer badly through the introduction, as Teng Hsiao-ping had urged, of professionalism and technical qualifications. This group was no longer a powerful force in academic institutions after 1975; the majority of its members had graduated and been replaced by students who had received a reasonable secondary education and were not intimidated to the same extent by proper academic standards. The use made by "gang of four" of the students was brought out by the vast outpouring of anti-Teng vituperation from the universities, when the rest of the country tried to ignore the anti-Teng drive, and, according to official provincial reports, by the employment of students from Peking's colleges as emissaries on behalf of the "gang of four."

The second source of potential support was the factions. Their leaders had wielded power in 1966 and 1967 when the "gang of four" had appeared to dominate Peking. A return of the quartet to control of the Government promised a revival of the factions' fortunes. In addition, some members of the factions were genuine Maoist extremists who believed the "gang" enjoyed Mao's unreserved confidence. Individuals associated with the late Lin Piao, who had escaped the dragnet which followed his death in September 1971 when fleeing Peking, also viewed the "gang of four" as more understanding than the rest of the Party Central Commitee of how individuals became associated with Lin Piao during his Maoist heyday. Unfortunately for the quartet, the factions were in a minority, hated by the public and under mounting pressure during 1975 and 1976 from central and local authorities.

The third group was more important. Any official appointed or promoted after 1966 could be looked upon as a Cultural Revolution beneficiary. Since the "gang of four" was accused of engineering the downfall of qualified veteran officials and promoting the "gang's" own toadies, new recruits to the bureaucracy and those who had climbed the ladder in the decade up to 1976 faced rigorous investigation of their records. Many in this category had been enthusiastic in their support of the Cultural Revolution and its radical innovations. The "gang of four" not only appeared to be closest in behaviour to the true Maoist ideals but they themselves had also been swept to high office by the Cultural Revolution. Thus, in the bureaucracy, a certain number still looked to the "gang" as their models. These bureaucrats, together with some factions, refused to surrender and criticise themselves after the "gang of four" had been arrested. What sparked this resistance to the rest of a jubilant nation when the quartet were under lock and key was the thought: if Mao's widow, Chiang Ching, could not claim immunity, who would be safe among the Cultural Revolution activists from the public's revenge?

However, not even all these various groups combined could summon up enough influence on behalf of the "gang" to sway Peking. The quartet were simply too hated to have more than the barest chance of salvation. Even teenagers had to pick the ancient leaders in the capital against the more youthful and dynamic "gang of four." Without the quartet to insist on radical experiments, youngsters could hope that the draconian measures to force secondary school graduates out of the cities down to the farms might be relaxed and direct entry to college and university reintroduced instead of being postponed for years of manual labour.

The official Chinese press at every level stressed consistently that Hua Kuo-feng was personally responsible for the arrest and destruction of the "gang of four." Hua has been presented as having been guided in his decision to detain the "gang" by Mao Tse-tung's personal advice. So insistent is the official line on the arrests being in obedience to Hua's own commands that an overwhelming impression is created of genuine feuds between Hua Kuo-feng and each of the "gang of four." A survey of Hua's experience after being summoned to Peking in 1971 to work in the central administration reveals considerable evidence of old scores to settle between the quartet and the man who claimed to have been nominated by Mao as his ultimate heir.

Chiang Ching is the most interesting case since her arrest devalued Mao Tse-tung's prestige on which Hua Kuo-feng relied heavily in support of his status as legitimate successor to Mao's authority. In 1973, a film was produced with Hua's blessing by Hunan province based on a local opera. Its theme was educational reform and the ideal relations between teachers and students. Called *Song of the Gardner*, the film has been described as very popular with the public and applauded by Mao himself. In 1974, duriny the national campaign to criticise operas and other artistic works in which Chiang Ching was hailed (for the last time) as the standard-bearer of revolution in the dramatic world, *Song of the Gardner* was condemned. The first press criticism emerged in Hunan itself and was then picked up by the national papers. As the opera had been endorsed by Hua and could be closely identified with his own views, condemnation of the opera was a direct assault on Hua's credentials in his own province. (He was still Hunan's senior Party and government official.)

Hua Kuo-feng had substantial reasons in 1974 for suspicions that he was no favourite with Chiang Ching. He had also to ensure that he maintained his hold over Hunan Province, no easy feat when he was burdened with duties in Peking on behalf of the central Government. The quarrel with Chiang Ching almost certainly began privately long before the open bid before the entire country to discredit Hua. While Hua may have earned golden opinions from Mao Tse-tung in 1969 for erecting a mausoleum to honour Mao's second wife, Yang Kai-hui, executed in the Civil War, Mao's current wife, Chiang Ching, did not share this sense of respect for the revolutionary martyr. Hua must have weighed in advance how for his gesture of admiration for one of Mao's previous spouses would arouse hostility in Chiang Ching but win the gratitude of Mao. To honour the Mao family's heroine thus was almost calculated defiance of Chiang Ching and a symbol of the distinction Hua was able to make between Mao Tse-tung as China's greatest leader in modern times and Mao the husband of Chiang Ching.

Hua Kuo-feng's quarrel with Wang Hung-wen was partly a straight clash over authority and policies and partly mutual irritation. In 1974, Wang had spent October, November and December with Mao in Hunan. With nothing more pressing to occupy him, Wang had taken in hand the local militia and given its commanders instructions on its reorganisation. Provincial militia are the responsibility of provincial Party Committees (although as a military force, the militia structure is linked to the regular army). Wang's intervention in the affairs of militia units under Hunan Province implied the provincial Party was unable to cope and that it was under Wang's authority. As with the opera, *Song of the Gardener*, Hua Kuo-feng had been given grounds to suspect that an attempt was underway to undermine his prestige in his own parish. In the same year, almost certainly before the militia question arose, an argument had erupted in a different field between Wang and Hua. This dispute could only have reinforced Hua Kuo-feng's misgivings about Wang Hung-wen's intentions towards him. The dispute occurred over the correct way to conduct criticism of Lin Piao and Confucius in the Commission for Physical Culture and Sports. Hua had been appointed to oversee this political movement in the Commission but Wang Hung-wen interfered with Hua's instructions, implying they could be ignored. Wang lacked a proper sense of Hua's true importance.

Mutual irritation seems to have been caused by the problem of law and order in 1975 and 1976. Final responsibility for suppression of factions and disorder rested with the Minister of Public Security, the post in which Hua Kuo-feng had been confirmed in January 1975. Yet a great deal of Wang Hung-wen's time was spent on visits to different parts of the country for protracted negotiations with factional leaders. Wang clearly had been ordered to play a major role in finding permanent and peaceful settlements to the local disorders which caused serious economic and political disruption during these years. By and large, Wang's efforts to restore harmony among the cliques hungry to win a portion of the power which the Communist Party branches and local bureaux of the Government arrogated increasingly to themselves met with little success. His main problems seem to have resulted from attempts to win over the dissidents by seeking to show he understood and sympathised with their outlook. This bid to gain the cooperation of ambitious faction leaders by references to his own climb to power through rebel activities in the Cultural Revolution backfired. Wang's remarks were seen as discreet expressions of support for those brave enough to defy local officials even after the return to normal Government with the end of the Cultural Revolution. In addition, he had a grave disadvantage in coping with unruly factions because of the antagonism he had aroused among the military commanders and the leadership of the public security forces associated with the army establishment at the national level (in contrast to the basically police duties performed by local public security bureaux).

Wang Hung-wen appears to have felt cut off from reliable information about what was happening in the provinces and unable to rely on the normal channels of communication. To overcome this obstacle, he established his own liaison network, which proved a further handicap. The existence of a second, separate communication channel with the capital encouraged the idea that the Party bosses were at odds in Peking. Individuals frustrated in their search for power at the provincial level came to believe they could ignore the conventional Party and government channels, in which they counted for so little, and use Wang's network to appeal for support from Peking. Quite often, appeals along this parallel chain of command, which became closely involved in the separate Party structure which Chiang Ching built as a Maoist bastion, proved very effective. Through such appeals, men condemned as dangerous malcontents or criminals either by the central or provincial authorities found themselves exonerated or, in many cases, simply released from prison or police custody. In one instance, Mao Tse-tung's own verdict on an individual was reversed in this way.

Such an independent set-up threatened ordinary police procedures and legal processes which were Hua Kuo-feng's domain. Furthermore, every failure to quell factionalism and every fresh encouragement given to local dissidents raised the question of how Public Security Minister Hua was spending his time. The more factionalism fostered anarchy and outright crime, the greater the criticism which could be made of Hua's efficiency. By choice, design or accident, Wang's failures in dealing with factions threatened Hua's reputation as an adroit administrator.

In 1970, Mao Tse-tung had instructed that his native province of Hunan should transform the local economy and become industrialised by 1980. This directive demanded the mechanisation of agriculture as well as the erection of sufficient factories to shift the balance from peasant cultivation to mechanical and manufacturing production as the chief source of Hunan's income. The official expected to shoulder the burden of organising a programme to comply with Mao's desires was the province's chief administrator, Hua Kuo-feng. He took the idea seriously and felt what was good for Hunan could be applied with profit to the rest of the nation. The next year, Hua was called to the capital to work for the central administration. One of the first tasks given to Hua was to head a National Conference on Farm Mechanisation in August and September 1971. The delegates approved the aim of completing the bulk of agricultural mechanisation throughout China by 1980. Hua had an editorial drafted to announce the Conference's conclusions to the nation but found an insurmountable obstacle to the publicity he anticipated for this major innovation in farm policy.

Yao Wen-Yuan was not in favour of Hua Kuo-feng's editorial on farm mechanisation. Yao had doubts about the peasants' capacity to achieve the 1980 target. But of no less importance was the crisis which rocked Peking in September 1971 when Lin Piao, Mao Tse-tung's heir, fled from the capital only to crash in the Mongolian Republic. The headaches involved in editing the news media to adjust to this dangerous drama were grave enough. Yao was not eager to launch a publicity drive at this time to sell to the rural population an ambitious scheme to replace traditional cultivation techniques with new-fangled machines, fertilisers and other chemicals, especially as the villagers would have to be induced to finance this agricultural revolution from their own resources. Hua's editorial went into the waste-paper basket. However good Yao's reasons for not putting Hua Kuo-feng's message into print, the incident was viewed in retrospect as a deliberate slight by Yao.

Yao Wen-yuan also failed to pay the proper deference to Hua after his appointment as Acting Premier in February 1976. When Hua Kuo-feng took foreign guests to visit Mao Tse-tung, the accusation ran, Yao deliberately prevented Hua from receiving the personal coverage in films and photographs which he rated by convention. Worse still, Yao allegedly ignored Mao's instruction to promote a personality cult around Hua Kuo-feng when he had been confirmed in the rank of prime minister after the April 1976 riots. Thus, apart from direct clashes on policy matters (as in 1971), the picture presented of relations between Yao and Hua was that of a struggle for exposure in the national news media, with the former frustrating the efforts of the latter.

The evidence for an outright quarrel between Hua Kuo-feng and the fourth member of the "gang," Chang Chun-chiao, is slight. At one major conference after Hua had been appointed Acting Premier, Chang took objection to what he regarded as Hua's habit of seeking to silence dissident voices by invoking Mao Tse-tung's authority. Chang refused to be so intimidated. After his arrest, Chang's private papers revealed some cryptic observations on the downfall of Teng Hsiao-ping and the elevation of Hua Kuo-feng in February 1976. The precise significance of Chang's comments is obscure, even though officially represented as proof positive of Chang Chun-chiao's dismay at Hua's promotion to the premiership.

Hua Kuo-feng perhaps needed no personal rupture with Chang Chun-chiao to feel that Chang ought to be in custody rather than still free to attend Politburo sessions. Wall posters went up after the deaths of both Chou En-lai and Mao Tse-tung in favour of Chang's appointment as prime minister. Rumours circulated widely that Chang would take over as premier particularly when Mao lay in state during September 1976. Chang Chun-chiao had been named, the country believed, by Chou En-lai before his death as second only in competence to Teng Hsiao-ping among the nation's administrators. The potential threat from Chang to Prime Minister Hua Kuo-feng was undisguised, whether or not Chang Chun-chiao himself entertained dreams of taking over the premiership by toppling Hua.

Chang Chun-chiao's fatal flaw, however, was the excuse he provided Hua Kuo-feng for believing that Chang stood shoulder to shoulder with the rest of the "gang." On October 2, 1976, the Politburo was in session to consider the text of a speech which Foreign Minister Chiao Kuan-hua was to deliver at the United Nations. It contained a reference to a "final instruction" from Mao Tse-tung, widely quoted since September 16 of the same year. Hua deleted the reference on the grounds that he had checked what Mao had written down for him and discovered the directive had been distorted (for the evil ends of the "gang of four" was the subsequent charge). In the margin beside Hua's own note explaining the deletion, Chang scribbled a request that the mistake in the Mao directive should not be revealed outside the Politburo to avoid embarrassment. Hua apparently acceded on the unspoken understanding that Chang Chun-chiao would guarantee that the erroneous version of the Mao quotation appeared no more. Only two days later, Peking's *Kwang-ming Daily* carried a lengthy article built up entirely around the misquotation. Yao Wen-yuan has been accused of trying on the same day to amend a similar article due for publication on October 7. Possibly the Chinese press is so ponderously edited that Chang Chun-chiao could not stop the offensive article from appearing on October 4. In the event, realities were immaterial. Chang became the final conspirator; the "gang of four" was complete and ready for denunciation.

The separate conflicts between Hua Kuo-feng and the individual members of the "gang of four" are important pieces of evidence. An astonishing feature of the first months of daily denunciation of the "gang of four" was the failure to point to a single occasion on which the quartet could be alleged to have acted in concert as a united group. The "gang" was shown pairing off to undertake various diabolical stratagems but not joining forces to act as a single unit. Heilungkiang Province in January 1977 commented on the way the "gang" usually acted separately. Yet the quartet did share certain common characteristics: a public image based on identification with Cultural Revolution extremism; long association with the city of Shanghai; careers which prospered through Mao Tse-tung's patronage; Mao's denunciation of them for forming a clique; and their personal and policy differences with Hua Kuo-feng.

The combination of the personal and policy factors is significant. On the personal side, the "gang" were not the only dignitaries pictured as evil conspirators against Hua Kuo-feng, Mao Tse-tung and Chou En-lai. Since drama and films are the responsibility of the Ministry of Culture, the fall of the "gang of four" was the prelude to a clean-up of that ministry's upper echelons. This purge was hardly a surprise after Hua's embarrassment over *Song of the Gardener* whose condemnation could be blamed in part on cultural officials. The Sports Minister was also cast into oblivion. The sexual athletics he had allegedly provided for Chiang Ching's entertainment were only half the charge against him. He should also have ensured Wang Hung-wen was not permitted to interfere with Hua's work in the Commission for Physical Culture and Sports during the campaign against Lin Piao and Confucius. Another figure to disappear was the Health Minister. This event was an enigma until the revelation that the central administration had given Hua overall charge of the population planning programme whose success required the cooperation of Health Ministry personnel. Hua seemingly felt the assistance rendered him had been less than adequate. When these clues are put together with the charges against the "gang of four" that they had slighted Hua and neglected to foster public adulation for him, an image is created of an insecure individual, hungry for publicity and unable to forget any differences of opinion which could be read as a personal slur.

As it happens, this image is very much at odds with Hua Kuo-feng's own record when attacked over the years by political extremists and with his previous preference for privacy. This attitude is plain enough from the almost total lack of information about his origins and family life when appointed Premier. Hua had deliberately kept out of the limelight in the past just as he had swallowed the insults of radical hotheads. A large quantity of gall, therefore, had been stirred into the honey poured over Hua Kuo-feng by the press and radio from September 1976 by the innuendoes about his personal touchiness and desire to settle old scores. Hua could not take his position for granted, which would explain why he supported the decision to move so hastily and with such disregard for Chinese cultural traditions to arrest Chiang Ching and the other three.

The knowledge that even the personality cult around his name was an indirect threat must have made Hua determined to show through his treatment of the "gang of four" that he was not a man to be trifled with. Furthermore, any personality cult in China is inauspicious. The tactic is associated first with Stalin, whose grossness is well known to the Chinese despite Peking's refusal to condemn this Soviet monster. Mao Tse-tung and Lin Piao are the other examples of men whose images were artificial creations. Neither figure basked in the country's affections by 1977. The true folk heroes, Chou En-lai, Chu Teh and Chen Yi, for instance, spurned contrivances to accentuate their popularity. Teng Hsiao-ping was invariably blunt to the point of rudeness, but no leader since 1949 had matched the appeal his name possessed by 1976 when the masses rioted for his return to power. Thus, the Hua cult was a two-edged weapon and not just a symbol of strength.

This reasoning helps to explain another extraordinary development. Under Hua Kuo-feng's leadership, the Party Central Committee brusquely removed the Foreign Minister, Chiao Kuan-hua. Peking is extremely sensitive about its international image: ministers and officials responsible for relations with the outside world generally have a special immunity from open criticism or disgrace. Chiao was not merely cast aside with

barely an initial pretence of indisposition. The background to
his downfall was allowed to circulate very quickly. The Chinese
public was ready to accept his dismissal for he had almost
exulted in Teng Hsiao-ping's downfall. Chiao was the only
official of his rank to exhibit pleasure for public consumption at
Teng's removal.

The Chinese masses would readily assume Foreign Minister
Chiao Kuan-hua had fallen because he was opposed to Teng
Hsiao-ping. This view is an additional complication in the
situation which emerged after Mao Tse-tung's death. Although
the various leaders arrested or dismissed could be portrayed
(as the press eagerly did in Peking) as involved in personal
quarrels with Hua Kuo-feng, they had also fallen out just as
seriously with Teng. But Teng was omitted from the official
story, perhaps because the public would not have tolerated
allegations against their hero of personal vindictiveness. But the
facts are that Chiao Kuan-hua attacked Teng in public as did
Chang Chun-chiao. Chiang Ching had not suppressed her
animosity towards Teng on her visit to Tachai in September
1976. Teng had first come under fire from the universities
under the Ministry of Education, now being punished. Teng's
demands for improved standards of medicine had led to a
stream of abuse from the Health Ministry. He had also been
attacked by members of the Sports and Culture Ministries. On
reflection, the true test of who was a threat to the men who had
taken over China on Mao's death was not Hua's opinion of individuals but how they had behaved in the anti-Teng campaign.
This conclusion made Hua Kuo-feng's position as national
leader seem shakier still and all the more dependent on the
goodwill of the old guard who had soldiered with Mao and
Chou En-lai and come to power with them in 1949.

Yet to Hua Kuo-feng and the rest of the Politburo, Foreign
Minister Chiao Kuan-hua was a serious case. He had been party
to a trick to protect Chiang Ching and Chang Chun-chiao with
the aid of his wife. Communist Party members were told how
Kang Sheng, who sat in the Politburo as representative of the
national security and intelligence machines, had lost trust in
Mao's wife and in Chang Chun-chiao. Kang Sheng had been
close to Mao Tse-tung, and he decided to send a deathbed
message to Mao in 1975 to warn him that Chiang Ching and

Deputy Premier Chang were no longer persons for whom Kang Sheng could vouch as he had done originally. The message was given to a pair of young women on Mao's private staff. At a loss to know what to do with Kang Sheng's message, the couple approached Chiao Kuan-hua for advice. The Foreign Minister induced the pair to write down Kang's charges, and he gave their manuscript to his wife, a close friend of Chiang Ching. Kang Sheng's warning ended up in the hands of Mao's wife, who naturally did not pass the message on to her husband. The two young women found themselves transferred from Mao's immediate entourage. Foreign Minister Chiao had put petticoat politics before Maoism. His loyalty was suspect after the "gang of four's" arrest. His retention in office could not be tolerated until his own wife's dominance over him had been investigated thoroughly.

CHAPTER FOURTEEN

ECONOMIC DEBATES AND
THE STRUGGLE FOR POWER

WHEN POLITICIANS GATHER to arrange the dismissal, denunciation and destruction by public criticism and self-criticism of former colleagues, a degree of animosity, if not genuine hatred, helps to still consciences and smother recollections of past favours received. Personal struggles for power are a natural outcome of human ambition. Politicians, nevertheless, like most individuals forced to work in group situations, learn to tolerate the less pleasant side of their fellows and to suppress irritation and anger. The condition for such collective patience and moderation is that the group achieves its goals successfully without any members being forced to totally sacrifice pet ideas or schemes. As long as business proceeds with reasonable smoothness, debate and argument are not only permissible but valuable as a means of removing suspicions and frustrations, with frankness used to symbolise mutual confidence.

The personal rancour between Hua Kuo-feng and the "gang of four" and the disgust which the rest of the top Chinese leadership felt for the quartet by October 1976 were important. Such emotions eased the way for the "gang's" overthrow. An important question, however, is why the rulers of China found the "gang of four" so intolerable that they had to be removed with almost indecent haste after Mao Tse-tung's memorial services. Personal differences had existed for too long to be a good explanation of the impetuous decision to take the foursome into custody. The Party Central Committee felt obliged, in fact, to arrest the "gang" because their ideas about how to administer the country had become completely and menacingly at odds with the plans of their colleagues. Quarrels over major policies decided the fate of the "gang of four." Yao Wen-yuan's failure to arrange enough TV coverage of Hua Kuo-feng, Chiang Ching's taste in French clothes and Chang Chun-chiao's imports of permissive foreign films only ranked as mortal sins when the "gang" had fallen out with the rest of the Party leadership over issues which revealed dangerous political preferences rather than private tastes.

The exact cleavages in the debate between the "gang of four" and the rest of the leadership are hard to identify. Their details remain obscured, by design, in the flood of denunciations aimed at the personal sins and character defects of the quartet. The refusal to clarify the issues over which disputes reached such intensity that Mao Tse-tung's own wife had to be condemned in the most savage terms is no accident. If the debate were made plain for all the nation to follow, the "gang of four" might rally some support even after their bitter, nationwide execration.

The main lines of the argument can be uncovered, all the same. Inevitably, in a poor country, the sharpest disputes centred around economic problems. The old issues of timing, balance and priorities, which have always vexed the Chinese Politburo, came to the fore. The debate started as a genuine search for consensus, seemingly, and was carried on without much rancour for most of 1974 and 1975. In this context, the charges against Teng Hsiao-ping are worth recalling. He was accused of advocating economic programmes which conflicted with Mao Tse-tung's doctrines. But the documents for which Teng was flayed have never been represented as programmes for action. They were documents drawn up for Teng, which he revised and then used as material for speeches and conferences. In other words, Teng was putting forward his side of an argument. He was not engaged in trying to ram his views into practice over objections from the rest of the Party Central Committee. Teng's career is a clear indication that, even in late 1975, open discussion was in progress within the Politburo and the rest of the Central Committee on major economic policies.

As the debate dragged on in the Politburo, views began to harden and patience to wear thin. The various groups looked for support outside the ranks of the Politburo. The Party Central Committee was lobbied by the main rivals. The arguments were not resolved satisfactorily in this larger forum. An effort began to recruit support from the lower echelons of the

Communist Party. The desire to appeal to a wider audience brought the factions to life once more in 1975. The factions could both exploit and be exploited as the circles involved in the debate widened to embrace subordinate Party organisations.

When Teng Hsiao-ping was denounced for his heretical policies in January 1976 and failed to win the premiership the following month, the arguments seemed to have been settled by Mao Tse-tung's intervention against the Chou club and programmes they favoured. But Teng was too popular within the Party and the Government and too respected by the masses for Mao to be able to break the deadlock so simply. Teng's supporters of every rank refused to capitulate and took to the streets in April 1976 on his behalf. The factions were running wild, too. Their leaders saw the popular confusion caused by the Teng controversy as a new chance to seize power. Even Teng Hsiao-ping's public dismissal in April 1976 did not put a stop to the dissensions. Battle was joined in the Politburo and in the streets and refused to die down. The debate had gone to the nation.

The 1976 riots over Teng Hsiao-ping and the unrest which followed started a chain reaction in Chinese political life. Formal official denunciation of a leader, even in Mao's name, no longer convinced the masses. Indeed, in Teng's cause, the more intense the criticism, the more popular opinion rallied to Teng and what he represented. To break this vicious circle, Hua Kuo-feng and the Politburo hit upon a clever strategy after Mao Tse-tung's death. They tried to reverse history and blot out the bitter clashes and denunciations of 1976. Hua and the Politburo tried to take the nation back to 1975 and its promises of a future filled with progress and ultimate prosperity. They convened national agricultural and coal conferences identical in aims and spirit with those held in 1975. This return to the past was possible because the "gang of four" were in custody, and the Chou club no longer had opponents capable of arousing agitation on any large scale over questions of policy or principle.

The removal of the "gang of four" from political life gave the Politburo a free hand in deciding the future of Maoism. Hua

Kuo-feng took credit for publication of a Mao Tse-tung speech, "Ten Great Relations," made in 1956 but not released officially before December 1976 except within the Party ranks. Hua was engaged in a redefinition of Mao Tse-tung Thought. The stress was on Mao's teachings which had brought the country progress very successfully until the disastrous 1958 Great Leap Forward. The same policies had formed the foundations of China's recovery both from the Great Leap catastrophe and from the chaos of the Cultural Revolution.

Against this background, Peking was unable to prevent a rough outline of what was at stake in the debates with the "gang of four" from circulating outside the Communist Party elite.

The first issue in the argument was over management of the economy at all levels, but especially at the farm and factory stages of production. Involved was a pair of quite distinct difficulties, although the two became confused in the wrangles. The first was simple discipline. With disorder threatening output in the towns and rural indifference to official decrees a challenge to state agricultural plans, authority was an issue which could not be ignored. Teng Hsiao-ping's views were well known: managers were paid to get things done and professionals should be entrusted with the solution of technical problems. Hua Kuo-feng had made his similar but more guarded opinions clear in October 1975 when he addressed the National Agricultural Conference. His speech was approved by Mao Tse-tung and published after a short delay. Hua wanted the eradication of corruption and maladministration in the countryside and the enforcement of law and order throughout China as a whole.

Practical sentiments of this obvious kind seem almost clichés for a poor nation. However, they conflicted with a very different set of ideas about human behaviour. In dispute with men such as Teng Hsiao-ping and Hua Kuo-feng (the Chou club in fact) was a group which did not want the nation to collapse in anarchy. But it feared three things. The first was genuine anxiety over popular reaction to tough law-and-order policies after so many years of almost unfettered freedom to defy everyone in power except Mao Tse-tung himself. Factory workers saw no reason to return to the pre-1966 era when they had been no more than obedient pawns of the management class. The revelations of the Cultural Revolution and the Lin Piao scandal had not provided

the peasants with any good reason for abandoning their traditional mistrust of the capital's designs on the villages. Was it not
better, the anti-authoritarians argued, to trust the workers and
peasants and lead them gradually to impose law and order
through systems of their own design? Was this approach not only
more Maoist but also what the Cultural Revolution had been all
about?

The basic difference between the Chou club and its critics was
over administrative methods and could have been settled by
assessing which offered the most effective solution to the authority problem. In many ways, the ideal approach would have been
to let the public evolve its own solutions for disorder and for
disruption of output. However, to wait for the public meant a
sacrifice of economic growth, which was the second strand in the
debate. How long could the nation put up with unruly and
insubordinate behaviour? The more time involved meant slower
progress towards the abolition of poverty. The ordinary citizens
wanted higher living standards. Their desire was constantly
proved by the ruses to obtain unlawful bonuses in factories and
by the black markets flourishing in both town and country.
Popular discontent could be stirred up if economic growth were
delayed. Yet, equally, popular resentment could be aroused by
tough management to make the economy more efficient.

The "gang of four's" stand in the debates had a simple consis-
tency. The danger, in their view, was that the bad harvests of the
1970s, the failure of industrial production to grow at a rapid even
rate (because of factional and political disruption) and the difficulties in financing imports of key plant and machines would be
used as excuses to betray the Cultural Revolution and basic
Maoism. Their line, as far as it can be disentangled, was that the
performance of production in the short run was not the real test
of China's progress. Political awareness, mass management and
direct participation of workers and peasants in administration
were the immediate targets towards which the country should be
steered. In the world at large, the richest nations and strongest
economies were those of the United States and similar capitalist
states and of the Soviet Union which had swopped Marxism for
"social fascism" and "social imperialism." The outside world was
ample testimony that if life were to be reduced to success in meeting the physical and profit quotas in state plans, China might

reject Maoism and take to the same degraded paths as the Americans and Russians.

The "gang of four" were prepared to argue, therefore, that trains behind schedule and factories in which output had come to a halt were not necessarily to be condemned. Rather, the Maoist zeal of the train or factory workers should be examined. Production could be legitimately halted, the "gang" felt, to allow the labour force to take part in revolutionary activities and strengthen control over the authorities. Within reasonable limits, time off for political activities and study is essential for truly democratic management of society. The issue is how much time can be afforded and where is the line to be drawn between work-shy agitators who get their mates to down tools for the day and the idealist with a genuine grievance to air before the local community.

The response from the "gang of four's" critics was that Maoism and democracy had been reduced to a farce by anarchy. Without sufficient wealth, China could make only the slowest progress towards a society in which differences in living standards between peasants and workers, intellectuals and manual labourers, and bureaucrats and the masses could be abolished. Until China had advanced significantly towards such equality, the nation could not hope to move forward to the Marxist Utopia. Economic development was a material necessity in a poor country such as China and an ideological virtue for its Marxist rulers, the opponents of the "gang of four" maintained.

In response, the "gang" argued that constant practice of revolutionary politics broke down the mental, cultural and traditional barriers to the social and economic transformation of China; through revolution, production would rise automatically. The counter-argument was to point out the impact since 1966 of mass chaos on the pace of Chinese economic growth. References to the costs of anarchy implied a criticism of Mao Tse-tung's Cultural Revolution, which the "gang of four" felt obliged to defend. Such a debate must end up by pushing into the arena the most fundamental Maoist notions about human beings, society and the true goals of Marxism. Of such stuff are ideological heresies made.

In 1975, Wang Hung-wen quarrelled with the conclusions of the National Coal Industry Conference. He was in total disagreement with its suggestions on ending factionalism and restoring unity. Since China's miners number a mere three million, they form too tiny a group over which to engage in a power struggle. Wang was arguing over the principles of law and order. At a 1974 national economic conference, Chang Chun-chiao disagreed that railway disruption menaced the entire economy. Chang was against coercive measures to restore order among recalcitrant railwaymen, as was Chiang Ching. Yet low productivity and outright sabotage were constant threats to national communications. At the same conference, Wang Hung-wen wanted a veto on discussion of the iron and steel industry. Steel remains a semiprecious metal in China. The most modern production facilities have been erected in such centres of political agitation and unrest as Wuhan in central China and Liaoning Province in the north. Wang was against draconian measures to boost the iron and steel sector which could have crushed bases of fervent Maoism. Chang Chun-chiao wanted the 1974 meeting to hear nothing on the subject of finance. The reason is not hard to surmise. Ledger books reveal in terms of dollars and cents what costs and benefits will flow from different policies. Cold cash distracts attention from even the most noble ideals.

The "gang of four" were in a minority in the Party Central Committee and at conferences attended by government officials. To overcome such lack of support, Chang Chun-chiao and Yao Wen-yuan were forced to insist in April 1975 that a proposed national industrial conference be left to the Politburo to arrange. In effect, this move prevented the conference's convention.

On the agricultural front, the "gang" opposed spare-time activities for personal profit by peasant households and wanted tighter controls over the free rural markets. They maintained that the peasants would be tempted back into capitalism unless such breeding grounds for selfish profit interests were abolished or at least rigorously restricted. China's peasants, as Mao Tse-tung had warned, are very sensitive to incomes and profits. Without cash inducements to grow vegetables and to raise livestock and poultry in their free time, the peasants would not supply these key food items to the towns and cities. At the same time, a real difficulty existed in some areas where villagers did not bother to work their obligatory eight hours in the communal fields; they could make too much money from private enterprise. The views of the "gang of four" were not without some rational basis.

Similar difficulties arose in another sector of the economy, foreign trade. Here the arguments highlighted most clearly, perhaps, the clash between idealism and harsh economic truths. The "gang of four" opposed the expansion of oil exports. They claimed that through increased oil shipments, China would join in the exploitation of oil-hungry nations by taking advantage of world shortages and high prices. On general sales policies, could China claim to be any better than the capitalists if exports were sold at world market prices, asked the "gang"? During 1974, the Chinese encountered balance of trade problems (with American Government estimates of a balance of payments deficit at around US$1,000 million). The immediate cause was errors in grain purchases; the long-term problem was the number of contracts signed for deliveries of foreign factories to be erected in China. To the "gang of four," the solution to the trade gap was to cut back imports and adhere more closely to the Maoist principle of self-reliance. The "gang" set their faces against efforts to boost exports because they felt such a solution would encourage even greater dependence on imported resources. The "gang of four's" critics pointed to the nation's need to buy sophisticated foreign technology to accelerate the pace of economic modernisation. China was desperately hungry for advanced plant and equipment from overseas.

In the battle over economic policy, the "gang of four" attacked the model oilfield of Taching which Mao Tse-tung had held up for imitation by Chinese industry. Chang Chun-chiao was especially bitter on the subject, arguing that political ideals had been forgotten by Taching and that its only current concern was increased output. The "gang" also regarded Taching as heretical because it used foreign equipment. Taching was an old battleground. During the Cultural Revolution, one of the few occasions on which Chou En-lai and Chiang Ching had been openly at loggerheads was in a discussion of Taching and its loyalty to Mao. Chiang Ching had argued that the oilfield's leaders were not loyal to Mao; Chou fought to insulate Taching from the storms of the Cultural Revolution. The quarrel was inconclusive and ended with a sort of tacit compromise. Red

Guards appeared in Taching, but the oil industry stayed relatively untroubled by the Cultural Revolution.

The oil arguments involved more than Taching's political morals, the ethics of oil exports and ancient grudges. A national fuel plan was worked out for 1976 on which Wang Hung-wen had been very voluble at the 1975 National Planning Conference. The Politburo, including Mao Tse-tung, Chou En-lai and the "gang of four," managed to agree on the production, distribution, domestic consumption and export quotas for each type of fuel including oil. The plan broke down in practice because its targets had miscalculated demand from places which were modernising their industrial plants. Shanghai and Liaoning Province, on the whole, contain the country's most advanced factories. Coal boilers no longer met their production requirements, and they were switching to oil. A spurt in their demand for oil emerged in 1976, which both areas were able to meet at the expense of less industrially strategic districts such as Kwangtung Province. Disruption of the national fuel plan by diversion of oil to Shanghai and Liaoning has been used as evidence of deliberate sabotage by the "gang of four".

On agricultural modernisation, the "gang of four" did not speak with a single voice. Yao Wen-yuan had been sceptical about China's capacity to mechanise farming by 1980. Wang Hung-wen allegedly proposed in 1975 such a complete mechanisation of rice cultivation that the farm modernisation policy would have become absurd. Chang Chun-chiao has been attacked for lack of enthusiasm about top priority in every sphere for the needs of agriculture. Chang insisted that this policy pampered the peasants at the expense of industry and the towns. Chang Chun-chaio had touched a sensitive issue. Agriculture is more backward than industry and grows more slowly. Resources devoted to the peasants are lost to the development of the most efficient sectors of the economy. Nevertheless, with 700 million peasants against some 200 million urban inhabitants, Peking is no position, politically or economically, to ask the village population to take second place.

On the subject of the overall economy, the reality is that some districts are better organised, more sophisticated and more successful in industrial production. Why should they be drained of supplies to aid the more backward areas? At this sort of point, the idealistic "gang of four" became as hardheaded and growth-conscious as the rest of the leadership. This diversity of economic capacity and efficiency from one area or sector to another involved a fundamental economic problem never solved by Mao Tse-tung: the correct balance between central control and provincial autonomy and self-sufficiency. In times of economic difficulty, Peking's temptation is to leave the provinces to solve their own difficulties. The central authorities thus avoid the politically sensitive task of commandeering supplies and redistributing them between areas traditionally resentful of each other. Teng Hsiao-ping thought that provincial autonomy was outdated. He argued for a national concept of the economy, with Peking's ministries in charge. This central control would replace the way in which districts were left to their own devices, with local factories communally owned by the peasants frequently engaged in open competition with state enterprises.

The "gang of four" got into this argument. The prosecution admitted the "gang" came down sharply on neither one side nor the other. The quartet was alleged to have backed ministerial control when they were in control of a government department's staff. But when the "gang" wanted to take over a district, they were said to have backed the local official against Peking. This account is probably the strict truth: the "gang of four" supported those ministry officials they trusted and backed the development projects of individual districts with whose political climate they felt in sympathy. The "gang" need not necessarily have been guilty of bad faith here; Mao Tse-tung himself never found a satisfactory solution to the balance of power between the capital and the provinces.

However, the power implications of the debate over central versus local control cannot be ignored. The "gang of four" suspected, apparently, that emphasis on economic success would buy local support for their opponents in the Politburo and Party Central Committee. For this reason, the "gang of four" needed to protect their right as Peking's representatives to inspect local conditions and ensure that output was not flourishing as a result of cutting out political study or paying illegal bonuses. The "gang" also wanted to be able to intervene in specific areas to prevent local Communist Party machines from being dominated by career bureaucrats and technical personnel. The "gang" had to retain the authority to dispatch emissaries with the power to force Party branches and committees to invite individuals trusted by the "gang" to take part in their deliberations as true Maoist representatives. At the same time, the "gang of four" wanted the masses to supervise (and dismiss if they pleased) their local bosses. The dilemma was a difficult problem for the "gang", all the more so because Chiang Ching and Wang Hung-wen were far more concerned with what happened at the grass-roots than Chang Chun-chiao and Yao Wen-yuan. The "gang's" approach clashed with the idea of orderly administration implied by tight control from the capital. Peking could not be responsible for local administration unless it could prevent its officials from being harried at will by the masses.

These economic quarrels were not abstract philosophical discussions. They had an immediate effect on the Chinese economy. Wang Hung-wen was against harsh measures to improve the performance of the iron and steel sector. Yet several instances could be cited of serious disruption of output. The Wuhan Iron and Steel Company, for example, is one of China's largest, with a work force of 80,000. Its 1974 output slumped below the 1973 level because of factionalism and political dissensions.

Hangchow was the best-known example of a city torn apart by political differences. Its silk printing and dyeing mill lost enough money in the 30 months up the end of September 1976 to construct another two mills of equal size and efficiency. In Heilung-kiang Province, the backlash from debates in Peking caused one motor plant in 1976 to suffer 40 days of total and partial strikes. The city of Chengchow in the central province of Honan is known as the "heart of the country's railway system." In 1976, the volume of coal moved by rail through Chengchow dropped by 12 million tons. Yet Chiang Ching and Chang Chun-chiao were not in favour of getting tough with railwaymen.

The Kiangsi Tractor Plant became notorious because all production ceased between February and October 1976 in the wake of disputes over the correct economic policies to follow. This enterprise is one of the largest producers of farm machines in the country. Not all of industry suffered on this scale. Oil production did not grow as rapidly in 1976 as in previous years but the Manchurian province of Kirin could boast of record output despite transfers of skilled personnel and equipment to other oil fields.

Agriculture appears to have been more directly affected than the rural economy had been by the Cultural Revolution, a good indication of the significance of the economic dissensions. In December 1976, six provinces, with a total population of 220 million (a quarter of the national figure), were listed as victims of serious disruption on the farm front for several years. With agriculture the chief bottleneck to Chinese economic progress, this statement was a grave admission. As with industry, however, not all the rural sector was in a sorry state. A total of six provinces and regions were listed at the same time (their combined population of 288 million being almost a third of the national total) as examples of rapid progress. The material losses which resulted from disunity in Peking and growing antipathy between the "gang of four" and the rest of the leadership were a further reason for the decision to place Chiang Ching and the "gang" under arrest.

The "gang of four" was cut off from a majority in the Politburo and the Party Central Committee by another clash of opinions. This dispute centred on the lengths to which China should go to produce a version of the Marxist gospel different from that found in the Soviet Union. Chang Chun-chiao dramatised this aspect of the quarrel by claiming that a prime reason for the Kremlin's betrayal of the true Marxist creed was its obsession with technical progress and the skilled personnel who create new technologies. Chang was prepared to sacrifice education, culture and even scientific advance to prevent China from imitating the Soviet Union. Chang Chun-chiao was no more violently patriotic than any other member of the Party Central Committee; he was merely more extreme in his hunt for anything which smelled of Soviet "revisionism" than his colleagues other than the "gang of four." The "gang" expressed serious reservations about any project which stressed increased output on the grounds that obsession with production had lured the Soviet Union into a form of capitalism. Not only was the Maoist model of Taching attacked but grave doubts were expressed about the validity of Tachai's performance although Mao Tse-tung had proclaimed the village to be the nation's model farm community. Chou En-lai's January 1975 call for modernisation of the whole

country by 2000 A.D., based on a 1964 Mao directive, was highly
suspect in the "gang's" eyes.

On defence policy, the "gang of four" clung to the notion of
"people's war," with the enemy to be drowned in a sea of hostile
masses. The "gang" believed that gigantic armies would neutra-
lise the sophisticated technology adopted by the Soviet Union
which had given power to the Kremlin's defence establishment.
The "gang" was accused of seeking to expand the militia to
create a rival army; more accurately, they sought to use the militia both to provide the masses for "people's war" and to prevent
the armed forces from winning too powerful a voice in the
councils of state.

The "gang of four" attacked every form of material incentive
for production. The idea that workers and peasants can be moti-
vated indefinitely to ever higher physical productivity without
personal rewards is a distorted version of Mao Tse-tung's comments on labour management. The "gang" stressed self-reliance
in solving such difficulties as food shortages to forestall any bid
to practise "goulash" communism. When northern China was
struck in July 1976 by one of the worst earthquakes in Chinese
history, the "gang" refused to budge from the principle of self-
reliance, apparently. The interests of the seven million people at
the epicentre of Tangshan could not take precedence over the rest
of the nation's needs or over the drive to criticise Teng Hsiao-
ping. Belief in the ability of ordinary people to solve even the
most dreadful calamities through their own efforts without outside help is Maoist in origin. But here the "gang" took Mao
Tse-tung Thought to extremes.

Such distortions were not deliberate perversions of Mao Tse-
tung's precepts nor based on an unfeeling inhumanity. They arose,
it is clear, because the "gang of four" insisted that whatever was
diametrically opposed to Soviet practice was the right course for
China. Thus, Russian children are selected for college by
competitive academic tests; China should abolish examinations.
Russian workers are tied to a complex system of wage incentives;
China should move towards the abolition of income differentials.
Free peasants' markets flourish in the Soviet Union; China should
bring such markets under rigid state control. Russian workers
have no right to strike, denounce managerial mistakes or protest
politically; such activities ought to be encouraged in China. The

Kremlin's main measure of success is annual growth in output; China should consider first its political salvation. The Soviet army is encased in steel and lives by electronics; China should rely on a citizen army reinforced by a vast, patriotic militia.

Another Soviet characteristic to which the "gang of four" paid special attention was the power of public security and judicial officials. Peking believes that Soviet tyranny, through an arbitrary and unjust administration, intimidates its citizens. To ensure such an evil did not infect China, the "gang" took great interest in persons arrested in areas whose leadership was not notably Maoist in the "gang's" judgment. This concern to see that the innocent were not incarcerated by all-powerful bureaucrats brought the "gang" into direct contact with the factions. The only groups eager to denounce the local authorities for wrongful imprisonment of political activists were factions. They had good reason to seek outside help in 1976. In the drive to quell the pro-Teng riots of April 1976 and arrest his supporters, most local administrations ignored Teng Hsiao-ping's sympathisers (the mass of the people) and arrested faction members who had used violence for political ends since 1974. Hence members of groups which regarded themselves as closer to the "gang of four" than to any other segment of the Peking establishment were placed in custody. The only remedy was for their comrades to appeal to the "gang," which often secured the release of imprisoned unlucky firebrands. This assistance identified the "gang" more than ever with those responsible for fomenting violence and disorder.

The "gang of four" saw no flaw in their attempts to prevent the "dictatorship of the proletariat" (as Marxists call police and legal activities) from growing into a monstrous tyrant of the Stalinist variety. The Party Central Committee saw a trap. Defiance of authority may be valuable and deter officialdom from riding rough-shod over the populace. But anarchy can create its own tyranny, in which the loudest voice and wildest slogan win the day. The masses become a mob; the frenzied crowd rules the individual as viciously as a secret police backed by terror. Affairs become even more despotic when the mob is manipulated by small groups on behalf of some individual's personal interests.

The "gang of four" were sucked into just such a situation. The majority of officials, both Party and state, opposed them. The Party Central Committee and provincial leaderships were out of sympathy with the "gang." Quite rightly, the "gang of four" believed that at the grassroots, large numbers were subject to harassment, extortion and persecution because of their records during the Cultural Revolution or their dedication to extreme Maoism. With little support in the upper parts of the administration and anxious to aid their humbler supporters, the "gang of four" had no other allies in many areas except the factions. These bands far too often were composed of worthless criminals or men of unbridled ambition. The "gang's" connection with a faction gave it a certain respectability and some political credentials. The faction then felt free to practise its own style of mob rule which, on balance, the public found more terrifying than the abuse of power by some local mandarin. The "gang of four" thus managed to reinforce its reputation for supporting the most unsavoury and depraved elements in Chinese politics.

At the end of January 1977, Peking was being quite explicit about the implications of the "gang of four's" brand of politics. China would have ended up with a fascist regime had the "gang" come to power, it was alleged. This charge is not so far-fetched. The "gang" never appreciated how its hostility to everything for which a parallel could be found in the Soviet Union created a tyranny as repugnant as Soviet abuses once the "gang" relied on anarchy and unlawful factions. Mob rule is a form of despotism. Peking in 1977 also linked the "gang of four" to the quarrels between Lenin, Stalin and Trotsky. The "gang" was accused of imitating Trotsky by refusing to accept economic realities. The "gang of four" became the modern Chinese version of Trotsky. Mao Tse-tung was identified with Lenin. Both Chou En-lai and the new Premier and Communist Party Chairman, Hua Kuo-feng, were cast in the role of Stalin. Quite unintentionally, it seems, Peking was revealing the similarity between Chou, Hua and Stalin. All three believed in efficient administration; a disciplined population; order imposed from above; and a smooth Communist Party apparatus backed by effective penal sanctions.

Thus, the "gang of four" opposed Stalinist-type oppression but terrified the nation through the chaos and violence they provoked. The "gang's" opponents were basically the Chou club who favoured a trend towards the authoritarianism out of which Stalinism was born. But the Chou club ended up by toppling the "gang of four" whose policies and tactics had alienated most of the Politburo and the Party Central Committee as well as a majority of the population. The irony of this switch in roles was macabre.

The final question is why the somewhat impersonal debates of 1974 and most of 1975 exploded into such a bitter power struggle in 1976. One reason is that the debates dragged on too long: individuals lost patience; and the numbers involved increased as the contestants looked for support at the grassroots. Secondly, the growing physical weakness of Mao Tse-tung and Chou En-lai in 1975 meant that frustrations mounted as there was no obvious umpire to settle disputes and reconcile the disputants by his personal authority. Thirdly, genuine confusion existed as to what line China should follow and also about Mao's economic ideas. Chang Chun-chiao, for example, wanted to know in early 1976 who could guarantee that the agricultural modernisation programme approved by Mao in October 1975 still remained in force. Fourthly, the lower levels of the administration and the Communist Party rank and file were perplexed by events in Peking. They knew of the disputes at the top and were wary of making a false move. Hence, when only one of the "gang of four" attended the National Planning Conference in July 1976, many timid spirits felt terrified of accepting the Conference's decisions. If the "gang of four" came out on top in the struggles in the capital, would the National Planning Conference be denounced as an anti-Maoist plot?

Even more important was the need to finalise the five-year development plan which began in January 1976 but whose detailed implications would be spelled out during the rest of the year. The debates had a special importance in this context, for their outcome would decide which areas, industries and sectors of the economy got the lion's share of the nation's investment funds and other resources until the end of the decade. The April 1976 riots saw demands for more development and less ideology. They were followed by natural disasters, especially the July earthquake. A re-examination was essential of the priority to be given to welfare and living standards.

This question involved too many principles and personalities for the arguments to remain dispassionate. The 1976 emergencies were too grave for any more time to be wasted on talk or slogans; immediate practical remedies were required. This urgency brought the ideologues (exemplified by the "gang of four") into direct conflict with the professional administrators and technocrats.

Finally, the deaths of both Chou En-lai and Mao Tse-tung left no single figure who could compel a measure of obedience from all groups. The factions claiming the patronage of individual members of the "gang of four" were power bases independent of Party Central Committee control and threatened national security. The Chinese had long ceased to dream of open rebellion against Mao or Chou. Their disappearance from the scene meant that even indirect defiance of conventional authority could not be tolerated because there was no longer an extraordinary authority (namely Mao or Chou) to take command when the Communist Party or Government buckled under the strain.

Possibly the most human element in the equation was the disappearance of Mao Tse-tung who had ruled so long and, in his later years, so much according to his personal whims. Once the yoke could be thrown off, the arrest of the "gang of four"—the group most intimately associated with Mao's era—symbolised a fresh start towards a very brave new world. Their detention was the most concrete evidence for all levels of the nation as to which side had finally won the debate; it was the most positive indication of the direction in which to expect the economy to move in the future. An arrest is a most persuasive conclusion to a major dispute among politicians over policy priorities.

CHAPTER FIFTEEN

THE CHAIRMAN'S EPITAPH

THE NATION WENT wild with joy at the fate of the quartet. All the hatred for the Cultural Revolution, for the suppression of individual opinion, for the subordination of material progress to abstract slogans spilled over in mass galas complete with endless parades everywhere. Rightly or wrongly, the "four," and Chiang Ching most of all, were regarded as the demons who had taken possession of the body politic exactly ten years earlier and driven the people on a wild and evil course. Their arrest signalled a new era, China believed, in which the excesses of the Cultural Revolution could never be repeated.

For Chiang Ching, the arrest and indictment against her were bitter ironies. In 1966, the wife of Head of State Liu Shao-chi had been seized by the Red Guards. She was vilified and accused of seeking to sabotage Tachai, Mao's favourite village; of lavish taste in clothes; and of never having been a true communist, among other things. Now similar charges were made against Chiang Ching. Her fashion sense became wild extravagence; visits to Tachai, an attempt to interfere with its Maoist operations. Her success in acting as Mao's eyes and ears and, sometimes, his voice when he could no longer move with any ease, was a bid to split the Party. Her interviews with Professor Roxane Witke, to which Yao Wen-yuen had been privy, were secret contacts with foreign powers to the detriment of China's national interests. The charges did not matter. The very fact that the Government had locked up Chiang Ching and three men with national reputations for extremist sentiments won massive popularity for the post-Mao leadership. This step alone had proved its right to rule.

While Mao Tse-tung's widow languished in detention, Peking's leaders continued to lavish praise on Mao Tse-tung

Thought. Even the arrest of his widow was carried out in his name. To the intellectuals would fall the task of writing the last word on Mao who had failed to crush the freedom of spirit of Chinese academics. Chou En-lai had always come to their aid and encouraged Teng Hsiao-ping to do likewise in 1975. Chou En-lai was now mentioned constantly in terms of deep affection, and the "four modernisations" were respectable again. Mao Tse-tung was used to destroy his wife and her friends.

Mao Tse-tung had declined to appear at Chou En-lai's funeral rites. Mao's final verdict on his prime minister would seem to be obvious. Chou's view of Mao Tse-tung could not be revealed until the disgrace of the "gang of four" and, even then, only indirectly. On January 2, 1976, according to the official press, Chou asked for two poems by Mao to be read to him once more. The poems had been composed in 1965 but only published on the eve of New Year 1976. When the final lines of the second poem were recited yet again to Chou, only a week from his death, the Premier laughed with delight. He never laughed again in this world. The lines which filled the dying man with glee have an earthy quality not normally associated with Chinese poetry and modestly concealed in the official translation. The couplet also contained a prophecy which could be interpreted as a prediction that Mao's world would be turned topsy-turvy before long.

Chou En-lai certainly knew that history is the final judge of a nation's leaders. History's verdicts in China are controlled by the intellectual elite whom Mao Tse-tung had come to regard as successors to the mandarins of old. Chou En-lai on his deathbed, many Chinese believed, was confident that Mao's own words would be seized upon with a cynical and undeserved ingratitude and transformed by the intellectuals into their epitaph for Mao Tse-tung:

> Stop your windy nonsense!
> Look you, the world is being turned upside down.

THE INDICTMENT AGAINST
THE "GANG OF FOUR"

THE MAJOR CHARGES hurled at the "gang of four" are the case for the prosecution. The Peking propaganda machine feels under no obligation to report impartially on the background to the arrest of the quartet or to suggest that anything could be said in their defence or even in mitigation on their behalf. But Peking's allegations are not as persuasive or watertight as is implied by the vehemence of the abuse showered on the "gang." Peking is merely the prosecutor, intent on presenting the best case which will leave both China and the outside world convinced of the total guilt of Mao Tse-tung's widow, Chiang Ching, and her three alleged accomplices.

The various accusations can be examined in two different ways. The first is to put together the various charges made in different versions since the "gang's" arrest in October 1976 and see how far the indictment is consistent. The second is to look at some of Peking's key assertions in the light of the historical record.

A joint editorial in the *People's Daily, Liberation Army Daily* and *Red Flag* journal described on October 25, 1976, how Mao Tse-tung had condemned the "gang of four" specifically for acting as a faction and clique on July 17, 1974; December 24, 1974; and May 3, 1975. The same article reported Mao as condemning the political ambitions of Chiang Ching and Wang Hung-wen, ascribing his rebuke to "November and December" of 1974. Honan Radio Service stated on November 17, 1976, that Mao had expressed his distaste for the attitude of the quartet in a written note on April 23, 1975.

The implication is that the four had forfeited Mao Tse-tung's trust as early as 1974 and that he continued to struggle against them thereafter. The first problem is that, with the exception of May 3, 1975, Mao' comments on the "gang of four" could not have been intended as formal denunciations made in his capacity as Chairman of the Chinese Communist Party. In the case of the May 1975 criticism, it is merely said that Mao expressed his anxiety about the "gang" at a Politburo meeting but the joint editorial of October 25, 1976, shows Mao did not regard them as a critical problem. He is quoted in these terms: "If this is not settled [i.e. 'the gang of four'] in the first half of this year, it should be settled in the second half; if not this year, then next year. If not next, then the year after." The casual attitude towards the time available for dealing with the "gang" it not what might be expected of a man who feels he has nurtured a nest of vipers in his bosom. The criticisms ascribed to Mao in November and December must be viewed as less than formal since no Communist Party meeting could have been in progress because Premier Chou En-lai did not arrive in Hunan where Mao and Wang Hung-wen were staying until December 27, 1974 (according to the *New China News Agency* January 12, 1977).

Wang Hung-wen was "severely denounced by Chairman Mao" after Wang presented Mao "with a statement of accusation against Premier Chou" in October 1974. Despite this calumniation of Chou En-lai, now described as Mao's loyal friend, Mao did not dismiss Wang from his entourage. He was still in residence with Mao when Chou En-lai arrived at the end of December 1974. (These facts are narrated in *Red Flag* 12/1976 and Hunan Radio Service November 11, 1976.) Also of some interest is the fact that Chou took Wang to task for a speech made to a study class. Hunan Radio Service (November 11, 1976) states that Chairman Mao supported Chou and "criticised Wang Hung-wan face-to-face." More important was Wang's reaction as portrayed by the broadcast: "Wang was still annoyed in March [1976], saying 'What mistakes were there in my speech? I uttered nothing except in Marxist-Leninist terms *with the agreement of Premier Chou.*'" (Emphasis added, although the broadcast implies Wang was a liar on this point.) Mao's tolerance of a young man who had attacked Chou behind his back seems remarkable.

The case of Yao Wen-yuan is even more astonishing. Yao was presumably as strongly condemned by Mao Tse-tung in his various rebukes of the "gang of four" as the other three. On

August 14, 1975, according to the *People's Daily* (December 12, 1976), Mao gave instructions for a public attack on a famous novel, *Water Margin*. The date of the instructions is most revealing, a bare three and a half months after Mao had attacked the "gang of four" at a Politburo session. The instructions seem to have been transmitted to Yao personally (or, indisputably, to some member of the "gang") and Yao took the directive to the news media without consulting the Politburo (*Kwang-ming Daily* 16 December, 1976). Here is another example of Mao's tolerance of the "gang of four" despite his unfriendly comments about them. Similarly, it is a fair construction on the published accounts of Mao Tse-tung's endorsement of Hua Kuo-feng as his successor (*People's Daily* December 17, 1976 and *Kwang-ming Daily* December 24, 1976) when he wrote on April 30, 1976, "with you in charge, I'm at ease," that Yao Wen-yuan was present in the same room (although not so recorded by the press on the day in question). He alone of the "gang of four" is alleged to have seen Mao's written comment, which Hua read but did not circulate at a subsequent Politburo meeting.

A couple of lesser points about Yao Wen-yuan may be taken conveniently here. He is described as having enjoyed "control over the propaganda media" (*People's Daily* November 20, 1976). As will be shown, he could not arrange publication of a Chiang Ching speech. In addition, he allowed the news media to be filled with pro-Teng Hsiao-ping slogans even though this man was the object of great suspicion to Chiang Ching (*People's Daily* December 15, 1976). He is accused of preventing the proper press and media coverage of Chou En-lai's obsequies. *Red Flag* journal was stopped from publishing the memorial speech made at the Premier's funeral service. This allegation demands, for its credibility, a convenient refusal to recall the speech was delivered by Teng Hsiao-ping who, by the appearance of the February issue of *Red Flag* in 1976, was out of political favour though not yet openly identified in the virulent criticism campaign already launched against him. Peking Radio in its home service of January 6, 1977, can be interpreted without gymnastics as evidence that Yao was under Mao Tse-tung's personal control in deciding what should be relayed about the late Chou En-lai to China by television. The Party Central Committee intervened only to ensure the outside world was given access to a televised obituary for Chou. As for Yao's loyalty or otherwise, the *People's Daily* January 14, 1977) quoted Yao Wen-yuan as expressing his worries about the broadcasting staff's readiness to "follow the instructions of the Party Central Committee." Despite the *People's Daily's* best endeavours, this statement cannot be read as testimony to a secret Yao plot.

Did the "gang of four" even exist as an identifiable clique except in Politburo deliberations? A conspiracy in which all four shared should be demonstrated by instances of them acting in unison. Yet such examples are not to be found. The *Heilungkiang Daily* (January 29, 1977) asserted that they usually operated individually. The "gang's" common bonds seem to have been more spiritual than based on a mutual conspiracy.

At this point, the question of the freedom of the "gang of four" to act as they pleased can be raised. If guilty, as alleged, of a bid to sabotage the authority of Mao Tse-tung and Chou En-lai and then to seize power, the four would have needed some independence of movement and freedom from supervision. Hunan Radio Service on January 7, 1977, said Wang Hung-wen had described his trip to Hunan to see Mao Tse-tung in the following way: "He had managed to leave Peking when Premier Chou was taking a rest. Wang Hung-wen said that it was pretty risky for him to come." Such a sentiment sounds more like a recruit slipping out of camp without a pass and terrified of his platoon commander's wrath than the attitude of a conspirator who had the power and status of a Vice Chairman of the Communist Party (Wang's rank). It is very likely, nevertheless, that Chou En-lai kept the youthful Wang on a tight leash.

Chang Chun-chiao made some critical comments about the work of military units. Mao Tse-tung took a completely different line in a subsequent speech. Chang promptly apologised in person to the officers concerned (Shantung Radio Service, January 30, 1977). This act hardly showed disloyalty to Mao.

Mao Tse-tung's own wife, Chiang Ching, was not immune to the normal discipline of the Communist Party even during her husband's life. She complained bitterly that the Politburo had crushed her during a three-month struggle in 1975 (Hupeh Radio Service, November 10, 1976). On approximately August 30, 1976, she complained of the Politburo: "They do not allow me to go out. It is Chairman Mao who suggests I go out and meet the workers, peasants and soldiers" (Shantung Radio Service, November 21, 1976). She got into serious trouble over her condemnation of a film, *Pioneers*, which Mao liked; and Chiang Ching sought desperately to clear her name on this score (*Red Flag* 11/1976 and *Kwang-ming Daily* November 8, 1976). Mao criticised her for sending out political documentation to various parts of the country on her own authority, bypassing normal channels of communication. She appears to have felt very nervous over Mao Tse-tung's rebuke, stating: "Sending materials has become a great charge against me" (Hupeh Radio Service, November 10, 1976). She made a speech at the National Agricultural Conference held in September-October 1975 which she wanted published. Hua Kuo-feng reported to Mao the contents of her address. Her husband forbade its publication (*Red Flag* 1/1977). Chiang Ching was certainly no law unto herself.

In Liaoning Province, Mao Tse-tung's nephew occupied a senior administrative post. Nevertheless, Mao vetoed the appointment to the Communist Party Ninth and Tenth National Congresses of a supporter of the "gang of four" from Liaoning (Liaoning Radio Service, November 21, 1976). The quartet's power to manipulate appointments from behind the scenes was not unrestricted, apparently, provided Mao chose to intervene.

Another set of charges refers to Chiang Ching's loyalty to her husband. Mao Tse-tung twice in 1974 and twice the following year impugned his wife's devotion to his political ideals (*Liberation Army Daily* November 8, 1976 and *People Daily* December 22, 1976). She so infuriated him, the *People's Daily* recounted (December 7, 1976), that Mao had commanded on March 20, 1974: "It is better not to see you. You have not implemented much of what I have told you for years in the past." This condemnation seems categorical enough. Chiang Ching had been expected to follow Mao's guidance and neglected to do so very fully for some years. Yet Mao did not call for her expulsion from the Communist Party's ruling elite, and she was a full Politburo member when he fulminated against the "gang of four" in May the following year.

More tell-tale is Chiang Ching's reaction. Did she take umbrage at Mao's irate denunciation of her uselessness and cease all support for him? Quite the contrary. She grew very perturbed about his position. In the movement to criticise the classic,

Water Margin, Chiang Ching is depicted in such a way as to indicate she believed she had to protect Mao Tse-tung against his enemies. The *People's Daily* (December 15, 1976) quoted her as having stated in September 1975: "The crux of *Water Margin* is to kick Chao Kai upstairs. . . . There are now people in the Central Committee who are trying to kick Chairman Mao upstairs." The *New China News Agency* (December 24, 1976) reported her as vehement on the subject of an attempt in 1975 to make Mao a mere figurehead. On March 6, 1976, Hupeh Radio Service (December 12, 1976) declared that a conference unauthorised by the Party Central Committee was in session under the aegis of the "gang of four." At one point, Chiang Ching demanded of a veteran cadre: "Do you support Chairman Mao the most, in a vain bid thus to conceal her counter-revolutiouary features." Could not her concern to rally support for Mao have been genuine? Nothing else in this broadcast account about the conference suggests she was bent on Mao's betrayal.

Chiang Ching and the "gang of four" are attacked with special venom for their attempt to disgrace the late Premier Chou En-lai. Their aim was to isolate Mao Tse-tung by depriving him of his trusted Prime Minister. (*Kwang-ming Daily* December 2, 1976 and *People's Daily* January 12, 1977). Their principal weapon was the Lin Piao-Confucius criticism campaign of 1973-74 (*People's Daily* November 20, 1976). "It was only on the morning of January 25 [1975]," the *People's Daily* recounted on January 17, 1977, "that Premier Chou received a letter in Chiang Ching's name, and they compelled the Prime Minister to call a meeting on the same afternoon. They showed their attitude on the spot and launched a surprise attack against him. Before the meeting, Chiang Ching gleefully said: 'Ha! ha! We have forced the Prime Minister into a position where he can do nothing.' " The article, unfortunately, gives no explanation as to how Chou was forced against his will to call a meeting at such short notice nor, indeed, how it could be organised under his name and authority (for such is the allegation's plain meaning) in the face of Chou's opposition. The article describes Mao's reaction. He found the incident "a disgusting performance," and on February 24, 1974 (a belated reaction?), issued a statement which dealt "the 'gang of four' a blow on the head and caused their plot to fail." Mao's instructions amounted, it should be noted, to a command that nothing should be permitted to distract attention from direct criticism of Lin Piao and Confucius and their hidden disciples. Yet this movement, according to Peking after October 1976, was the very weapon by which the "gang" hoped to topple the Prime Minister. The critics of Chou En-lai were not rebuffed by Mao Tse-tung so energetically after all on this reading, unless the assumption is made that he misread the "gang's" overall strategy.

The extent of Mao Tse-tung's power is described in sweeping terms even within six months of his death. A fair assumption would be that Mao Tse-tung could have forbidden effectively further criticism of Chou En-lai under any circumstances. He could make far more important decisions in defiance of the "gang" according to the *People's Daily* (January 12, 1977): "After our beloved and esteemed Premier Chou died, the 'gang of four' tried to bring out their own man to become prime minister. But Chairman Mao did not yield power to them and, instead, personally nominated Comrade Hua Kuo-feng to be first Vice Chairman of the Party Central Committee and Premier of the State Council." Hua's backing against his opponents would appear to have been more solid than that proffered to Chou En-lai.

Another aspect of the drive to criticise Lin Piao and Confucius was the praise lavished on the Legalists, the philosophical rivals of the Confucian School. Chiang Ching and the "gang of four" are alleged to have sought to disguise themselves as Legalists to enhance their prestige while they attacked Chou-En-lai as a Confucianist (*Kwang-ming Daily* November 13, 1976). But the same accusation also reveals that Chiang Ching declared: "Legalists are only legitimate if their emperor is a Legalist." Unless Peking meant to imply after the "gang's" arrest that Mao Tse-tung was a Confucianist (most unlikely in view of the continued denunciation of the Sage, in the *People's Daily* of January 7, 1977 for example), Chiang Ching's motive might well have been to defend her husband's credentials. This explanation appears all the more acceptable since she has been accused (*New China News Agency* November 15, 1976) of the exploitation of her husband's reputation and prestige for her own purposes.

Another frequent charge is that persons were manipulated to write to Chiang Ching letters after the death of Mao Tse-tung to express their condolences and induce her to accept the leadership of the Communist Party. Of some interest is the assertion that Mao's widow was not prepared to be seen as acceding immediately to such petitions. She was not desperate to sit in Mao's seat while it was still warm (*Peking Daily* November 10, 1976 and *Kwang-ming Daily* December 23, 1976). Not without significance is the way in which a mere six out of the 29 major administrative units in China expressed their sympathy towards Mao's widow in the messages they sent on Mao's death to the Party Central Committee (and published by the *New China News Agency*); only four out of the eleven major military commands offered their condolences to the widow; and a lone province mentioned Chiang Ching in local mourning services. Even if Chiang Ching and her friends had to rely on the published news agency reports to assess local attitudes towards her, by September 12, 1976, the national score card on who shared Chiang Ching's sorrow was complete. The manufacture of letters of condolence makes small sense in this context.

Chiang Ching and her accomplices are accused of refusing to have anything to do with the violent earthquake which struck northern China in July 1976 and whose tremors destroyed buildings in the capital and in the major port of Tientsin (*New China News Agency* November 8, 1976). The *People's Daily* (December 24, 1976) carried a spirited account of a visit by Hua Kuo-feng to Tientsin where he braved the perils of new tremors and crumbling buildings to inspect the damage. Who is accused in the same account of sneaking into Tientsin as if part of this official comfort mission headed by Hua? Chiang Ching. Her alleged lack of interest in the natural disaster cannot be sustained.

The charges against Chiang Ching in particular look very tattered when they relate to history. On January 9, 1977, the *Peoples Daily* hailed Chou En-lai's defence of his Foreign Minister, the late Chen Yi, during 1967 and the Cultural Revolution. Chiang Ching was accused of having plotted to trap Chou into an 18-hour confrontation over the Foreign Minister's fate during which the Premier "neither ate nor slept." Chiang's accomplice was named as Chen Po-ta, a former intimate of

Mao who fell into disgrace because of his connections with Lin Piao, Mao's official heir mysteriously killed in a 1971 plane crash over Mongolia. In 1967, no group had any special interest in showing Chen Po-ta on the side of a "reactionary" figure such as Chen Yi or of presenting Chiang Ching as out of sympathy with young Maoist firebrands, however misguided their extremism. It is peculiar, therefore, that the Red Guard publication, *Wen-ko Tung-hsin* (October 9, 1967), quoted Chen Po-ta as declaring in public: "I am the greatest royalist. I defended Chen Yi several times. The Premier has never protected Chen Yi." The 1977 allegation needs fuller and better particulars to make this charge stick, given the written record at the time.

Much the same pattern comes to light when Chiang Ching's connections with the violent Red Guards are examined. The worst of these formed themselves into the "May 16 Group" which seized the Foreign Ministry physically and burnt down the British Embassy in the summer of 1967. The "gang of four" collaborated with the "May 16" elements, it has been stated (*People's Daily* January 7, 1977 and *Honan Daily* the next day). A full account of the "May 16" conspiracy was published during the Cultural Revolution in a pamphlet by Red Guards in the Peking College of the Iron and Steel Industry. The document contains several comments by Chiang Ching on the "May 16 Groups," which "would not be tolerated" she declared. "There is also a 'May 16', which is clandestine and conspiratorial body," she went on, "Its spearhead is directed at Chou En-lai but is actually aimed at the Central Committee because opposition to Premier Chou is opposition to the Central Committee. . . . Those in the 'May 16' adopt the appearance of the radical 'left'. Their principal aim is to oppose Premier Chou and compile incriminating material about us."

The same pamphlet reported that Chiang Ching had been the target for members of the "May 16" in 1966 before they turned their fire on the Premier. The contemporary record compiled in the Cultural Revolution is either total fabrication (which seems a meaningless exercise unless its authors were gifted with prophetic vision) or Chiang Ching stands cleared of conspiracy with this illegal group. A second member of the "gang of four" can cite in his behalf similar evidence. A Red Guard paper,

Chu-ying Tung-fang-hung (October 1, 1967), quoted Chou En-lai as having remarked: "Comrade Yao Wen-yuan has exposed in his article the 'May 16' as a counter-revolutionary, covert organisation."

Another serious charge against the "gang of four" is that from the Cultural Revolution onwards, they stirred up violence and tried to undermine the armed forces through the slogan "drag out a handful in the army" which emerged in 1967 (*People's Daily* December 4, 1976). In a speech made in 1967 and distributed to the whole country, Chiang Ching condemned this slogan and said: "We can only talk about dragging out a handful of capitalist-roarers in authority and nothing else." A pamphlet circulated by the Canton Red Guard Headquarters and dated October 1967 quotes Chou En-lai as describing Chiang's speech as a declaration that "our Chinese People's Liberation Army must be strengthened and no one is allowed to weaken it." This very sentence was used, without identification of its author or context, to attack the "gang of four" after their disgrace (Peking Home Service, January 31, 1977). History was clearly being manipulated.

In the same address, Chiang Ching employed the slogan: "Attack with words [or reason] and defend by force," interpreted after October 1976 as deliberate instigation to violent anarchy (*Liberation Daily* November 17, 1976). In her speech in 1967, Chiang Ching explained very carefully that the slogan was not to be exploited as an excuse for violence: "Comrades, I am not in favour of armed struggle, and you must not think I like it because I am firmly opposed to it." So much for this charge.

Even less significant issues such as Chiang Ching's interference with Chinese opera look rather unimpressive when checked against the historical record. The *People's Daily* (August 13, 1967), for instance, made it plain that Chiang's ban on traditional opera was not a permanent measure.

There are three different traditions about the proper attitude to adopt towards persons charged with the grave offences alleged against the "gang of four." The first is the tradition of common-law states which insists that accused persons must be presumed innocent until proved guilty and that the prosecution must not struggle to obtain a verdict of guilty. The second is the inquisitorial process adopted by nations influenced by the Napoleonic Code. Here the prosecution is supposed to be concerned not so much with the individual as culprit but with establishing the truth of what actually occurred in connection with the alleged crimes. Such investigations and interrogations of the accused are Peking's preference. But Peking also shares a Soviet tradition by which persons fall into groups where guilt is a matter of definition (they belong to a certain social class); of confession; or of popular denunciation. Stalin adapted such measures from the Reign of Terror in which the French Revolution had devoured its own children over a century before his era. Mao Tse-tung eschewed the physical extermination practised by Stalin. But self-incrimination as criminals and submission to mass condemnations, Mao found politically useful.

The problem is that popular denunciations can be organised by the current power-holders and, over the long run, are less persuasive than hard evidence. The smaller the investment of time in the construction of a public case against the "gang of four" which is based on a chain of consistent and verifiable facts and the greater the devotion to vitriolic abuse of the quartet, the stronger suspicions will become that either the case against the "gang of four" is essentially a matter of politics or that grave national embarrassment might result from the open publication of the full facts.

The dangers to Peking's credibility were all the more substantial in 1977 since the previous year had seen ten months of remorseless abuse of Teng Hsiao-ping whose sins were tranferred subsequently and without exception to the heads of the "gang of four." This switch in the treatment of Teng makes it impossible not to hasten slowly to judgement on the "gang of four" without abandoning all pretence at impartiality. This "gang of four" may prove to have been monsters. To so assert is not enough; their demoniac features must be made manifest, a task yet to be accomplished.

INDEX